"I've long been impressed by the breadth of Wyatt Graham's reading, but this book shows a corresponding depth of insight. The message of the kingdom is not only a major theme in the Psalter but also in the preaching of Jesus, and Graham effectively draws a collection of psalms together—with a particular focus on the enigmatic Psalm 108—to reveal its message of the Messiah's eschatological kingdom. May this book help readers of Scripture attain a greater breadth and depth of engagement with the canon and its inner coherence and meaning."

IAN HUGH CLARY, associate professor of historical theology, Colorado Christian University

"Graham's insightful study of the Psalms is very rich theologically. His introduction to the various interpretations of the Psalter's macrostructure—and its reuse and recontextualization of individual psalms—is extreme- ... and important contribution to Psalter studies."

...PSTER, professor emeritus of religious studies, ...lall University; author of *Dominion and Dynasty: A Biblical Theology of the Hebrew Bible*

"This fresh study of Psalm 108—a psalm frequently overlooked in Psalter studies—is most welcome. Psalm 108 is shown to entail profound theological reflection on other psalms as they pertain to the Davidic kingship. Graham's study provides vital insights into the historical construction of the Psalter."

MICHAEL A. G. HAYKIN, chair and professor of church history, The Southern Baptist Theological Seminary, Louisville, KY

"Since pioneering work by Childs and Wilson on the canonical shape of the book of Psalms, scholars have supported, refined, and challenged their ideas. As the discussion continues, testing theories about the Psalter's macrostructure, with depth-work on particular psalms or groups of psalms, is an important next step, and this is where *The Promised Davidic King* fills an important gap in scholarship. Graham's treatment of Psalm 108 argues that the editor of Psalms was a biblical theologian, and his research bolsters evidence for a Davidic and eschatological reading of book five. It also provides an important model for the way that reading individual psalms in light of the shape and flow of the book sheds significant light on their meaning. Far from a random conjoining of portions of Psalms 57 and 60, Graham convincingly argues that Psalm 108 leads readers to hope in an eschatological Davidic king. I warmly recommend this helpful book."

IAN J. VAILLANCOURT, associate professor of Old Testament and Hebrew, Heritage Theological Seminary; author of *Treasuring the Psalms: How to Read the Songs that Shape the Soul of the Church*

The Promised Davidic King

Psalm 108's Canonical Placement and Use of Earlier Psalms

The Promised Davidic King

Psalm 108's Canonical Placement and Use of Earlier Psalms

WYATT A. GRAHAM

STUDIES IN SCRIPTURE & BIBLICAL THEOLOGY

The Promised Davidic King: Psalm 108's Canonical Placement and Use of Earlier Psalms
Studies in Scripture and Biblical Theology

Lexham Academic, an imprint of Lexham Press
1313 Commercial St., Bellingham, WA 98225
LexhamPress.com

Print ISBN 9781683596790
Digital ISBN 9781683596806
Library of Congress Control Number 2023935083

Lexham Editorial: Derek R. Brown, John Barach, Katrina Smith
Cover Design: Joshua Hunt
Typesetting: Mandi Newell

To my wife, Leanne Graham,

with gratitude and thankfulness in my heart

Contents

Contents

Abbreviations

AOTC	Abingdon Old Testament Commentary
ATANT	Abhandlungen zur Theologie des Alten und Neuen Testaments
BBB	Bonner Biblische Beiträge
BJSUCSD	Biblical and Judaic Studies from the University of California, San Diego
CahRB	Cahiers de la Revue biblique
DCH	*Dictionary of Classical Hebrew.* Edited by David J. A. Clines. 9 vols. Sheffield: Sheffield Phoenix, 1993–2014.
FAT2	Forschungen zum Alten Testament 2. Reihe.
HALOT	*The Hebrew and Aramaic Lexicon of the Old Testament.* Ludwig Koehler, Walter Baumgartner, and Johann J. Stamm. Translated and edited under the supervision of Mervyn E. J. Richardson. 4 vols. Leiden: Brill, 1994–1999.
HBS	Herders Biblische Studien
IBHS	*An Introduction to Biblical Hebrew Syntax.* Bruce K. Waltke and Michael O'Connor. Winona Lake, IN: Eisenbrauns, 1990.
JSOT	*Journal for the Study of the Old Testament*
JSOTSup	Journal for the Study of the Old Testament Supplement Series
LHBOTS	The Library of Hebrew Bible/Old Testament Studies
LXX	Septuagint
MT	Masoretic Text
NICOT	New International Commentary on the Old Testament
OTE	*Old Testament Essays*
StBibLit	Studies in Biblical Literature (Lang)
SBS	Stuttgarter Bibelstudien
SBB	Stuttgarter biblische Beiträge

SBJT	*The Southern Baptist Journal of Theology*
TBSS	Tools for Biblical Study Series
THOTC	Two Horizons Old Testament Commentary
VT	*Vetus Testamentum*
WBC	Word Biblical Commentary

Preface

I can vividly remember sitting in my university classroom while reading my Bible. Memories can sometimes prove unreliable, but I think that I was reading the book of Psalms. These poems or songs for many years felt elusive to me. The words of each psalm melded together in my mind. The ideas they presented seemed locked away except perhaps as proof texts for dogmatic reasoning. In many ways, I still struggle to understand the language of the book of Psalms. But I have been reading them for about fifteen years now, and I would like to think that I have grown in my understanding.

The book in your hands represents part of that growth. I had the privilege of studying under James Hamilton for my doctorate. Since he was working in the psalms, I decided to do so also. I am glad that I did, not least because it allowed me to complete my dissertation and earn my doctorate. I also grew in my understanding of the art of research, which has continued to help me in both academic and regular life.

I should also give my thanks to Peter Gentry and Michael Haykin who also served on my dissertation committee. Stephen Dempster kindly served as my external reader. My wife stood by me during my studies, moving not only to a new state but even to a new country before I finished my dissertation.

I wrote it knowing that I might publish it one day. While much of it interacts with the necessary scholarly sources, I tried to communicate with lucid clarity. Thank you for reading this book, and I hope it benefits you in your intellectual pursuits.

Wyatt A. Graham
Hamilton, Ontario
December 2020

Introduction

The Psalter can feel like a labyrinth. Sections of psalms seem to blend together. At other times, the oddity of individual psalms makes it hard to imagine the psalms could fit into a coherent whole. Yet readers have often discerned some sort of order to the Psalter, and recent scholarship has found ways to demonstrate the plausibility of the idea that editors shaped the Psalter into a coherent work.

Building upon earlier research into the shape of the Psalter, this book shows how editors may have organized psalms within the Psalter. In particular, it discusses Psalm 108, an often ignored psalm compared to its neighboring psalms, Psalms 109 and 110. These two psalms often receive attention because of their use in the New Testament. Psalm 110 particularly played an important role for the earliest Christians in understanding the person of Jesus.[1] Psalm 109 is associated with Judas. Psalm 108 is not explicitly cited in the New Testament, nor does it have an obvious association with a figure in the New Testament. Yet it appears within a Davidic trilogy alongside Psalms 109 and 110. This grouping, marked by Davidic authorship, suggests that Psalm 108 should be read together with these two psalms. This work, then, not only shows how Psalm 108 relates to its neighboring psalms but also makes a plausible case for its intentional placement in the Psalter.

In a sentence, this book argues that Psalm 108 introduces the eschatological notions of the king and of the kingdom into its canonical group (Pss 108–110) through its inclusion of a non-historically specific superscription, its quotation and paraphrase of earlier psalmic material (Pss 57 and 60), and its canonical placement in Book V of the Psalter. While the scope of this work limits itself to Psalm 108 in its canonical setting, it will (I hope) allow readers to think about how each psalm contributes to the greater whole.

1. A helpful overview of how early Christians in both the New Testament and the early church understood Psalm 110 can be found in Matthew W. Bates, *The Birth of the Trinity: Jesus, God, and Spirit in New Testament and Early Christian Interpretations of the Old Testament* (Oxford: Oxford University Press, 2015).

With that said, the argument here takes a more minimalistic approach to the organization of the Psalter than some other works do.[2] Chapter 1 outlines this approach to organization. It presents this study's thesis along with three undergirding assumptions: (1) the Psalter is a book; (2) individual psalms should be read in sequence; and (3) the Psalter progressively tells a story along redemptive-historical lines.

Chapters 2 and 3 provide histories of the interpretation of Psalm 108 and of research into inner-biblical exegesis and canonical approaches to the Psalter. Chapter 2 shows differences among interpreters' views of Psalm 108. Chapter 3 then shows how this work's approach engages inner-biblical exegesis and Psalter exegesis (a canonical approach) to clarify the meaning of Psalm 108.

Chapter 4 interprets Psalm 108 in its canonical context. It reveals how Psalm 108 participates in the narrative flow of the Psalter. It concludes that Psalm 108 continues the story of eschatological redemption that began in Psalm 107, which records the eschatological return of Israel to the land. In continuation of this story, Psalm 108 speaks of the eschatological conquest of the land. In response to the king's prayer, God will go out with Israel's armies and conquer the land, and through the king's prayer, the kingdom comes.

Chapter 5 compares Psalm 108 with Psalms 57 and 60 to clarify the message that Psalm 108 conveys by its quotation and paraphrase of these two earlier psalms.

Chapter 6 highlights certain themes that Psalm 108 shares with Psalms 109 and 110, noting the development of these themes across the three psalms. Psalm 108 introduces the eschatological notions of the king and the kingdom to this Davidic triptych (Pss 108–110). Before discussing these psalms, this chapter also explores the theoretical tools of willed types and pregnant meaning to explain how the Psalter's editor(s) could have organized Davidic psalms into a sequence while honoring David's authorial intent.

Finally, Chapter 7 summarizes this book's argument and proposes lines for future research into other psalms which similarly have their content doubled in the Hebrew Bible.

---

2. For example, Peter C. W. Ho recently published a well-researched and detailed set of arguments for the unity of the Psalter. While I sympathize with his approach, his maximalist approach potentially over-reads the evidence for the unity of the Psalter. See *The Design of the Psalter: A Macrostructural Analysis* (Eugene, OR: Pickwick, 2019).

1

Thesis And Method

Psalm 108 combines Psalms 57:8–12 and 60:7–14 to form a new psalm in the Psalter's fifth book, which puzzles those who study the Psalter. Some argue that Psalm 108 uses earlier material for historical-critical reasons,[1] while others see Psalm 108 as a discrete psalm with its own unique purpose.[2] Both groups, however, fail to account for Psalm 108's citation of earlier psalmic material in its new canonical setting. They miss the significance of Psalm 108's placement in the Psalter, its contribution to the redemptive-historical storyline of the Psalter, and its meaningful citation of Psalms 57 and 60.

A third group recognizes that Psalm 108's use of earlier material and its canonical placement have interpretive significance. Hossfeld and Zenger, for example, interpret Psalm 108 as a discrete psalm whose use

1. For example, see G. W. Anderson, "The Psalms," in *Peake's Commentary on the Bible*, ed. Matthew Black and H. H. Rowley (New York: Thomas Nelson, 1962), 437; Sigmund Mowinckel, *The Psalms in Israel's Worship*, trans. D. R. Ap-Thomas, 2 vols. (Oxford: Basil Blackwell, 1962), 1:218; Cyril S. Rodd, *Psalms 73–150*, Epworth Preacher's Commentaries (London: Epworth, 1964), 70; Hans-Joachim Kraus, *Psalms 60–150*, trans. Hilton C. Oswald (Minneapolis: Augsburg, 1989), 333–35; Mitchell Dahood, *Psalms III: 101–150*, Anchor Yale Bible Commentaries (Garden City, NY: Doubleday, 1970), 93; Ernst Axel Knauf, "Psalm LX und Psalm CVIII," *VT* 50, no. 1 (2000): 55–65; Konrad Schaefer, *Psalms*, Berit Olam (Collegeville, MN: Liturgical, 2001), 269; Richard J. Clifford, *Psalms 73–150*, AOTC (Nashville: Abingdon, 2003), 168; Walter Brueggemann and William H. Bellinger Jr., *Psalms* (New York: Cambridge University Press, 2014), 469–70.

2. For example, see James Luther Mays, *Psalms*, Interpretation (Louisville, KY: John Knox, 1994), 347–48; Leslie C. Allen, *Psalms 101–150*, WBC (Nashville: Thomas Nelson, 2002), 94; Willem A. VanGemeren, *Psalms*, rev. ed., vol. 5 in *The Expositor's Bible Commentary*, eds. Tramper Longman III and David E. Garland (Grand Rapids: Zondervan, 2008), 804; Nancy deClaissé-Walford, Rolf A. Jacobson, and Beth Laneel Tanner, *The Book of Psalms*, NICOT (Grand Rapids: Eerdmans, 2014), 821.

of earlier material and canonical context generate meaning.[3] O. Palmer Robertson also finds meaning in what Psalm 108 omits from its previous material.[4] While these investigations mark improved interpretations of Psalm 108, they provide only the initial steps toward explaining why Psalm 108 cites earlier material and why it is placed in its current canonical context. This book goes further to discover the fuller meaning of Psalm 108.

THESIS

Psalm 108 introduces the eschatological notions of the king and of the kingdom into its canonical group (Pss 108–110) through its inclusion of a non-historically specific superscription, its quotation and paraphrase of earlier psalmic material (Pss 57 and 60), and its canonical placement in Book V of the Psalter.

Psalm 108 was intentionally placed after Psalms 57 and 60, and readers are meant to notice how Psalm 108 differs from these two psalms. Psalm 108 also follows Psalm 107, which celebrates Israel's eschatological return and sets out a pattern of eschatological redemption. Psalm 108 then narrates the next step of Israel's redemption, namely, that YHWH and the coming Davidic king will conquer the nations who inhabit Israel's land. Psalms 109 and 110 further develop and clarify these eschatological notions.

METHODOLOGY

Three premises support this study: (1) the Psalter is a book; (2) individual psalms should be read in sequence; and (3) the Psalter progressively tells a story along redemptive-historical lines. In the following paragraphs, I argue for the plausibility of these premises by surveying and criticizing relevant literature.

THE PSALTER AS A BOOK

Is the Psalter a book? In other words, is the Psalter a coherent literary work with a unified message? This seemingly simple question has a

---

3. Frank-Lothar Hossfeld and Erich Zenger, *A Commentary on Psalms 101–150*, vol. 3 of *Psalms*, ed. Klaus Baltzer, trans. Linda M. Maloney, Hermeneia (Minneapolis: Fortress, 2011), 115.

4. O. Palmer Robertson, *The Flow of the Psalms: Discovering Their Structure and Theology* (Phillipsburg, NJ: P & R, 2015), 191.

contested set of answers. Some scholars have answered "Yes" to this question because they see evidence of editorial arrangements in the Psalter as a sufficient basis for reading it as a book with a coherent message. Others have answered "No" because they see insufficient evidence for reading the Psalter as a literary work with a unified message.

The following paragraphs briefly survey scholarly arguments in favor of each position. On the basis of this discussion, I will conclude that the Psalter is an edited book that conveys a coherent message.

The Psalter Is a Book

Modern scholars who affirm that the Psalter is a book[5] can trace their roots to Brevard Childs's canonical approach to Scripture.[6] Childs advocated an approach that studies the Bible's content in its canonical form. Earlier scholars had studied biblical passages in isolation, attempting to find their historical origin or define their literary layers. In the realm of Psalter scholarship, Hermann Gunkel had argued that a psalm's form or *Gattung* had its origins in Israel's ritual ceremonies.[7] Hence, one could study the formal features of a psalm to understand not only the psalm itself but also its origin. Arguing that individual psalms were performed during Israel's cultic ceremonies, Sigmund Mowinckel went beyond Gunkel's program and especially highlighted a yearly enthronement festival.[8] The form-critical and cult-functional methods of Gunkel and Mowinckel aim to interpret individual psalms within their life-setting.

Childs's approach to the Bible widens the focus of biblical study from individual passages to the canonical composition of biblical books. In 1985, Gerald Wilson, a student of Childs, applied his teacher's method to the Psalter in the monograph *The Editing of the Hebrew Psalter*.[9] Wilson provided a comprehensive proposal explaining how the Psalter is a book with a coherent message.

---

5. The term "book" is anachronistic, since early Psalm manuscripts would have been scrolls. By book, I mean a coherent literary work.

6. Brevard S. Childs, *Introduction to the Old Testament as Scripture* (Philadelphia: Fortress, 1979).

7. Hermann Gunkel, *Die Psalmen*, 5th ed. (Göttingen, Germany: Vandenhoeck & Ruprecht, 1968). *Die Psalmen* was first published in 1929.

8. Mowinckel, *Psalms in Israel's Worship*. The English edition translates Mowinckel's Norwegian work published in 1951.

9. Gerald Henry Wilson, *The Editing of the Hebrew Psalter*, Society of Biblical Literature Dissertation Series (Chico, CA: Scholars, 1985).

Gerald Wilson

Wilson identifies external and internal evidence verifying that the Psalter is the product of an editorial venture. In terms of external evidence, Wilson has studied Ancient Near Eastern texts and found evidence of editorial shaping.[10] Consequently, Wilson concludes that the same editorial concerns existed for the collection and organization of the Psalter.

Internally, Wilson identifies a number of examples of editorial work in the Psalter. First, psalm superscriptions organize psalms into large groups: "For Books One through Three of the Psalter (Pss 3–89) the primary organizational concern is apparently authorship. This is clearly demonstrated in Book One (3–41) where every Ps is attributed to David, either explicitly in its [superscriptions] or by implied combination with its predecessor (Pss 10, 33)."[11] Of the 61 psalms in Books IV and V, "only 19 bear attributions of authorship."[12] Books IV and V do not, therefore, rely on authorship to organize their material as much as Books I–III do.

Second, Wilson identifies changes of authorship at the seams of the Psalter as further evidence.[13] Psalm 41 closes Book I of the Psalter, and Psalms 42 and 43 open Book II with a change in authorship from David to the Sons of Korah. Book II ends with a psalm of Solomon (Ps 72), and Book III opens with an Asaphite collection (Pss 73–83). Book III ends with a Korahite collection (Pss 84–85, 87–88), to which Psalm 89 is related because its superscription is similar to Psalm 88's superscription. Book IV opens with a psalm of Moses (Ps 90), representing another change of authorship.

Third, the first four books evince editorial activity because they each conclude with doxologies (Pss 41:14; 72:19; 89:53; 106:48).[14] Together, the doxologies and the authorship-changes at key junctures in the Psalter "represent conscious editorial activity either to introduce such author-changes in order to indicate disjuncture between such divisions or to make use of such existing points of disjuncture in the divisions of the Psalter."[15] In other words, the editor either inserted the author-changes

10. Wilson, *Editing of the Hebrew Psalter*, 13–61. He also studied Qumran Psalter scrolls, which I mention later in my exposition of Wilson's argument.

11. Wilson, *Editing of the Hebrew Psalter*, 155.

12. Wilson, *Editing of the Hebrew Psalter*, 155.

13. Wilson, *Editing of the Hebrew Psalter*, 157.

14. Wilson, *Editing of the Hebrew Psalter*, 185–86.

15. Wilson, *Editing of the Hebrew Psalter*, 157.

and doxologies at the conclusion of Psalter Books or took advantage of their existence to create divisions between Books of the Psalter.

Fourth, psalm genres reveal editorial activity because they soften the transition between psalm groups. For example, Psalms 42–49 form a Korahite collection, which transitions to an Asaphite psalm (Ps 50) and then to a Davidic collection (Pss 51–70/1).[16]

Psalms 47–51 soften the disjunction caused by the changing of authorship, because the five psalms share similar genres:

Ps 47 לַמְנַצֵּחַ לִבְנֵי־קֹרַח מִזְמוֹר
Ps 48 שִׁיר מִזְמוֹר לִבְנֵי־קֹרַח
Ps 49 לַמְנַצֵּחַ לִבְנֵי־קֹרַח מִזְמוֹר
Ps 50 מִזְמוֹר לְאָסָף
Ps 51 לַמְנַצֵּחַ מִזְמוֹר לְדָוִד

These five psalms are *mizmorim*, and Psalm 47 (Korahite), Psalm 49 (Asaphite), and Psalm 51 (Davidic) include the phrase לַמְנַצֵּחַ. The use of *mizmor* in Psalm 47 is particularly striking because no earlier Kohathite psalms are *mizmorim* and the term does not appear again until Psalm 62.[17]

Fifth, Wilson demonstrates that the lack of superscriptions in Qumran Psalm manuscripts provides evidence of editorial arrangement. He likewise believes that the lack of superscriptions in Psalms 1 and 2, 9 and 10, 32 and 33, 42 and 43, and 70 and 71 also supplies evidence of an editorial arrangement.[18]

Sixth, Book IV opens with the only psalm attributed to Moses (Ps 90). Outside of Book IV, Moses's name only occurs once (Ps 77:21), "[y]et here, in the space of only eight pss, his name is mentioned *seven* times (90:1; 99:6; 103:7; 105:26; 106:16; 106:23; 106:32)."[19] This suggests a level of organization that would require an editor.

Seventh, Book V is structured around a pattern of הַלְלוּ־יָהּ (*halleluyah*) and הודו (*hodu*) psalms. For example, Psalm 107, a *hodu* psalm, opens a section in Book V; Psalm 117, a *halleluyah* psalm, ends it (Pss 107–117). Psalm 118 opens the next section as a *hodu* psalm; Psalm 135, a *halleluyah* psalm, concludes the section (Pss 118–135). Psalm 136, a *hodu* psalm, opens the final section of Book V, which closes with Psalm 145, a *halleluyah* psalm

16. Wilson, *Editing of the Hebrew Psalter*, 163.
17. Wilson, *Editing of the Hebrew Psalter*, 163.
18. Wilson, *Editing of the Hebrew Psalter*, 173.
19. Wilson, *Editing of the Hebrew Psalter*, 187.

(Pss 136–145).[20] Psalms 146–150 are, according to Wilson, a separate liturgical section, responding to Psalm 145:21.[21]

Eighth, Wilson points to psalms that are thematically grouped. For example, Psalms 65–68 bind together around the idea of praise, Psalms 93 and 96–99 around the idea of enthronement, Psalms 105–106 around YHWH's action in Israel's history, and Psalms 146–150 around the praise of YHWH.[22]

Ninth, other techniques exist, such as adjacent psalms with the same initial word, adjacent psalms with the same catch phrases, and adjacent psalms that use a particular designation for God (e.g, the Elohistic Psalter).[23] Such techniques suggest the existence of an editor who would have employed them.

After identifying numerous signs of editorial work in the Psalter, Wilson also interprets the data. He argues that Psalm 1's introductory function, the five-book division of the Psalter, and the final Hallel (Pss 146–150) are obvious places to begin uncovering the meaning of the Psalter's editorial arrangement.[24] Psalm 1, as an example, indicates that the Psalter should be read and not performed, and the psalm also supplies hermeneutical principles for reading the Psalter.[25]

Books I–III are marked by author groupings as well as royal psalms that appear at the seams of these books (Pss 2, 41, 72, 89). The royal psalms advance a progressive message about kingship and the Davidic covenant. According to Wilson, however, Psalm 89 portrays the Davidic covenant as having failed: "The Davidic covenant introduced in Ps 2 has come to nothing and the combination of three books concludes with the anguished cry of the Davidic descendants."[26]

Book IV features a large number of untitled psalms—thirteen out of seventeen have no title—and distinctive traits (e.g., a focus on Moses).[27]

---

20. Wilson, *Editing of the Hebrew Psalter*, 187, 190.

21. Wilson, *Editing of the Hebrew Psalter*, 189.

22. Wilson, *Editing of the Hebrew Psalter*, 190–94.

23. Wilson, *Editing of the Hebrew Psalter*, 194–97.

24. Wilson, *Editing of the Hebrew Psalter*, 204.

25. Wilson, *Editing of the Hebrew Psalter*, 207.

26. Wilson, *Editing of the Hebrew Psalter*, 213. Wilson assumes that readers will read the psalms in their canonical sequence. Ps 89 follows Pss 2, 41, and 72, and the sequence matters for determining the meaning of the editorial arrangement of the Psalter.

27. Wilson, *Editing of the Hebrew Psalter*, 215.

Consequently, Wilson calls Book IV the editorial center of the Psalter. Book IV answers the question of the Davidic covenant's failure in Psalm 89 by proposing that YHWH is Israel's king and refuge.[28] The focus on Moses in Book IV reflects that God has always been Israel's refuge, even before the monarchy.[29]

According to Wilson, Book V resists easy interpretation due to its size (44 psalms) and its inclusion of collections that existed prior to the final form of the Psalter because the existence of earlier collections would have prevented editorial manipulation.[30] Wilson sees Book V as a response to the plea of the exiles to return from the *diaspora* (Ps 107:1–3 with Ps 106:47).[31] Further, the two Davidic collections (Pss 108–110; 138–145) present David as a model of faithfulness to follow. Psalm 119 guides readers to follow YHWH in obedience, and Psalms 145 and 146 put forward YHWH as king and as one worthy of trust. In essence, Book V shows Israel how to live without a Davidic king on the throne.

In summary, Wilson comprehensively identifies evidence of editorial arrangements in the Psalter. His interpretation of the evidence reveals that the Psalter is a book with a message that progresses across the five Books of the Psalter. Books I–III chronicle a story of kingship and the failure of the Davidic covenant. Books IV and V instruct readers how to live without a Davidic king on the throne. The answer is to obediently follow and trust in God.

Other scholars have followed Wilson's example and have discovered further signs of editorial work or clarified how the editorial arrangements in the Psalter communicate theological meaning.

Walter Brueggemann

Building on Wilson's proposal, Walter Brueggemann focuses on the theological purpose of the Psalter's editorial shape. He argues that Psalms 1 and 150 frame the Psalter around the ideas of torah obedience (Ps 1) and praise (Ps 150).[32] Part of his justification for reading these two psalms as framing the Psalter is their peculiar character.[33]

---

28. Wilson, *Editing of the Hebrew Psalter*, 215.
29. Wilson, *Editing of the Hebrew Psalter*, 215.
30. Wilson, *Editing of the Hebrew Psalter*, 220.
31. Wilson, *Editing of the Hebrew Psalter*, 227–28.
32. Walter Brueggemann, "Bounded by Obedience and Praise: The Psalms as Canon," *JSOT* 16, no. 50 (1991): 64–66.
33. Brueggemann, "Bounded by Obedience and Praise," 68.

Psalm 150, for example, lacks the normal characteristics of praise psalms in the Psalter:

> Psalm 150 is remarkable because it contains no reason or motivations at all. It is the only Psalm which completely lacks motivation. It is the most extreme and unqualified statement of unfettered praise in the Old Testament. Psalm 150 is situated literally at the end of the process of praise; it is also located theologically at the end of the process of praise and obedience, after all of Israel's motivations have been expressed and no more reasons need to be given.[34]

Psalm 150 ends the Psalter with praise, and Psalm 1 begins a process of torah obedience. The psalms between Psalms 1 and 150 chronicle the movement from obedience to praise. According to Brueggemann, Psalm 73 particularly functions as the theological and canonical center of the Psalms.[35] Brueggemann thus sees a theological purpose to the canonical shape of the Psalter.

David Mitchell

Like Brueggemann, David Mitchell argues for a theological purpose behind the Psalter. He proposes that "the Hebrew Psalter was designed by its redactors as a purposefully ordered arrangement of lyrics with an eschatological message."[36]

Mitchell marshals the following evidence. First, the Psalter "originated within an eschatologically conscious milieu."[37] Second, Mitchell writes, "the figures to whom the Psalms are attributed were regarded as future-predictive prophets even in biblical times."[38] Moreover, some psalms exceed the historical realities of ancient Israel (i.e., they are about eschatological events).[39] Further, royal psalms point to a messianic redaction, since David was already dead and thus their inclusion would not make sense unless they refer to a future royal figure:[40] "After

34. Brueggemann, "Bounded by Obedience and Praise," 67.

35. Brueggemann, "Bounded by Obedience and Praise," 81.

36. David C. Mitchell, *The Message of the Psalter: An Eschatological Programme in the Book of Psalms* (Sheffield: Sheffield Academic, 1997), 15.

37. Mitchell, *Message of the Psalter*, 82.

38. Mitchell, *Message of the Psalter*, 83.

39. Mitchell, *Message of the Psalter*, 85.

40. Mitchell, *Message of the Psalter*, 86.

the extinction of the kingdom psalms referring to the king or *mashiah* would have been understood as referring only to the anticipated future deliverer."[41]

Brueggemann and Mitchell interpret the same or similar evidence that Wilson uncovered, but they expand on Wilson's canonical reading of the Psalter in theological ways. Subsequent studies on the Psalter also follow Wilson's basic identification of editorial arrangements in the Psalter and attempt to refine or extend his argument.[42]

Michael Snearly

One recent proposal for reading the Psalter as a book appears in Michael Snearly's 2016 monograph, *The Return of The King.*[43] Snearly contributes to the discussion of the Psalter as a book through the use of poetics.[44] The discipline of poetics involves describing various levels of communication. For example, J. P. Fokkelman outlines the levels of signification of poetic texts:

---

41. Mitchell, *Message of the Psalter*, 87.

42. James Luther Mays, "The Place of the Torah-Psalms in the Psalter," *Journal of Biblical Literature* 106 (1987): 3–12; John H. Walton, "Psalms: A Cantata about the Davidic Covenant," *Journal of the Evangelical Theological Society* 34, no. 1 (March 1991): 21–31; J. Clinton McCann, "Books I–III and the Editorial Purpose of the Hebrew Psalter," in *The Shape and Shaping of the Psalter*, ed. J. Clinton McCann (Sheffield: JSOT, 1993), 93–107; David M. Howard Jr., "A Contextual Reading of Psalms 90–94," in McCann, *Shape and Shaping of the Psalter*, 108–23; Jerome F. D Creach, *Yahweh as Refuge and the Editing of the Hebrew Psalter* (Sheffield: Sheffield Academic, 1996); David M. Howard Jr., *The Structure of Psalms 93–100*, BJSUCSD 5 (Winona Lake, IN: Eisenbrauns, 1997); M. D Goulder, *The Psalms of the Return (Book V, Psalms 107–150)*, vol. 4 of *Studies in the Psalter*, JSOTSup 258 (Sheffield: Sheffield Academic, 1998); Robert L. Cole, *The Shape and Message of Book III*, JSOTSup 307 (Sheffield: Sheffield Academic, 2000); Jean-Marie Auwers, *La Composition Littéraire du Psautier: Un État de la Question*, CahRB 46 (Paris: Gabalda, 2000); Erich Zenger, "The God of Israel's Reign over the World (Psalms 90–106)," in *The God of Israel and the Nations: Studies in Isaiah and the Psalms* (Collegeville, MN: Liturgical, 2000), 161–90; Jamie A. Grant, *The King as Exemplar: The Function of Deuteronomy's Kingship Law in the Shaping of the Book of Psalms* (Atlanta: Society of Biblical Literature, 2004); Robert E. Wallace, *The Narrative Effect of Book IV of the Hebrew Psalter*, StBibLit 112 (New York: Peter Lang, 2007); Terrance Randall Wardlaw, *Elohim within the Psalms: Petitioning the Creator to Order Chaos in Oral-Derived Literature*, LHBOTS 602 (New York: Bloomsbury, 2015).

43. Michael K. Snearly, *The Return of The King: Messianic Expectation in Book V of the Psalter*, LHBOTS 624 (New York: Bloomsbury T&T Clark, 2016).

44. The discipline of text-linguistics is also important to Snearly's discussion. Text-linguistics provides the language of cohesion and coherence, which are elements of texts.

Poetry: Levels of Signification

collection or book
sections/groups of songs
poems
stanzas
strophes
verses
half-verses/cola
phrases
words
syllables
sounds[45]

The poetic strata climb the ladder from the sound level to the book level. Each level connects with the one before and after it. A sound makes up a syllable, and a word is made up of syllables. Sections exist in books, and a book includes sections. If the Psalter thus presents a coherent and cohesive narrative, from the level of sound to book, then it is a book. This is precisely what Snearly argues.

To make his argument, Snearly uses text-linguistics to explain how the Psalter can make connections from the level of a sound to the level of a book. In their introduction to text-linguistics, Robert-Alain de Beaugrande and Wolfgang Ulrich Dressler show how text-linguistics pinpoints what constitutes a text. They define a text as an act of communication that attains certain standards of textuality.[46] These standards include cohesion, coherence, intentionality, acceptability, informativity, situationality, and intertextuality.[47] The first two standards define a text, while the five that follow illustrate how a text expresses coherence.[48]

A text is thus cohesive and coherent. If the Psalter is a book, it too will present cohesive and coherent elements. A key cohesive element in the

45. In the original work, the spacing is different than presented here. See J. P. Fokkelman, *The Crossing Fates*, vol. 2 of *Narrative Art and Poetry in the Books of Samuel* (Dover, NH: Van Gorcum, 1986), 4. The word "Poetry" does appear in all capital letters in the original text.

46. Robert-Alain de Beaugrande and Wolfgang Ulrich Dressler, *Introduction to Text Linguistics* (New York: Longman, 1981), 3.

47. Beaugrande and Dressler, *Introduction to Text Linguistics*, 4–10.

48. Snearly, *Return of The King*, 43.

Psalms is repetition.[49] Adjacent psalms and psalms within groups repeat the same or similar words, phrases, and clauses. These repetitions bind psalms together. For example, Psalm 1 opens with, "Blessed is the man," while the last verse of Psalm 2 reads, "Blessed are all who take refuge in him" (2:12). Since the end of Psalm 2 repeats the link-word "blessed," an element of cohesion glues the two psalms together.[50]

Snearly's proposal advances the discussion in Psalter studies by using poetics to show how a piece of writing can be defined as a book. At the same time, Snearly appears to argue too much. Can the entire Psalter fit cohesively and coherently combine together from the level of the sound up to the level of a book? The Psalter is a work of theological poetry, not a letter of Paul. Overly specific approaches to the book of Psalms are not tenable, and they provide easy foils for those who argue that the Psalter is not a book.

The Psalter Is Not a Book

Some scholars are not convinced that the Psalter is a book with a coherent message. They question whether the evidence of editorial arrangement in the Psalter warrants the conclusion that the Psalter is a book.

Roland Murphy

One such scholar, Roland Murphy, has contributed a chapter to a multi-author book that studies the psalms "as a coherent literary whole."[51] In his chapter, Murphy attempts to explain what it means to read a psalm in the context of the Psalter as a book. He proposes six theses to shape his explanation. His first thesis cautions against reading the Psalter as a book without a strong historical basis. All contextual interpretation requires some historical reconstruction, and canonical approaches to the Psalter are no exception. Consequently, reading the Psalter in the context of the canon does not make the approach "more 'objective' than other approaches."[52]

49. Another important element of cohesion is genre repetition. Pss 57 and 60, for example, are both *miktamim*, which ties the two psalms together.

50. For many other links between Pss 1 and 2, see Robert Luther Cole, *Psalms 1–2: Gateway to the Psalter* (Sheffield: Sheffield Phoenix, 2013).

51. J. Clinton McCann, preface to McCann, *Shape and Shaping of the Psalter*, 7.

52. Roland E. Murphy, "Reflections on Contextual Interpretation of the Psalms," in McCann, *Shape and Shaping of the Psalter*, 21.

Murphy views the pre-history of the Psalter from its earlier collections to its final form as requiring a fair level of historical reconstruction. He further argues that relationships between psalms, like the connection between Psalms 1 and 2 or the so-called echo between Psalm 2:1 and Psalm 89:51, may simply be free associations.[53] Put another way, when a later psalm (Ps 89) references an earlier psalm (Ps 2), the reference may simply represent a non-intentional and synchronic relationship (i.e., what is commonly called an intertextual relationship).

He further avers that theological readings of the Psalter are reader-responses to the text.[54] In other words, the theological unity of the Psalter occurs in the mind of the reader and not objectively in the text. The text is primarily a historical rather than a literary or theological work, although he grants that both literary (the Psalter as a book) and theological readings have their place.

Murphy is a cautious proponent of reading the Psalter as a book. His commitment to historical criticism prevents him from fully embracing a canonical reading of the Psalms. Oddly, he argues that all historical readings involve hypothetical reconstruction, but he appears to give form criticism an uncritical pass. One illustration of this is his treatment of the superscriptions, which he calls misleading and which, he claims, point to an unhelpful context (e.g., the life of David).[55] Murphy appears to favor reading individual psalms as discrete entities that have a cultic origin.[56] As a consequence, the psalm titles mislead readers because they function at the canonical level and do not point to an original *Sitz im Leben*. But his claim seems to assume the truth of form criticism before evaluating the evidence that would show how the superscriptions function within the book of Psalms.

Erhard Gerstenberger

Objecting to the notion that the Psalter is a book, Erhard Gerstenberger states, "The Psalter is not a book, but a collection of extraordinarily rich, theologically and anthropologically profound and insightful prayers

53. Murphy, "Reflections on Contextual Interpretation of the Psalms," 23.
54. Murphy, "Reflections on Contextual Interpretation of the Psalms," 25–26.
55. Murphy, "Reflections on Contextual Interpretation of the Psalms," 26–27.
56. Murphy, "Reflections on Contextual Interpretation of the Psalms," 23–24.

and songs from various life situations."[57] In his article, Gerstenberger argues that canonical approaches to the Bible are full of problems.[58]

According to Gerstenberger, canonical readings devalue the historical origin of traditional faith. Canonical approaches make exegesis easier because interpreters can ignore a text's *Sitz im Leben*. In addition, the canonical form of the Hebrew Bible is bound to the historical experiences of post-exilic Jews in Palestine and in the diaspora. Consequently, the Hebrew Bible is the result of various random influences and concerns.

Gerstenberger goes on to argue that, of all the books in the Bible, the Psalter most strongly resists a canonical or coherent reading.[59] Gerstenberger admits that synonymous words, formulas, and phrases appear in the Psalter, which might invite an integrated reading of the Psalms.[60] However, he cautions interpreters against a simple identification of words, forms, and structures as evidence of the Psalter's composition and as evidence that the Psalter is a book. Each text must be examined to see whether the related expressions are from the original text or the redactor's hand.

Consequently, some psalms and psalm-groups should be read together at the canonical level. Gerstenberger explains that some psalms are meant to be read together, such as Psalms 111 and 112 or 105 and 106.[61] Other psalms obviously form groups (Pss 3–7; 96–99; 120–134; 146–150).[62] He further admits that the Psalter's editors inserted Psalms 1 and 2 as an introduction and Psalms 146–150 or just 150 as a conclusion.[63] He observes, however, that these psalms and psalm-groups show only that some psalms are meant to be read together. They do not prove that the Psalter is a book with a coherent message.

---

57. My translation of "Der Psalter ist kein Buch, sondern eine Sammlung von außerordentlich reichen, theologisch und anthropologisch tiefsitzenden und tiefblickenden Gebeten und Liedern aus unterschiedlichen Lebenssituationen." Erhard S. Gerstenberger, "Der Psalter als Buch und als Sammlung," in *Neue Wege der Psalmenforschung*, ed. Klaus Seybold and Erich Zenger, HBS 1 (New York: Herder, 1994), 12.

58. Gerstenberger, "Psalter als Buch und als Sammlung," 3–4.

59. Gerstenberger, "Psalter als Buch und als Sammlung," 5.

60. Gerstenberger uses the language of an "integrated" reading of the Psalter. I take him to mean by this term a kind of reading that views the Psalter as a book with a coherent message or something similar to this.

61. Gerstenberger, "Psalter als Buch und als Sammlung," 6.

62. Gerstenberger, "Psalter als Buch und als Sammlung," 6.

63. Gerstenberger, "Psalter als Buch und als Sammlung," 6–7.

Additionally, link-words, textual links, and theological links do not create the kind of cohesion that would make the Psalter a book. Link-words, for Gerstenberger, are not reliable ways to create uniform meaning in the Psalter. Individual psalms spring up in collections, whose process is broken, incoherent, and does not constitute a single line of thought. He, therefore, denies that there is a theological unity in the Psalter.[64]

Norman Whybray

In *Reading the Psalms as a Book*, Norman Whybray opposes the idea that the Psalter is a book with a coherent message.[65] Key to Whybray's argument is that insufficient evidence exists within the Psalter to discern any comprehensive redactional effort to unify the Psalter into a coherent work. According to Whybray, the Psalter presents wisdom, torah, and royal redactional emphases, but the emphases fail to unite the Psalter around a coherent message. Instead, they are different voices interpreted throughout an unorganized collection of psalms. He concludes:

> Unfortunately there is no direct evidence (except Ps. 72.20), internal or external, about the process by which the Psalter received its shape. All hypotheses about this basic question are purely speculative, based on inferences drawn from textual data that can be, and often have been, interpreted in quite different ways by different scholars (so Murphy). All that can be said with reasonable certainty about the process is that it was extremely complex, took place over a considerable time, and was influenced at its various stages by different editorial policies (Millard).[66]

Whybray critiques various proposals in favor of the Psalter fitting together, leading him to conclude that the Psalter is not a book with a coherent message. First, Whybray avers that insufficient evidence exists to support the idea that the Psalter is a book with a coherent message. For example, he surveys Mathias Millard's work on the Psalter's composition in which Millard argues for a comprehensive post-cultic

64. Gerstenberger, "Psalter als Buch und als Sammlung," 8.

65. Norman Whybray, *Reading the Psalms as a Book*, JSOTSup 222 (Sheffield: Sheffield Academic, 1996).

66. Whybray, *Reading the Psalms as a Book*, 119.

reading of the Psalter.[67] Whybray concludes that "The main weakness of Millard's argument lies in the fact that the evidences of composition are too sparse and too ambiguous to support his contentions."[68]

Whybray also rejects the position that the Psalter progresses from lament to praise, a theory based on the distribution of lament and praise psalms across the Psalter. The only part of this theory that Whybray affirms is that the Psalter ends with praise.[69] Whybray argues that no single theme dominates Book I (sixteen psalms are not laments).[70] In his view, there is no progression from lament to praise in Books II–IV. Furthermore, Book II does not differ from Book I so as to show progression, and Book III differs from Books I and II because only one psalm is attributed to David (Ps 86).[71] Book IV also does not demonstrate progression, but he admits that Book V contains no lamentations.[72]

A major weakness of Whybray's critique of the lament-to-praise theory—and of the theory itself—is that it relies too heavily on form criticism. The dispersion of lament and praise psalms across the Psalter is itself an unhelpful way to describe the Psalter's progression. Many psalms mix and match genres. Whybray's critique seems to assume psalms consistently express form-critical genre, but that is not the case. For example, Psalm 73 contains elements of wisdom, lament, and praise.

Whybray also rejects a comprehensive torah or wisdom redaction of the Psalter.[73] He claims that the scattered nature of wisdom psalms (e.g., Pss 1, 8, 73, 119) shows that editors did not shape the psalms around the

67. Whybray, *Reading the Psalms as a Book*, 30–31; Matthias Millard, *Die Komposition des Psalters: Ein formgeschichtlicher Ansatz*, Forschungen zum Alten Testament 9 (Tübingen: J.C.B. Mohr, 1994).

68. Whybray, *Reading the Psalms as a Book*, 30.

69. Whybray, *Reading the Psalms as a Book*, 34.

70. Whybray, *Reading the Psalms as a Book*, 34.

71. Whybray, *Reading the Psalms as a Book*, 34.

72. Whybray, *Reading the Psalms as a Book*, 35.

73. James Mays has detailed the ways in which torah psalms influence the shape of the Psalter in "The Place of the Torah-Psalms in the Psalter." Gerald Wilson states, "Without question, the final shape of the Psalter, with its dominant wisdom elements, suggests that the Psalter assumed final form at a time when the sages had the upper hand in restructuring the community's perception of these cultic traditions. The result is a collection of psalms loosened from their 'historical moorings' and allowed to continue to speak with power in an almost unlimited series of circumstances in the lives of the reader." Gerald H. Wilson, "The Shape of the Book of Psalms," *Interpretation* 46 (1992): 138.

theme of torah or wisdom.[74] While Whybray's critique is compelling, he again overvalues the nature of form criticism in regard to the Psalter's possible editorial shape.

Whybray's skepticism also stems from a doubt that Psalm 1 functions as the introduction to the Psalter, as Wilson and others have argued.[75] Whybray admits that Psalm 1 encourages readers to meditate on a written corpus (Torah), but he finds no evidence that the torah in Psalm 1 refers to the Psalter as a new torah.[76] According to Whybray, Psalm 1 leads individuals to follow YHWH's torah, but the psalm itself says nothing about the structure of the Psalms: "It must, indeed, be acknowledged that the opinion, venerable as it is, that Psalm 1 was intended to function as an introduction to the Psalter is no more than an inference and is not susceptible of demonstration."[77] He further asserts that "the notion that the Psalter should have an introduction or 'preface' at all is not based on anything in the text: it is derived, in modern discussion at least, from a prior conviction that the Psalter must have a logical, or at least comprehensive, 'structure.' "[78]

Actually, the argument that Psalm 1 introduces the Psalter is based on something in the text. Further, Psalm 1 and Psalm 2 function together to introduce the Psalter, and numerous lines of evidence verify their introductory nature. First of all, Psalms 1 and 2 are both untitled, yet almost every other psalm in Book I of the Psalter features a title. Additionally, Psalms 1 and 2 share numerous linguistic and thematic connections, showing that they were intended to co-introduce the Psalter. For example, Psalm 1:1 begins with "blessed is the man," while Psalm 2:12 ends with "blessed are those who take refuge in him," enclosing the two psalms within a blessing frame.

Psalms 1 and 2 also introduce common Psalter themes, such as the king, God's kingdom, the wicked and the righteous, and meditation on YHWH's Torah. Whybray claims that Psalm 1 does not comprehensively introduce themes to the whole Psalter, and he further claims that Psalm 2 cannot relate to Psalm 1, partly because Psalm 2 does not contain the wisdom concepts that are in Psalm 1.[79] As to his first claim, his objection

74. Whybray, *Reading the Psalms as a Book*, 38.
75. Wilson, "Shape of the Book of Psalms," 133.
76. Whybray, *Reading the Psalms as a Book*, 40.
77. Whybray, *Reading the Psalms as a Book*, 41.
78. Whybray, *Reading the Psalms as a Book*, 41.
79. Whybray, *Reading the Psalms as a Book*, 40, 80.

makes sense only if Psalms 1 and 2 do not function together as an introduction to the Psalter. But they do function in this way. Together, Psalms 1 and 2 introduce key themes that pervade the whole Psalter.

Regarding his second claim, his reliance on form criticism impedes his analysis of the text. Form criticism clouds his vision to the extent that the phrase "take refuge" in Psalm 2:12 bars the psalm from relating to Psalm 1 because "[t]o take refuge in Yahweh is not a wisdom concept."[80] His reliance on form criticism also leads him to make questionable statements such as "The immediate impression that the reader receives from reading [Psalms 1 and 2] together is one of total dissimilarity."[81] Actually, the opposite is true, and Robert Cole's 2013 work *Psalms 1–2: Gateway to the Psalter* has clearly demonstrated the numerous connections between Psalms 1 and 2.[82]

Furthermore, Whybray calls superscriptions late additions to the Psalter that provide no evidence for a torah-orientated redaction of the Psalter.[83] He admits that superscriptions link groups together but notes that readers have no reason to believe that the superscriptions were added at the time of the Psalter's composition.[84] Consequently, even if superscriptions tie psalms together, he claims that these groups cannot shed light on the meaning of the final form of the Psalter.

An alternative reading of the evidence is that an editor included psalm-groups and used superscriptions to link psalm-groups together intentionally. Whybray rightly claims that we cannot know when superscriptions were added to psalms; yet it seems possible—even probable—that superscriptions were added before the editor shaped the final form of the Psalter. If Wilson is essentially correct in his reading of the Psalms and the Psalter progresses along a coherent trajectory, then readers are almost forced to assume that an editor organized the final form of the Psalter and used superscriptional psalms as an organizing principle because the superscriptions fit into that trajectory so well.

Next, Whybray asserts that there is no eschatological message in the Psalter on the basis of a failed monarchy (see Pss 2, 72, 89):

80. Whybray, *Reading the Psalms as a Book*, 80.

81. Whybray, *Reading the Psalms as a Book*, 80.

82. Cole, *Psalms 1–2*.

83. Whybray, *Reading the Psalms as a Book*, 74.

84. Whybray, *Reading the Psalms as a Book*, 119.

> There is no evidence that redactors set themselves deliberately to document the failure of the Davidic monarchy and to draw theological conclusions from this: rather the contrary. The setbacks experienced by various kings are not concealed; but this did not, apparently, exclude hopes, so frequently expressed in many of the royal psalms, for the fulfilment of God's promise to David in an eschatological future.[85]

While eschatological or messianic elements exist, Whybray sees them as existing within singular psalms, such as Psalm 110.[86] Therefore, the appearance of eschatological psalms does not lead to an eschatological purpose to the Psalter. Whybray also avers that as the appearance of wisdom psalms does not mean there was a systematic wisdom redaction, so also the existence of royal psalms does not mean that there was a systematic royal or eschatological redaction.[87] He concludes that there are at least two different theological influences in the Psalter (wisdom and royal theological influences).[88]

Whybray rightly criticizes Wilson's argument that Psalm 89 chronicles the failure of the Davidic covenant and Books IV and V extol YHWH's kingship. The existence of Davidic psalms in Book V and particularly Psalm 110 clearly articulate hope in a Davidic king after Psalm 89. At the same time, Whybray wrongly concludes that the existence of

85. Whybray, *Reading the Psalms as a Book*, 99. Whybray suggests that reinterpretation of royal psalms in eschatological ways occurs in the mind of the reader, not in the text itself, at least in the case of Psalm 73. Whybray, *Reading the Psalms as a Book*, 42. Roland de Vaux provides an alternative explanation for an eschatological or messianic sense in royal psalms, which I find to be plausible:

> It has been maintained that Ps 2, 72, and 110 were at first royal psalms, and were modified after the Exile in a Messianic sense; but it is very hard to say what the revisions were. It is more reasonable to suppose that these psalms, like Nathan's prophecy and other texts referring to royal Messianism, had a twofold meaning from the moment of their composition: every king of the Davidic line is a figure and a shadow of the ideal king of the future. In fact, none of these kings attained this ideal, but at the moment of enthronement, at each renewal of the Davidic covenant, the same hope was expressed in the belief that one day it would be fulfilled. All these texts, then, are Messianic, for they contain a prophecy and a hope of salvation, which an individual chosen by God will bring to fulfilment. Roland de Vaux, *Ancient Israel: Its Life and Institutions*, trans. John McHugh (London: Darton, Longman, and Todd, 1961), 110.

86. Whybray, *Reading the Psalms as a Book*, 96.

87. Whybray, *Reading the Psalms as a Book*, 99.

88. Whybray, *Reading the Psalms as a Book*, 99.

both wisdom and royal psalms reveal divergent themes in the Psalter. Whybray seems to prioritize psalm-forms (*Gattungen*) as the primary evidence for a possible purpose within the Psalter. I am not convinced, however, that defining psalm-forms is the best or even an appropriate way to uncover the theological purpose of the Psalter. Even assuming for a moment that Whybray rightly focuses on psalm-forms, could not the final editors have included both wisdom and royal psalms into the final form of the Psalter in a complementary way?

For example, Psalm 107 chronicles God's redemption of Israel from exile and ends with a note of wisdom: "Whoever is wise, let this person attend to these things. Let them understand the faithfulness of God" (107:43).[89] Psalms 108, 109, and 110 immediately follow Psalm 107:43, highlighting the faithfulness of God (108:5; 109:21, 26). These psalms are Davidic and focus on the king (Ps 110 is a so-called royal psalm). The wisdom element in Psalm 107 seems to lead naturally into the following three Davidic psalms, which highlight God's faithfulness. Psalm 110, a royal psalm, does not use the term "faithfulness," but it clearly communicates God's faithful fulfillment of his promises to David and Israel. Consequently, the royal and wisdom elements in the Psalter can work together for a common end. Whybray's reading of the Psalms has created an either-or situation, but, in actuality, the Psalter presents a both-and situation.

Moreover, Whybray attacks Wilson's organizational principles for Books I–III (organized by author) and Books IV–V (organized by genre superscriptions):

> The difficulty with such theories—Wilson's is only one of several—is that they paint on a very broad canvas paying insufficient attention to the contents of most individual psalms, whose apparent randomness of arrangement (for instance the mingling of psalms of praise with psalms of lament) remains a stumbling-block for those who fail to find any consistency or overarching structure or plan to the book. Any theory of a coherent pattern ought surely to provide some explanation of the arrangement of the *whole* collection.[90]

89. All translations are mine unless otherwise noted.

90. Whybray, *Reading the Psalms as a Book*, 120.

A number of studies have shown how the placement of individual psalms are intentional since the time of Whybray's publication.[91] Additionally, his evidence of the Psalter's random arrangement is weak: the mingling of praise and lament psalms testifies only to the inadequacies of form criticism for explaining the meaning of the Psalter's final form.

Whybray also finds verbal and thematic links between psalms to be unreliable evidence for a comprehensive redaction of the Psalter. He claims that verbal links are simply common vocabulary that the psalmists drew upon, making them coincidences that occur for non-editorially significant reasons.[92] Thematic links bind psalms into groups, but Whybray alleges that they do not point to a major redaction of the Psalter: "Only if it could be shown that every psalm is linked to its immediate neighbours could such a theory be tenable."[93]

As noted, many studies have uncovered these links, and this makes the theory of a systematic redaction tenable. Additionally, although Hebrew poets may have used a repository of common language, their common repository hardly explains why neighboring psalms share vocabulary that is uncommon elsewhere in the Psalter. For example, יְשִׁימוֹן appears four times in the Psalms, and two of those appearances are in Psalms 106 and 107 (Pss 68:8; 78:40; 106:14; 107:4). The verbal link, coupled with thematic links between Psalms 106 and 107, binds these psalms together. Therefore, similar verbal links can bind other psalms together.

In summary, Whybray finds no evidence for a systematic redaction of the Psalter; he finds no evidence that the Psalter possesses a coherent message. But his criticisms of the introductory nature of Psalm 1, of the Psalter as a book, and of thematic and verbal links binding the Psalms together fail to convince.

---

91. Howard, *Structure of Psalms 93–100*, 90; Mitchell, *Message of the Psalter*; Erich Zenger, "The Composition and Theology of the Fifth Book of Psalms, Psalms 107–145," *JSOT*, no. 80 (1998): 77–102; Cole, *Shape and Message of Book III*; Frank-Lothar Hossfeld and Erich Zenger, *A Commentary on Psalms 51–100*, vol. 2 of *Psalms*, ed. Klaus Baltzer, trans. Linda M. Maloney, Hermeneia (Minneapolis: Fortress, 2005); Jean-Luc Vesco, *Le Psautier de David: Traduit et Commenté*, 2 vols. (Paris: Cerf, 2006); Hossfeld and Zenger, *Commentary on Psalms 101–150*.

92. Whybray, *Reading the Psalms as a Book*, 121.

93. Whybray, *Reading the Psalms as a Book*, 121.

David Willgren

In *The Formation of the "Book" of Psalms,*[94] David Willgren argues that the Psalter is an anthology and not a book. Willgren claims that canonical approaches to the Psalms wrongly define the Psalter as a literary book, and he asserts that the material evidence (e.g., DSS, LXX, etc.) demonstrates that the Psalter's creation process happened over a long period of time and that individual psalms had multiple orders and arrangements in various collections.[95]

The strength of Willgren's argument is its foundational outlook toward material evidence, as it shows how one might conceive of the book of Psalms and how one might think of the Psalter's purpose. Willgren describes the book of Psalms as an anthology, like other ancient collections. As an anthology, the Psalter is like a garden with various flowers and paths that the reader might take.[96] As for the anthology's purpose, Willgren avers that there is no single purpose to the Psalter. Rather, the Psalter is "a multivocal work where each psalm contributes to an ongoing interaction between God and God's people ultimately hoping that the entire creation would one day join the choir in praise of YHWH, for he is good, for his steadfast love endures forever."[97]

Willgren's theoretical critique of the idea of a book is a serviceable contribution to the canonical study of the Psalter. The Psalter is composed of many psalms, and the concept of an anthology may be amenable to this study's approach, if the Psalter could still possess a coherent message as an anthology.

The primary weakness of Willgren's proposal, however, is that it precludes the Psalter from possessing a coherent message. He reasons that

94. David Willgren, *The Formation of the "Book" of Psalms: Reconsidering the Transmission and Canonization of Psalmody in Light of Material Culture and the Poetics of Anthologies*, FAT2 88 (Tübingen, Germany: Mohr Siebeck, 2016).

95. Willgren, *Formation of the "Book" of Psalms*, 131–32.

96. Willgren explains it this way: "Like a garden of flowers, the anthology invites you to enter into it, to look upon flowers of various kinds, to linger the longest by the flowers you enjoy the most, perhaps even encouraging you to pick some into a bouquet." He continues: "While some flowers would be appreciated by many, others are rarely picked. To facilitate the strolling, there would be paths guiding the visitor to various parts of the garden, and providing various ways through it. Signs would describe different kinds of flowers, and fences could sometimes be put up to protect delicate flowers from careless feet." Willgren, *Formation of the "Book" of Psalms*, 28.

97. Willgren, *Formation of the "Book" of Psalms*, 392.

editorial evidence, such as the Psalter's introduction (Pss 1–2),[98] superscriptions,[99] and the concluding Hallel (Pss 146–150), do not lead to the conclusion that the Psalter is an edited work with a unified message.[100] Wilgren's reasoning here stems from his findings that parallel anthologies and the Dead Sea Scrolls developed over time without literary organization. He, thus, infers that the same must be true of the book of Psalms.

A number of brief responses to Willgren's argument are warranted. First, Willgren overplays the importance of other versions than the MT Psalter for understanding the formation of the Psalter. Parallels to the MT Psalter in Qumran provide important historical information, but the Qumran sect was one unique group; what they did with their Psalter manuscripts does not necessarily mean the same thing happened to the MT Psalter.

Additionally, Willgren's manuscript evidence seems to disprove the argument that smaller versions of the Psalter existed and were later combined (e.g., Pss 1–89 combined later with Pss 90–150).[101] He has arrived at this conclusion because he observed various canons and arrangements of psalms in Qumran manuscripts, and he also saw that superscriptions did not bind psalms together. But he seems to overlook the possibility that an editor(s) could have compiled many psalms over a short time to form the MT Psalter on the basis of some organizing principle. That organizing principle, I will shortly suggest, is Israel's history of redemption.

In conclusion, I recognize that the Psalter is not a book like Paul's letter to the Romans or a narrative as seen in the book of Joshua. Instead, the Psalter may well be a text akin to an ancient anthology. Even as an anthology, as I am defining it, the Psalter can express cogent theological ideas and organization. Willgren's monograph certainly advances the discussion concerning the canonical Psalter, but he fails to overturn the reality that the Psalter presents cogent theology and organization in its final form.

98. Willgren, *Formation of the "Book" of Psalms*, 136–71.
99. Willgren, *Formation of the "Book" of Psalms*, 172–95.
100. Willgren, *Formation of the "Book" of Psalms*, 244–83.
101. Willgren, *Formation of the "Book" of Psalms*, 192.

The Psalter Is a Book

The Psalter is a book with a coherent message.[102] The evidence that Wilson proposes for the editing of the Hebrew Psalter has been variously interpreted. But certain core pieces of his evidence lead to the conclusion that reading the Psalter as a book with a coherent message is more plausible than reading the Psalter as a random anthology of psalms.

First, Psalms 1 and 2 introduce Book I of the Psalter and Psalms 146–150 (or perhaps only Ps 150) conclude the Psalter. Psalms 1 and 2 lack superscriptions, even though almost all other psalms contain superscriptions in Book I. They introduce themes such as meditating on the Torah and walking in the path of righteousness rather than in the path of wickedness. They also introduce the themes of human happiness, the nations, Messiah, YHWH as King, and Zion.

Psalms 146–150 conclude the Psalter with praise. Psalm 150 is unique, according to Brueggemann, because it completely lacks motivation and communicates "unfettered praise."[103] Psalms 1–2 and Psalms 146–150 respectively introduce and conclude the Psalter. Their existence lends credence to Brueggeman's proposal that the Psalter progresses from obedience (Ps 1) to praise (Ps 150).

Wilson also observes that authorial superscriptions organize Books I–III, while genre superscriptions organize Books IV–V. I would add the caveat that this is a general pattern, and even Book V has a number of authorial designations (e.g., Pss 108–110; 138–145). The authorial superscriptions lead to certain conclusions about the books of the Psalter. Books I–III tend to focus on the Monarchy, as they are attributed to authors who lived during the Monarchy (e.g., David, Asaph, the Sons of Korah). Book IV looks to the past by its focus on Moses. For example, Psalm 90 is the only psalm written by Moses (90:1), and before Psalm 90 only Psalm 77:21 mentions Moses's name. But in Book IV of the Psalms (Pss 90–106), his name is mentioned seven times (90:1; 99:6; 103:7; 105:26; 106:16, 23, 32).[104] Book V organizes itself around the following themes: David (Pss 108–110; 138–145), the exodus (Pss 111–118; 120–134), and the Torah (Ps 119).

---

102. By "book," again, I mean a coherent literary work that aims to communicate a message.

103. Brueggemann, "Bounded by Obedience and Praise," 67.

104. Wilson, *The Editing of the Hebrew Psalter*, 187.

Consequently, the Psalter relies on a general historical and thematic structure. More specifically, the Psalter structures itself around Israel's history. Books I–III chronicle the Monarchy. Contrary to Wilson's claims, Psalm 89 does not signal the failure of the Davidic covenant, and Book IV does not point to YHWH as king on the basis of the failed Davidic covenant.[105] Book IV does shy away from a direct tie to the monarchical period of Israel's history, and Psalm 106 is clearly placed within the time-frame of the exile (106:47). It is reasonable to assume, then, that the Mosaic influence in Book IV aims to encourage exilic readers to obey and meditate on the Torah day and night while they await their return to the land (Jer 25:11–12; 29:10).[106]

The particular theories of Wilson, Brueggemann, Mitchell, and Snearly (among others) have merit. But some of their positions are more specific than the editorial evidence of the Psalter allows for. Gerstenberger, Whybray, and Willgren provide a counterbalance to these theories of the Psalter's message, but they have not overturned the weight of evidence that the Psalter is a book with a coherent message.

THE PSALTER IN SEQUENCE

If the Psalter is a book, should it be read in sequence like other books? One's position on form criticism partly influences the answer to this question. Brueggemann agrees that the Psalter is a book with a beginning and an end, moving from obedience to praise. He reads the Psalter along form-critical lines, however, meaning that its sequence is not of prime importance when understanding the Psalter's meaning. Although Brueggemann and William Bellinger in their commentary will "on occasion explore a particular psalm's place in the Psalter as a whole or its place in a collection of psalms,"[107] this approach is not the norm for them.

105. For a recent canonical approach that sees Book IV as a response to the failed monarchy chronicled in Book III and Psalm 89, see Michael G. McKelvey, *Moses, David and the High Kingship of Yahweh: A Canonical Study of Book IV of the Psalter* (Piscataway, NJ: Gorgias, 2014).

106. James Borger studies Moses in Book IV and concludes that "The cumulative effect of each psalm that refers to Moses is to create an overwhelming awareness of Israel's sin, need for forgiveness, and Moses' intercessory role in the past." James Todd Borger, "Moses in the Fourth Book of the Psalter" (PhD diss., Southern Baptist Theological Seminary, 2002), 148. Borger's conclusion seems to fit into the paradigm that I have proposed above. Through Israel's forgiveness, the people would enter into the Promised Land.

107. Brueggemann and Bellinger, *Psalms*, 8.

Brueggemann and others who concur with him read the Psalms as discrete texts from various times and places. The dispersion of various psalm-forms, whether lament or praise, matters little because the psalms recount "voices of faith in the actual life of the believing community."[108] The psalms are theological witnesses of a pattern of orientation, disorientation, and a new orientation.[109] Other than the introduction and conclusion of the Psalter, the primary organizing principle of the Psalter is not one of sequence but of theological ideas.

Like Whybray, Brueggemann has embraced form criticism as a primary way to read and understand the Psalter. Form critics, however, overlook that the Psalter itself has various genres, which the superscriptions identify. Psalms 56–60, for example, are *miktamim*, and Psalms 108–110 are *mizmorim*. The canonical Psalter itself has its own genres, and the genres unite sequential psalms into groups (e.g., Pss 3–6). In turn, groups of psalms develop ideas. Psalms 108–110 are all Davidic *mizmorim*, and they develop the idea of God's reign. Moreover, Psalm 108 highlights God's victory over the nations, Psalm 109 underscores the struggle of the king of God's kingdom, and Psalm 110 demonstrates how YHWH and a royal figure will bring about the kingdom.

If the Psalter is a book and if the canonical genres have priority over the form-critical genres, then the Psalter should be read in sequence.[110] The recent commentaries by Jean-Luc Vesco and by Frank Lothar Hossfeld and Erich Zenger have provided exegetical evidence that the Psalms should be read sequentially.[111] Their commentaries show that the editors of the final form of the Psalter intended the Psalms to be read in order. Furthermore, reading the Psalms in other ways will mislead interpreters of the Psalter, as their exegesis demonstrates.

---

108. Walter Brueggemann, *The Message of the Psalms: A Theological Commentary* (Minneapolis: Augsburg, 1984), 10.

109. Walter Brueggemann, *Spirituality of the Psalms* (Minneapolis: Fortress, 2002), x.

110. The canonical genres to which I refer are ones such as *mizmorim, miktamim*, and *tifalloth*, which are defined in the superscriptions of individual psalms. During a conversation on November 10, 2017, Peter Gentry referred to 1 Chr 16:4 as a text that defines three genres of psalms. The passage reads, "He appointed some of the Levites to minister before the ark of the LORD, to extol (וּלְהַזְכִּיר), thank (וּלְהוֹדוֹת), and praise (וּלְהַלֵּל) the LORD" (NIV). These three categories provide an overarching description of the psalms. Nevertheless, readers should first define a psalm by its own designation within its superscription.

111. Vesco, *Psautier de David*; Hossfeld and Zenger, *Commentary on Psalms 51–100*; Hossfeld and Zenger, *Commentary on Psalms 101–150*.

The notion of sequence is crucial to the present study. As I will argue, Psalm 108 is intended to be read after Psalms 57 and 60. Psalm 108's conspicuous differences from Psalms 57 and 60 and its canonical location signal to the reader that Psalm 108 typologically speaks of a future king and kingdom.

One possible objection to my argument is that readers may not have picked up on the differences between Psalm 108 and Psalms 57 and 60. In answer to this objection, I point out that some readers (or hearers) would have been able to notice the differences because the Psalter invites hearers to memorize it. Indeed, ancient readers and hearers would have memorized the Psalter in its canonical sequence.

Gordon Wenham's recent research into the Psalter is worthy of consideration at this juncture. He argues that "the Psalter is a sacred text that is intended to be memorized."[112] He draws on the earlier works of David Carr[113] and Paul Griffiths.[114] Both Carr and Griffiths show how ancient texts were meant to be memorized rather than merely to be read. In particular, Carr argues that literacy in the ancient world involved the mastery of oral-written texts.[115] And that mastery involved knowing the text by heart. The Bible's own witness is that readers ought to bind words to their hearts (Deut 11:8; Prov 3:3; 6:21; 7:3; cf. Exod 13:9). Psalm 1 enjoins readers to meditate on God's Torah day and night (Ps 1:2), further suggesting that readers would have memorized ancient texts.

Wenham outlines three features of the Psalter that allow for ease of memorization: its poetic form, its musical nature, and its thematic structure.[116] Readers and hearers would thus memorize the poetic psalms as they sang them and grasp the overall structure of the Psalter through its thematic structures.

If the Psalter is a work to be memorized and many hearers of the Psalter memorized it, then the probability further increases that readers would read the Psalms in sequence and observe the differences between Psalm 108 and Psalms 57 and 60.

---

112. Gordon J. Wenham, *Psalms as Torah: Reading Biblical Song Ethically* (Grand Rapids: Baker Academic, 2012), 41.

113. David M. Carr, *Writing on the Tablet of the Heart: Origins of Scripture and Literature* (New York: Oxford University Press, 2015).

114. Paul J. Griffiths, *Religious Reading: The Place of Reading in the Practice of Religion* (New York: Oxford University Press, 1999).

115. Carr, *Writing on the Tablet*, 13.

116. Wenham, *Psalms as Torah*, 49–50.

THE PSALTER AS REDEMPTIVE-HISTORY

The Psalter recalls Israel's redemptive history.[117] As noted above, Books I–III highlight the monarchical period of Israel's history, and Books IV–V relate to the exilic and post-exilic period. For example, 95 percent of psalms in Book I are attributed to David by their superscription, 58 percent in Book II, 6 percent in Book III, 12 percent in Book IV, and 32 percent in Book V.[118] This distribution is logical if Books I and II focus on David's reign, while Book III highlights a later point in the kingdom.[119] Internal evidence corroborates these observations. Book II ends with an explicit statement: "The prayers of David, the Son of Jesse, are concluded" (Ps 72:20 ESV); Psalm 72 concludes Book II with a psalm authored by Solomon; and Book III ends with a psalm of Ethan the Ezrahite (Ps 89), a contemporary of Solomon (1 Kgs 4:31). The effect of these psalms (Pss 72 and 89) highlights how Books I–III connect with the history of Israel.

Only two psalms in Book IV are Davidic (Pss 101 and 103), which would make sense if these psalms correspond to Israel's exilic era.[120] The final psalm of Book IV provides evidence for this observation, because the psalm explicitly calls for rescue from exile: "Save us, O Lord our God, and gather us from among the nations, that we may give thanks to your holy name and glory in your praise" (106:47 ESV). The next psalm, which opens Book V, celebrates God's salvation of Israel by gathering Israel from among the nations (Ps 107:2–3). The effect of Psalm 107's

---

117. Robert Wallace speaks of the "narrative impulse" embedded within the Psalter: "The canonical shape of the Psalter provides a hermeneutical setting in which one can productively read Book IV. While according to traditional form-critical categories the Psalter is not classified as 'narrative,' a narrative impulse exists within the Psalter, and Book IV is a part of that story." Wallace, *The Narrative Effect of Book IV*, 1. Other scholars also speak of the Psalter as a narrative (or having a narrative structure). See Egbert Ballhorn, *Zum Telos des Psalters: Der Textzusammenhang des Vierten und Fünften Psalmenbuches (Ps 90–150)*, BBB 138 (Berlin: Philo, 2004), 30, 32; Snearly, *Return of The King*, 1.

118. DeClaissé-Walford, Jacobson, and Tanner, *Psalms*, 27–28.

119. Pss 73–83 are Psalms of Asaph. David appointed Asaph to be a levitical singer (1 Chr 6:39); 2 Chr 5:12 indicates that Asaph participated in the dedication of Solomon's temple. Book III's initial author (Asaph) overlaps with both David's reign and Solomon's reign. It may be significant that Ps 72 is a psalm of Solomon that precedes the Asaphite collection (Pss 73–83).

120. Obviously the presence of Davidic psalms cannot be the only evidence that the Psalter follows a redemptive-historical trajectory. Davidic psalms appear even in Book V of the Psalter. Consequently, the distribution of authors in the five books of the Psalms can only be one form of evidence.

celebration is to situate Psalm 107 in a post-exilic setting. Furthermore, Psalms 108–110 are attributed to David and speak of God's victory and establishment of Israel. This hopeful perspective corresponds to a post-exilic setting as many Israelites had set their hope on God's saving action through a Davidic king (cf. Zech 12:7–9).

The historical specificity of certain psalms also suggests that Israel's redemptive-history functions as an organizing principle behind the Psalter's composition. Individual psalms point to specific historical events apart from which a psalm would not make sense. For example, Psalm 51's superscription relates the psalm to David's confrontation with Nathan over his affair with Bathsheba. If that superscription were not present, the psalm would lose its historical specificity. Psalm 57's superscription also connects the psalm to Israel's history, to a time when David fled from Saul and hid in a cave (1 Sam 24, 26). In Psalm 57, the superscription also presents the curious phrase "do not destroy," and the same phrase appears in 1 Samuel 26:9 in which David forbids Abishai from destroying God's anointed, Saul.[121] Psalm 57 clearly ties itself to Israel's history of redemption by its superscription.

Other psalms also link to Israel's history by their content rather than their superscriptions. For example, Psalm 106:47 concludes the psalm with a cry to God to gather Israel from the nations. In short, the entire psalm is set within the timeframe of Israel's exile and the psalmist's hope for redemption. Redemption comes to Israel in part as the books of Ezra and Nehemiah illustrate. Psalm 107 highlights the fullness of that redemption by praising God because he gathered Israel from the nations and redeemed Israel (107:1–3).

Not every psalm has a superscription or a direct reference to Israel's redemptive history within the psalm. In these cases, a psalm may be part of a group with a theme that fits into the redemptive-historical framework of the Psalter. For example, as a unit Psalms 96–99 praise God who reigns. God's reign seems particularly fitting in a context in which the monarchy has gone into decline (Ps 89) and the people are in exile (Ps 106).

---

121. For more on Ps 57's relationship to 1 Sam, see Gary A. Anderson, "King David and the Psalms of Imprecation," in *The Harp of Prophecy: Early Christian Interpretation of the Psalms*, ed. Brian E. Daley and Paul R. Kolbet (Notre Dame, IN: University of Notre Dame Press, 2015), 34–39.

At the same time, some psalms resist any neat connection to adjacent psalms or psalm-groups so that they do not fit neatly into a comprehensive message, such as Wilson or Mitchell proposed. Due to this fact, I do not subscribe to a particular reading of the Psalter that fits every psalm into a system. I do, however, subscribe to a reading that sees a general redemptive-historical pattern to the Psalms: Books I–III relate to the Monarchy, Book IV to the exile, and Book V to a post-exilic period.

The preceding observations concerning the distribution of Davidic psalms along with internal cues within the Psalter provide a plausible justification for reading the Psalter sequentially and along redemptive-historical lines as an editorially-shaped book. In chapters 3, 4, and 5 these methodological premises guide my interpretation of Psalm 108 in its canonical context.

2

History of Interpretation

This study interprets Psalm 108 by investigating how the psalm cites earlier Scripture and functions within its *Sitz im Literatur*. Consequently, this chapter sketches out Psalm 108's history of interpretation to demonstrate the need for this research project.

HISTORY OF INTERPRETATION

In the past, scholars often relegated Psalm 108 to being a historical oddity and did not directly interpret the psalm. They pointed to their earlier discussions of Psalms 57 and 60 instead of commenting directly on Psalm 108. Many contemporary scholars, however, interpret Psalm 108 as a discrete psalm with an independent meaning. Those who practice a canonical approach to the Psalms read Psalm 108 as a discrete psalm that contributes to the meaning of the whole Psalter.

PSALTER SCHOLARSHIP

George Phillips posits that the compiler of Psalm 108 started with Psalm 60. He then removed portions of Psalm 60 and inserted portions of Psalm 57, so that Psalm 108 would be appropriate for giving thanks over a victory.[1] Phillips does not comment on the text of Psalm 108, presumably because he sees the psalm as communicating the same meaning as Psalms 57 and 60. When mentioning the variants between Psalm 108 and the two earlier psalms, he tries to smooth out the differences. For example, he notes how "from above the heavens" in Psalm 108:5 and "unto the heavens" in Psalm 57:11 convey "the same sense."[2] Phillips does not read Psalm 108 as in independent psalm nor does he read the psalm within its canonical context.

1. George Phillips, *The Psalms in Hebrew: With a Critical, Exegetical, and Philological Commentary*, vol. 2 (London: John W. Parker, 1846), 400.

2. Phillips, *Psalms in Hebrew*, 401.

Joseph Addison Alexander argues that David combined Psalms 57 and 60 so that Psalm 108 would "be the basis of a trilogy (Ps. cviii—cx), adapted to the use of the church at a period posterior to the date of Ps. lvii. and lx."[3] In other words, David wrote Psalm 108 to preface Psalms 109 and 110. Alexander does not, however, explain why David combined Psalms 57 and 60 for this purpose.

Further, Alexander does not interpret Psalm 108 as he does other psalms but only points out the variants between Psalm 108 and Psalms 57 and 60. At two points, he discovers interpretive value in the variants. Psalm 108:5 inserts "from above" in place of "unto" (Ps 57:11). According to Alexander, the change in Psalm 108 suggests that God's mercy descends on mankind.[4] Furthermore, the addition of "I will shout aloud" in Psalm 108:10 indicates an "expression of triumph over a conquered enemy."[5] Alexander does not tease out the significance of David's expression of triumph in Psalm 108.[6]

Franz Delitszch argues that David compiled Psalm 108 from his earlier two psalms (Pss 57 and 60).[7] As a consequence, he sees Psalm 108 as a new psalm and interprets it as such. He also defines Psalm 108's structure in connection with Psalms 57 and 60. For Delitszch, Psalm 108 divides into two parts: 108:2–6 and 108:7–14.[8] This division corresponds to the two parts of the psalm, which were taken from Psalms 57 and 60. He also reads Psalm 108 within its canonical context. According to Delitszch, the phrase "I will praise you" in Psalm 108:4 echoes הדוּ from Psalm 107:1.[9] Although he does not interpret Psalm 108 as part of the story that the Psalter narrates, his canonical instinct is a precursor to canonical scholarship of the Psalter, which is discussed below.

J. J. Stewart Perowne argues that Psalm 108 is Davidic because it uses earlier Davidic psalms.[10] "But," he writes, "there is no reason for con-

3. J. A. Alexander, *The Psalms: Translated and Explained*, 3 vols. (New York: Baker and Scribner, 1850), 3:90.

4. Alexander, *Psalms*, 3:90.

5. Alexander, *Psalms*, 3:91.

6. In Ps 60:10, the imperative form of "shout aloud" is used. Alexander discusses Psalm 60:10 in *Psalms*, 2:70–71.

7. F. Delitzsch, *Psalms*, vol. 5 of C. F. Keil and F. Delitzsch, *Commentary on the Old Testament* (Peabody, MA: Hendrickson, 2006), 684.

8. Delitzsch, *Psalms*, 684.

9. Delitzsch, *Psalms*, 683.

10. J. J. Stewart Perowne, *The Book of Psalms: A New Translation with Introductions and Notes*, 3rd London ed., vol. 2 (Andover, MA: Warren F. Draper, 1879), 272–73.

cluding that these fragments were thus united by David himself."[11] As evidence, he cites the change between Psalm 108:10 and Psalm 60:10. In Psalm 108, the psalmist shouts in triumph over his enemies. In Psalm 60, the psalmist commands Philistia to shout. Accordingly, Perowne suggests that some later poet wrote Psalm 108 to celebrate a victory over Edom or Philistia.[12] When it comes to commenting on the text, Perowne translates the psalm but makes minimal comments. Instead, he instructs readers to refer to his earlier comments on Psalms 57 and 60.[13]

W. F. Cobb introduces, translates, and interprets the Psalms. When he comes to Psalm 108, however, he declines to comment. He translates Psalm 108 but tells readers to refer back to the portions of Psalms 57 and 60 that compose Psalm 108.[14] For Cobb, Psalm 108 repeats parts of the two earlier psalms and does not have an independent meaning apart from them.

Sigmund Mowinckel provides a historical rationale for the composition of Psalm 108. In his understanding, Psalm 60 belongs to the Davidic era, and David fulfills the words of that psalm's oracle by conquering Moab and Edom (cf. Ps 60:8–10).[15] In light of this fulfillment, the oracle becomes a promise for the future; God would again save David's house and Israel as he had in the past.[16] He cites appeals to Davidic promises as evidence for why the oracle would have persisted in the memory of Israel (See Pss 89:20–38 and 132:11–12).[17] The oracle, present in Psalm 60, became a word of promise to David, a word of future salvation. When a similar trial occurred later in the history of Israel, the oracle once again appeared in Psalm 108 (cf. Ps 108:8–10). Mowinckel suggests that this might have occurred during the reign of Jehoram (see 2 Kgs 8:20–22).[18] While Mowinckel's historical reconstruction is somewhat persuasive, he fails to deal with the claim of Davidic authorship that Psalm 108

---

11. Perowne, *The Book of Psalms*, 273.

12. Perowne, *The Book of Psalms*, 273.

13. Perowne, *The Book of Psalms*, 273.

14. W. F. Cobb, *The Book of Psalms: With Introduction and Notes* (London: Methuen, 1905), 312.

15. Sigmund Mowinckel, *Psalm Studies*, trans. Mark E. Biddle, History of Biblical Studies (Atlanta: Society of Biblical Literature, 2014), 565. This is a translation of Mowinckel's *Psalmenstudien*, which was originally published in 1921–1924.

16. Mowinckel, *Psalm Studies*, 565–66.

17. Mowinckel, *Psalm Studies*, 566.

18. Mowinckel, *Psalm Studies*, 567, 561.

makes.[19] David could have composed Psalm 108 after Psalm 60, citing God's earlier oracle as a promise of victory in a typological manner.

Mowinckel further comments on Psalm 108. He defines Psalm 108 as a psalm of national lament.[20] The earlier laments (Pss 57 and 60) become communal in Psalm 108. He notes, for example, that "[t]he suffering supplicant in Ps 57 has become reinterpreted in terms of a people suffering the attack of some enemy and the poison-spewing sorcerers in terms of this enemy."[21] Undoubtedly, Mowinckel has keenly observed how Psalm 108 focuses on the community rather than on the individual. One does not, however, have to embrace Mowinckel's form-critical definitions to appreciate his contribution to understanding the national focus in Psalm 108. Indeed, Psalm 108 speaks to a national victory in which Israel possesses the kingdom promised to her (Ps 108:8–10).

Even though Mowinckel advocated the cult-functional approach to the Psalter, he nevertheless interprets Psalm 108 as a discrete psalm. As this history of interpretation shows, many of Mowinckel's contemporaries who adopted the cult-functional approach ignored the discrete meaning of Psalm 108 by not commenting on the psalm and pointing readers back to their comments on Psalms 57 and 60.

Bernard Duhm calls Psalm 108 a new psalm (*neuer Psalm*) with its own superscription.[22] Duhm is unsure, however, of the psalm's function. He suggests that Psalm 108 was composed for some liturgical purpose (*zu irgend einem liturgischen Zweck*) but does not specify what that purpose is.[23] He refrains from commenting on Psalm 108, presumably because one can read his earlier comments on Psalms 57 and 60.

One reason why many commentators read Psalm 108 as a liturgical composition and simply refer readers back to their comments on Psalms 57 and 60 is the rise of the historical-critical method, especially the form-critical method of Hermann Gunkel. Gunkel himself sparingly comments on double psalms like Psalm 108.[24] Erich Zenger notes that

19. The superscription of Ps 108 identifies David as its author.

20. Mowinckel, *Psalm Studies*, 566.

21. Mowinckel, *Psalm Studies*, 566.

22. D. Bernhard Duhm, *Die Psalmen*, 2nd ed., Kurzer Hand-kommentar zum Alten Testament 14 (Tübingen, DE: Mohr, 1922), 393.

23. Duhm, *Psalmen*, 393.

24. Hermann Gunkel, *Die Psalmen: Übersetzt und erklärt*, 4th ed., Handkommentar zum Alten Testament 2 (Göttingen, Germany: Vandenhoeck & Ruprecht, 1926), 231–35, 300, 474–75.

"Regarding Psalm 14, Gunkel says simply, 'cf. Ps. 53' "[25] Gunkel provides more material in his notes on Psalm 108, although he still insufficiently interprets it, as Zenger recounts:

> At least Psalm 108 contains sixteen lines of explanation. The form-historical axioms, however, prevent Gunkel from positively appreciating this psalm, which is in fact composed, as a new, independent text. One can literally feel the contempt of the form-loving Gunkel for such compositions when he writes in the commentary on Psalm 108, among other things, "The song is to be understood as a revision of Psalm 60, which someone wanted to use again on some occasion for a worship-performance. To this end, the author has replaced the wailing lamentation (60:3–6) with a hymn-like song of thanksgiving (108:2–6): the mood or time of the reviser makes him feel that a confident song of thanksgiving is more suitable than lamentation at this point. But he made the work very easy for himself by not writing the missing song of thanksgiving himself, but by simply taking over Psalm 60 at a very unsuitable point for the new psalm." A work that, in terms of form-criticism, is so miserable naturally can only be dated very late: "The age of revision is to be reckoned at the end of Psalm composition."[26]

25. My translation of "Zu Ps 14 heißt es bei Gunkel einfach: 'vgl. Ps.53.' " Erich Zenger, "Psalmenexegese und Psalterexegese: eine Forschungsskizze," in *The Composition of the Book of Psalms*, ed. Erich Zenger, Bibliotheca Ephemeridum Theologicarum Lovaniensium 238 (Leuven, Belgium: Uitgeverij Peeters, 2010), 22.

26. My translation of "Ps 108 erhält immerhin 16 Zeilen Erläuterung. Allerdings hindern die gattungsgeschichtlichen Axiome Gunkel daran, diesen in der Tat zusammengesetzten Psalm als eigenen, neuen Text positiv zu würdigen. Man spürt buchstäblich die Geringschätzung des Gattungliebhabers Gunkel gegenüber derartigen Kompositionen, wenn er im Kommentar zu Ps 108 u.a. schreibt: 'Das Lied ist als eine Überarbeitung von Ps. 60 zu verstehen, den man bei irgend einer Gelegenheit für eine gottesdienstliche Aufführung aufs neue gebrauchen wollte. Zu diesem Zwecke hat der Verfasser das jammernde Klagelied 60:3–6 durch ein hymnisches Danklied 108:2–6 ersetzt: die Gemütsart oder die Zeitlage des Überarbeiters liessen ihn ein 'getrostes' Danklied passander als ein Klagelied an dieser Stelle empfinden. Er hat sich aber die Arbeit recht leicht gemacht, indem er has vermißte Danklied nicht selber dichtete, sondern einfach Ps. 60 an einer für den neuen Psalm sehr unpassenden Stelle mit übernommen hat.' Eine in gattungsgesichichtlicher Hinsicht so miserable Arbeit kann dann natürlich nur sehr spät datiert werden: 'Das Zeitalter der Überarbeitung ist am Ende der Psalmendichtung zu denken.' " Zenger, "Psalmenexegese und Psalterexegese: eine Forschungsskizze," 22–23.

According to Gunkel, the reviser took earlier material (Ps 60) and placed it in the middle of another song without much thought. It simply made better sense to the reviser to use a hymn of thanksgiving, because of his historical experience. On Gunkel's view, the reviser did not intentionally change Psalm 60 for a specific reason in Psalm 108.

T. E. Bird is rather muted in his commentary on Psalm 108. He makes a few observations about how Psalm 108 was edited.[27] He also notes certain textual features, such as the uses of *Elohim* and the single use of *YHWH* in Psalm 108:4. He adduces that the substitution is "obviously editorial" because *YHWH* replaces *Adonai*.[28] He does not, however, interpret the psalm. Instead, he expects readers to study his comments on Psalms 57 and 60.

Eduard König organizes his commentary by categorizing individual psalms rather than by commenting on them in the canonical order of the Psalter. Interestingly, he interprets Psalm 108 in two sections of his commentary. In a section that discusses patient suffering, König comments on Psalm 108:2–6.[29] In another section regarding prayers for God to act in history, he cites Psalm 108:7–14.[30] König reads Psalm 108 primarily as a parallel text to Psalms 57 and 60, providing little discussion of Psalm 108. Furthermore, he does not read Psalm 108 (nor any other psalms) as part of the redemptive-historical story of the Psalter.

W. E. Barnes argues that an editor intentionally created Psalm 108 out of Psalms 57 and 60. According to Barnes, the editor did so because he confronted a situation similar to the situation in Psalm 60.[31] He appears to assume that the editor had Psalm 60 in mind first but had to add Psalm 57 to supplement Psalm 60. The result was Psalm 108. In this new psalm, Barnes finds echoes to the exodus, and these echoes demonstrate that the editor of Psalm 108 pleads for salvation in a way that is similar

---

27. T. E. Bird, *A Commentary on the Psalms*, vol. 2 (London: Burns Oates & Washbourne, 1927), 226–27.

28. Bird, *Commentary on the Psalms*, 228.

29. Eduard König, *Die Psalmen: Eingeleitet, übersetzt und erklärt* (Gütersloh, Germany: C. Bertelsmann, 1927), 536–37.

30. König, *Psalmen*, 349.

31. W. E. Barnes, *The Psalms with Introduction and Notes*, vol. 2 (London: Methuen, 1931), 525.

to the exodus.[32] Instead of commenting on Psalm 108, Barnes points readers back to Psalms 57 and 60 for his notes.[33]

W. O. E. Oesterley does not comment on Psalm 108 but refers to his earlier comments on Psalms 57 and 60.[34] For Oesterley, Psalm 108 does not require an independent interpretation. He even updates the text of Psalm 108 by inserting phrases from Psalm 57.[35] By updating Psalm 108 with Psalm 57, Oesterley gives priority to the earlier psalm. Further, He does not find exegetical or theological value in the variants between Psalm 108 and the earlier two psalms with one exception. Psalm 108:4 uses the divine name YHWH, and this signals to Oesterley that Psalm 108 belonged to a psalm-group that used the divine name YHWH and not only Elohim.[36]

Artur Weiser notes, "Psalm 108 was probably compiled for liturgical purposes from ancient cultic traditions also used in Ps. 57.7–11 and in Ps. 60.5–12 (cf. the exposition of Pss. 57 and 60, especially that of Ps. 60.6–8)."[37] For Weiser, referring back to his comments on Psalms 57 and 60 is sufficient to understand Psalm 108. The psalm has no independent meaning, nor does it influence its canonical location (i.e., it is not related to Pss 107 and 109). Weiser does not translate Psalm 108 nor provide exegesis of it.

Like Weiser, Edward J. Kissane does not translate nor comment on Psalm 108. Kissane does, however, define Psalm 108 as a liturgical composition and points readers to his earlier comments on Psalms 57 and 60: "This psalm is a liturgical composition made up of fragments of two earlier psalms, namely, Ps. 57:8–12 and Ps. 60:7–14. For the commentary see these psalms."[38] Kissane is content to define Psalm 108 with cult-functional terms. He does not interpret the psalm as a unique contribution to the Psalter.

32. Barnes, *The Psalms with Introduction and Notes*, 525.

33. Barnes, *The Psalms with Introduction and Notes*, 525.

34. W. O. E. Oesterley, *The Psalms: Translated with Text-Critical and Exegetical Notes*, vol. 2 (London: Society for Promoting Christian Knowledge, 1939), 457.

35. Oesterley, *Psalms*, 457.

36. Oesterley, *Psalms*, 457.

37. Artur Weiser, *The Psalms: A Commentary*, trans. Herbert Hartwell, 5th ed., Old Testament Library (London: SCM, 1962), 688.

38. Edward J. Kissane, *The Book of Psalms: Translated from a Critically Revised Hebrew Text with a Commentary* (Dublin: Browne and Nolan, 1964), 500.

Joachim Becker claims that the author of Psalm 108 compiled his psalm from Psalms 57 and 60 in an odd whimsical way (*in wunderlicher Weise*).[39] Even so, Becker sees consistency in the psalm as it moves from an individual thanksgiving (108:2–6) to a communal lament (108:7–14).[40] Furthermore, Becker argues that God's glorious theophany in Psalm 108:7 leads to the salvation of the people and that this statement of glory explains why the author included Psalm 60 in his composition.[41] Psalm 108:7 (or Ps 60:7) is the connecting glue that ties Psalm 60 to Psalm 57 and thus creates Psalm 108. Becker uses form-critical categories to study the psalm, yet he interprets it as a new composition. Furthermore, Becker reads Psalm 108 as a theological work, as an eschatological poem.[42]

Louis Jacquet argues that Psalm 108 is a liturgical composition that was created to encourage the faithful.[43] A group of Israelites, in Jacquet's view, used earlier Davidic material to compose a new text.[44] The cult-functional approach of Jacquet leads him to posit a historical reconstruction for Psalm 108. His reconstruction, however, lacks concrete evidence and ignores the claim of Davidic authorship found in Psalm 108's superscription. On the positive side, however, Jacquet laments how commentators simply point back to Psalms 57 and 60 to interpret Psalm 108, and he exegetes the psalm.[45]

In his comments on Psalm 108, Hans-Joachim Kraus directs readers to Psalms 57 and 60: "For details, cf. the commentary on Psalm 57 and Psalm 60."[46] Kraus's comments on Psalm 108 comprise only two paragraphs of discussion, which focus on the form of the psalm. Agreeing with Schmidt, Kraus finds it "almost impossible" to explain the significance of Psalm 108's combination of Psalms 57 and 60.[47] In this way, Kraus leaves uncertain the function of the psalm, pointing readers to his earlier comments: "The interpretation of individual verses need not

39. Joachim Becker, *Israel deutet seine Psalmen: Urform und Neuinterpretation in den Psalmen*, SBS 18 (Stuttgart: Verlag Katholisches Bibelwerk, 1967), 65.

40. Becker, *Israel deutet seine Psalmen*, 66.

41. Becker, *Israel deutet seine Psalmen*, 67.

42. Becker, *Israel deutet seine Psalmen*, 66–67.

43. Louis Jacquet, *Les Psaumes et le Coeur de l'Homme: Etude Textuelle, Littéraire et Doctrinale* (Gembloux, Belgium: Duculot, 1979), 78.

44. Jacquet, *Les Psaumes et le Coeur*, 178.

45. Jacquet, *Les Psaumes et le Coeur*, 178.

46. Kraus, *Psalms 60–150*, 333.

47. Kraus, *Psalms 60–150*, 333.

be repeated here."[48] Kraus represents an older generation of traditional historical criticism. For him, it is sufficient to point back to Psalms 57 and 60 without commenting directly on Psalm 108.

Steve Cook studies apocalypticism in the Psalter and interprets Psalm 108 within this framework. According to Cook, Israel's eschatological promises did not come to pass. As a consequence, groups of Israelites became apocalyptic in their outlook. One group, argues Cook, wrote Psalm 108.[49]

While Cook creatively interprets Psalm 108, he misses the mark. Psalm 108 is not an apocalyptic psalm. Rather, Psalm 108 prophetically and typologically looks toward an eschatological fulfillment. Additionally, the superscription assigns Davidic authorship to the psalm. For that reason, one should interpret Psalm 108 as a Davidic psalm, not as a psalm spawned from an apocalyptic school.[50] Nevertheless, Cook's recognition of Psalm 108's so-called apocalyptic nature indirectly contributes to this book's argument that Psalm 108 is an eschatological text. Cook recognizes the future-orientation of this psalm, although he wrongly assumes that Psalm 108 is apocalyptic and does not speak of a future fulfillment of God's eschatological promises to David.

The preceding survey of scholarship on Psalm 108 has shown that many interpreters read Psalm 108 as a liturgical text whose meaning is no different than that of Psalms 57 and 60. Furthermore, they read Psalm 108 without recourse to its canonical context. Some commentators, however, exegete Psalm 108 and relate it to its canonical context albeit in a minimal way.

RECENT PSALTER SCHOLARSHIP

Recent scholarship generally reads Psalm 108 as a discrete psalm with a meaning that is independent of Psalms 57 and 60. For example, Leslie Allen sees Psalm 108 "as a composition in its own right"[51] and notes that "[t]he combination of earlier psalms illustrates the vitality of older Scriptures as they were appropriated and applied to new situations

48. Kraus, *Psalms 60–150*, 334.

49. Stephen L. Cook, "Apocalypticism and the Psalter," *Zeitschrift für die alttestamentliche Wissenschaft* 104, no. 1 (1992): 91.

50. Even if one doubts their historicity, the psalm superscriptions provide vital clues to canonical meaning of individual psalms. Ch. 3 provides significant detail on superscriptions and especially the superscription of Ps 108.

51. Allen, *Psalms 101–150*, 94.

in the experience of God's people."[52] Indeed, he appears to engage in Psalter-exegesis:[53] "The present task is to concentrate upon the reuse of the older material."[54] Yet Allen rarely comments on how Psalm 108 modifies its source material to communicate meaning.[55] He notes, for example, that the redactor replaced עַד־שָׁמַיִם (Ps 57:11) with מֵעַל־שָׁמַיִם (Ps 108:5) and that the change reflects a possible example of late Hebrew.[56] Notably, Allen fails to correlate changes from Psalm 108's source material with changes of theological intent on the part of the author or redactor.[57]

Samuel Terrien calls Psalm 108 a "copy" of Psalms 57 and 60.[58] Psalm 108 differs from these two earlier psalms because it has a new form: "The new psalm is an individual prayer, with a divine oracle followed by a supplication for a military victory."[59] Terrien does not comment on Psalm 108, presumably because readers should read his comments on Psalms 57 and 60. He does, however, discuss the psalm's date and theology.[60] He views Psalm 108 as a "traditionally Yahwistic" psalm and notes that the "rather grotesque nationalism within the context of praise may partly be explained by the memory of a long insecurity."[61]

John Eaton suggests that Psalm 108 speaks of an experience that is similar to the events surrounding Psalms 57 and 60. In Eaton's view, Psalm 108 is a combination of Psalms 57 and 60 and somehow fits the

52. Allen, *Psalms 101–150*, 96.

53. The term "Psalter-exegesis"refers to the practice of interpreting individual psalms within the context of the Psalter.

54. Allen, *Psalms 101–150*, 94.

55. Allen may be partially influenced by earlier historical-critical commentators who point readers back to earlier comments: "It is not necessary here or elsewhere in the discussion of Ps 108 to retrace ground already covered by M. E. Tate's commentary on the two earlier psalms, in *Psalms 51–100* ([WBC 20; Dallas: Word, 1990] 72–81,99–109)." Allen, *Psalms 101–150*, 94.

56. Allen, *Psalms 101–150*, 95.

57. Allen does helpfully show how Ps 108's structure relates to Pss 57 and 60. This study, however, is interested in how these changes shed light on the meaning of Ps 108.

58. Samuel Terrien, *The Psalms: Strophic Structure and Theological Commentary* (Grand Rapids: Eerdmans, 2003), 741.

59. Terrien, *Psalms*, 742.

60. He is uncertain of the date and is unsure if even a post-exilic situation can be assumed here. See Terrien, *Psalms*, 742.

61. Terrien, *Psalms*, 742.

situation of the king better than either of those two psalms alone would.[62] When Eaton interprets the psalm, Psalm 108's citation of Psalms 57 and 60 and its canonical location play no role.[63]

Howard N. Wallace defines Psalms 57 and 60 as lament psalms but sees Psalm 108 as something different: "in the combination a new psalm with a new message is created."[64] Psalm 108 has become "a psalm of trust."[65] While Wallace uses form-critical categories to speak of Psalm 108, he does not interpret Psalm 108 as simply being a liturgical poem. Rather, he sees Psalm 108 as part of the flow of the Psalter. Psalm 108 carries forward the theme of steadfast love from Psalms 105–107.[66]

While recent interpreters have embraced new approaches and realize that Psalm 108 constitutes an independent psalm, some contemporary critical scholars still read Psalm 108 merely as two conjoined psalms. For example, Walter Brueggemann and William H. Bellinger admit that Psalm 108 fits into a new exilic setting[67] but instruct readers that "The commentaries on Psalms 57 and 60 offer fuller expositions."[68] Brueggemann and Bellinger thus follow earlier critical scholars who say, "See my earlier comments," while adopting the view that Psalm 108 fits into its new setting. Unfortunately, they do not claim that Psalm 108 has gained meaning in its new context or that its changes are intentional, aiming to communicate something new. The historical-critical method continues to influence Psalms scholars, and the method tends to hide the richness of meaning that Psalm 108 conveys within its canonical context.

Nancy deClaissé-Walford follows Leslie Allen when she says that she will "examine Psalm 108 in its updated context in Book Five of the Psalter."[69] DeClaissé-Walford, nevertheless, fails to articulate the intentional inclusion or exclusion of Psalm 108's source material. Her interpretation of the psalm also follows historical patterns. After the Babylonian deportation, "The singers of Psalm 108 could do nothing

62. John Eaton, *The Psalms: A Historical and Spiritual Commentary with an Introduction and New Translation* (New York: T&T Clark International, 2003), 379.

63. Eaton, *Psalms*, 378–80.

64. Howard N. Wallace, *Psalms* (Sheffield: Sheffield Phoenix, 2009), 169.

65. Wallace, *Psalms*, 169.

66. Wallace, *Psalms*, 169.

67. Brueggemann and Bellinger, *Psalms*, 471.

68. Brueggemann and Bellinger, *Psalms*, 469.

69. DeClaissé-Walford, Jacobson, and Tanner, *Book of Psalms*, 821.

more than give thanks and learn to rely on their good God."[70] Although post-exilic singers may have sung Psalm 108, its superscription ascribes Davidic authorship to itself. On this reading, David himself is portrayed as relying on God totally for salvation. To understand Psalm 108 in its canonical context, it is vital to read the psalm as a Davidic psalm.[71]

Recent commentators go further than earlier historical-critical scholars when they interpret Psalm 108 in its canonical context, yet they overlook salient interpretive cues. Such cues may exist in the author's choices of what he kept, left, and changed from earlier psalmic-material.[72] Practitioners of Psalter-exegesis (i.e., canonical scholars) embrace these cues as meaningful and intentional theological signs in the context of the whole Psalter.

CANONICAL SCHOLARSHIP

Canonical approaches to the Psalter give researchers another tool to understand the meaning of Psalm 108.[73] When used on Psalm 108, the psalm's canonical meaning is unleashed. It frees the psalm from being a liturgical text whose meaning is no different than that of Psalms 57 and 60. It frees Psalm 108 to contribute to the meaning of the Psalter.

As a representative of the canonical approach, Frank van der Velden reads Psalms 108–110 together. For Van der Velden, Psalm 108 reenacts Psalms 57 and 60, and this reuse explains why Psalm 108 precedes Psalms 109–110.[74] Further, Van der Velden reads Psalm 108 alongside Psalms 109–110 and observes how themes develop across the three psalms.[75] For

70. DeClaissé-Walford, Jacobson, and Tanner, *Book of Psalms*, 826.

71. Chs. 3–5 of this book will demonstrate the claim made here.

72. It seems plausible that an editor(s) chose an already-existing psalm that differed from Pss 57 and 60 and inserted it into this Book of the Psalter. If so, then Ps 108's authorial integrity remains secure. At the same time, the differences between Ps 108 and the earlier two psalms can nevertheless represent editorially intended differences, which the editor(s) desired readers to understand in the course of reading the Psalter.

73. The canonical approach to the Psalter traces its modern origin to Wilson, *The Editing of the Hebrew Psalter*. Early Christian interpreters of the Psalter, however, read the Psalter canonically. For an example, see Gregory of Nyssa, *Gregory of Nyssa's Treatise on the Inscriptions of the Psalms*, trans. Ronald E. Heine (New York: Oxford University Press, 1995).

74. Frank van der Velden, *Psalm 109 und die Aussagen zur Feindschädigung in den Psalmen*, SBB 37 (Stuttgart: Verlag Katholisches Bibelwerk, 1997), 130.

75. Van der Velden, *Psalm 109*, 131.

Van der Velden, Psalm 108 is a new psalm in its own right[76] and deserves to be read within its canonical context.

Martin Leuenberger posits that Psalm 108 was composed to follow Psalm 107.[77] Furthermore, the oracles in Psalm 108:8–10 and Psalm 110:1 function to frame Psalm 109.[78] For Leuenberger, Psalm 108 is no longer a cultic text or merely a discrete psalm. Rather, Psalm 108 closely relates both to its preceding and succeeding canonical context. The psalm's meaning cannot be understood apart from its canonical location within the Psalter.

Jean-Luc Vesco also reads Psalm 108 within its canonical context, and he discovers meaning in the psalm's relationship to its surrounding context. For example, Vesco argues that David in Psalms 108–110 become a model of behavior for those redeemed from the exile, as described in Psalm 107.[79] Further, when Psalm 107:43 calls for the wise to consider God's work and love, Vesco argues that David does just that in Psalm 108.[80] In this way, Psalm 108 continues the message of Psalm 107. Vesco does not study Psalm 108 to find its *Sitz im Leben*. Rather, he seeks out the psalm's *Sitz im Literatur*, its place in the canon.

Geoffrey W. Grogan reads the Psalter as an edited whole, and he takes into account both the intention of the individual authors and the intention of the redactor of the Psalter.[81] Although Grogan follows earlier scholars by pointing readers back to his comments on Psalms 57 and 60, he finds meaning in how Psalm 108 differs from Psalms 57 and 60. Psalm 108 gives "a more positive emphasis by omitting the earlier part[s] of [Psalms 57 and 60]."[82] Psalm 108 selects the positive portions of Psalms 57 and 60, and this helps readers discern the meaning of Psalm 108.

---

76. Van der Velden, *Psalm 109*, 145.

77. Martin Leuenberger, *Konzeptionen des Königtums Gottes im Psalter: untersuchungen zu komposition und redaktion der theokratischen Bücher IV–V im Psalter*, ATANT 83 (Zürich: Theologischer Verlag Zürich, 2004), 286.

78. Leuenberger, *Konzeptionen des Königtums Gottes*, 287.

79. Vesco, *Le Psautier de David*, 2:1036.

80. Vesco, *Le Psautier de David*, 2:1036.

81. In his commentary, Grogan writes, "It is difficult to believe that the Psalter was put together without principles of selection or of order, so, in addition to the intentions of the individual authors, consideration should be given to the ultimate redactor's intention." Geoffrey W. Grogan, *Psalms*, THOTC (Grand Rapids: Eerdmans, 2008), 21.

82. Grogan, *Psalms*, 182.

Phil Botha pays close attention to Psalm 108's donor texts (Pss 57 and 60). For Botha, Psalm 108 is an anthology because it uses earlier canonical material, giving Psalm 108 special status during the post-exilic era.[83] In his interpretation, Botha studies the variants between Psalm 108 and the earlier two texts to elucidate the meaning of the psalm. Further, he ties Psalm 108 to its canonical context.[84] His approach shares many similarities to the present book's approach. At the same time, Botha's work is deeply flawed. Botha undervalues Psalm 108's superscription and its ascription of Davidic authorship. As this book will demonstrate, Davidic authorship clarifies the meaning of Psalm 108.

Erich Zenger interprets Psalm 108 as a specific contribution to the Psalter: "Psalm 108 was deliberately conceived as a composite psalm for the 'David triptych,' Psalms 108–110."[85] It is worth pausing here to contrast the historical-critical study of Psalm 108 with Zenger's canonical approach. Representing a traditional-historical critical reading, Ernst Axel Knauf notes how Psalm 108:7 changes Psalm 60:7's "answer us" to "answer me." Instead of looking to a canonical-intentional understanding, he uses historical reasoning to conclude that the change from the plural to the singular signals that Psalm 108:7 refers to John Hyrcanus.[86]

In contrast, Zenger, based partly on the "us" in Psalm 60:7 becoming "me" in Psalm 108:7, sees the "me" as David or a King who will rescue his people, which is also supported by the context of Psalms 108–110.[87] On this reading, Psalm 108 portrays an individual king who will rescue his people, whose identity and purpose receives further specification in Psalms 109 and 110. Additionally, Zenger sees the person-change as an intentional modification that transforms the meaning of Psalm 108 for its new context.

Another example within the psalm includes the phrase עוּרָה כְבוֹדִי ("arise, my glory") in Psalm 57:9 that changes to וַאֲזַמְּרָה אַף־כְּבוֹדִי ("I will make melody, even my glory [i.e. God]") in 108:2. Zenger argues that "my glory" refers to the psalmist in 57:9 but "my glory" refers to God in 108:2. He further notes that 108:2 does not represent a "shortening or simplification of Psalm 57; rather, the model is being deliberately

83. Phil J. Botha, "Psalm 108 and the Quest for Closure to the Exile," *OTE* 23, no. 3 (2010): 574–75.

84. Botha, "Psalm 108," 593.

85. Hossfeld and Zenger, *Commentary on Psalms 101–150*, 116.

86. Knauf, "Psalm LX und Psalm CVIII," 63–64.

87. Hossfeld and Zenger, *Commentary on Psalms 101–150*, 117.

altered. The anthropological accent in Ps 57:8 is changed in favor of a theocentric accent: 'indeed, you, my glory' is now a vocative addressed to God, analogous to the vocative 'God' in v. 2a."[88]

Additionally, the use of "my glory" in Psalm 108:2 as a name for God may allude to Psalm 3 in which God is also called "my glory" (Ps 3:4). Both psalms present the psalmist crying to God in the face of enemies, portray Yahweh answering and rescuing the psalmist, and refer to the morning.[89] If Zenger is correct, then the allusion to Psalm 3 may contribute to the theme of God's universal rule in Books IV and V.

Such connections show how Psalter-exegesis looks for intentional changes between Psalm 108 and Psalms 57 and 60 and demonstrate how Psalter-exegesis perceives these changes as communicating meaning within the canonical Psalter. It argues that these changes relate to intent; they create new meaning beyond their original context. Furthermore, Psalter-exegesis interprets Psalm 108 within its canonical context (e.g., Pss 108–110) to elucidate its meaning. Psalter-exegesis thus provides tools to understand Psalm 108 more fully, and its methodology plays an important role in this study.

CONCLUSION

This history of interpretation of Psalm 108 demonstrates the need for further research into Psalm 108, its unique citation of earlier psalmic material, and the effect of its placement in Book V of the canon. Psalter-exegesis reads the Psalter in its canonical form and discovers meaning in the context of the canon. This approach has laid the groundwork for a deeper understanding of Psalm 108, but it is a steppingstone. This book applies many of the insights of Psalter-exegesis and provides a fuller account of Psalm 108's meaning within the contours of the canon.

Additionally, this book differs from Psalter-exegesis because it not only affirms that an editor(s) shaped the Psalter and inserted individual psalms into it to create thematically united groups of psalms, but it also affirms that the editor(s) honored the authorial intent of individual psalms. The editor(s) placed psalms into psalm groups in ways which honored their intended meaning. Collectively, these psalm groups deepen and extend the meaning of individual psalms along

88. Hossfeld and Zenger, *Commentary on Psalms 101–150*, 115.

89. Hossfeld and Zenger, *Commentary on Psalms 101–150*, 119.

redemptive-historical lines.[90] Furthermore, this book argues that the Psalter narrates Israel's history of redemption. Accordingly, Psalm 108 is not only part of a canonical group (e.g., Psalms 108–110). It is also part of the redemptive-historical story of the Psalter.

90. Chs. 3, 4, and 5 of this book illustrate this in practice.

3

History of Canonical and Biblical Citation Research

The interpretive history of Psalm 108 sets up a discussion on recent scholarly advancements in biblical studies, such as the canonical approach to Scripture and inner-biblical citation methods. The canonical approach highlights how the Bible's canonical form communicates meaning beyond the level of verse and chapter. Inner-biblical citation methods trace how later Scripture uses earlier Scripture to develop theological ideas. By using the insights of canonical and inner-biblical citation approaches for understanding Psalm 108, this book will contribute to the scholarly investigation of the Old Testament.

CANONICAL SHAPING OF THE BIBLE

Canonical approaches understand the Bible as an authoritative body of literature and argue that a community of faith shaped the Bible. Before engaging current canonical scholarship, the discussion that follows recounts evidence that testifies to the canonical shaping of the Psalter. Such evidence is worth noting because it undergirds key assumptions related to this study's argument and will prepare readers to understand canonical scholarship on the Bible. The discussion that follows, therefore, first begins with the Psalter's early history before addressing the history of canonical scholarship.

The specifics of the Psalter's composition are hidden within the passage of time. A few pieces of historical evidence, however, furnish an understanding of the Psalter's composition: information from the psalm superscriptions, from Greek translations of the OT (LXX), from the Qumran scrolls, and from the New Testament's witnesses to its composition.

Superscriptions

Psalm superscriptions may have arisen after an individual psalm's composition because these superscriptions appear in the third person even when a psalm uses the first person within its body.[1] Furthermore, both the LXX and the Syriac translation of the Psalter contain different and additional superscriptions.[2]

Additionally, Daniel Estes avers that some superscriptions do not accurately represent the content of the psalm. He cites Psalms 3 and 30 as examples. According to Estes, Psalm 3 portrays David as confident even though he was depressed in the narrative to which the superscriptions point (2 Sam 15–18).[3] The superscription of Psalm 30 refers to the dedication of a house but its content underscores healing.[4] On this reading of the evidence, the superscriptions describe the body of their psalm from a distance and sometimes do not accurately describe the content of a psalm.[5]

One should not, however, discount the possibility that the superscriptions date back to the time of the Psalter's composition and, indeed, even to the hand of the actual authors. The authors may have penned the superscriptions and simply used the third person to introduce a psalm. But if the authors did not pen their own superscriptions, then whoever added the superscriptions likely had prophetic authority, since ancient Israelites frowned on changing or adding to a scriptural text improperly.[6]

---

1. Tremper Longman III and Raymond B. Dillard, *An Introduction to the Old Testament*, 2nd ed. (Grand Rapids: Zondervan, 2006), 241–42.

2. Daniel J. Estes, "Psalms," in *Handbook on the Wisdom Books and Psalms* (Grand Rapids: Baker Academic, 2005), 142.

3. Estes, "Psalms," 142.

4. Estes, "Psalms," 142.

5. It should be noted that Estes argues for the historical reliability of the superscriptions. But he does not confidently affirm Davidic authorship of the superscriptions nor does he affirm that the superscriptions of Pss 3 and 30 accurately describe the content of these psalms. Estes, "Psalms," 142–43.

6. Deut 4:2 forbids adding to Moses's words, which were God's communication to Israel. Yet Moses augments the tenth word from God in Deut 5:21 by adding "his field" to the original command in Exod 20:17. A prophetic person, therefore, can augment earlier canonical texts to uncover their intent and extend their meaning. Likewise, the psalm superscriptions may augment earlier canonical material to uncover the psalm's intent and extend its meaning.

Furthermore, even though the LXX and Syriac translation do not completely agree with the Hebrew text, this does not necessitate that the psalm superscriptions in the Hebrew text are not original. It may only mean that later translations paraphrased, added, or translated from a different base text.

Lastly, David could have written a confident psalm (Ps 3) while feeling depressed (2 Sam 15–18). People of faith frequently turn to God with great confidence in the midst of dark times. There is also no reason to assume that the superscription of Psalm 30 cannot fit into a context of healing. Based on these considerations, it is entirely possible that psalm superscriptions are part of the canonical text of Scripture.[7]

I favor the position that the psalm authors wrote the majority or all of their superscriptions because this appears to be the way that the canonical Psalter invites readers to understand it (see 2 Chr 29:30). Whatever one concludes about the historical reliability of the superscriptions, however, the argument of this study requires only that one read the superscriptions as part of the redemptive-historical story that the Psalter narrates. The superscriptions guide readers to understand the meaning of individual psalms within their canonical context. Psalm 51's body, for example, presents a non-historical account of the psalmist's repentance before God. No historically specific details accompany the body of the text.[8] The superscription, however, adds a specific historical context, controlling how the reader interprets Psalm 51: "To the end. A *Mizmor* by David when Nathan the prophet came to him because he had gone into Bathsheba." The reader thus receives new information about the psalm and its canonical meaning: it addresses Nathan's confrontation with David due to his affair with Bathsheba, canonically located in 2 Samuel 11.

Moreover, the body of the psalm details David's repentance to God concerning the affair. Whether an editor added this superscription or whether David penned it himself, it is an example of a superscription

7. Admittedly, this position runs against the stream of current scholarship. Speaking about the Davidic superscriptions in the Psalter, John Collins writes, "It is now generally accepted that these references were added by an editor long after the time of David, but they contributed to the tendency to see all the Psalms as Davidic." John J. Collins, *Introduction to the Hebrew Bible* (Minneapolis: Fortress, 2004), 461.

8. David does not mention Nathan, Bathsheba, or the particular sin in the psalm. Only in the superscription do these historically specific ideas appear.

that clearly interprets the content of its psalm. It also shows that superscriptions can point back to a canonical context.

Septuagint

Historical evidence concerning the Psalter's composition is also found in the Old Greek translation of the Hebrew Text, which witnesses to the shape and shaping of the Psalter. The translation occurred sometime around the second century BC. The Old Greek, or for simplicity's sake LXX,[9] largely agrees with what has become the Masoretic Text. This agreement suggests that the compositional process of the MT had become frozen before the LXX translated it in the second century.

Differences between the LXX and the MT involve order, number, and superscriptions. The differences in order between the LXX and the MT, however, are quite minor. Jennifer Dines explains, "Some psalms are divided differently from the MT, resulting in different numbering from 9 to 147 (MT 10–148) and there is an additional Psalm 151, quite different from the others; a similar Hebrew version has been found at Qumran."[10] The additional psalm in the LXX (Ps 151) indicates within its superscription that it falls outside the 150 authoritative Psalms, which is witnessed to in the LXX and the MT: "This psalm is written by the hand of David and is outside the number. When he fought in single combat with Goliath" (LXX 151:1).[11] By labeling itself "outside the number," Psalm 151 admits its non-canonical status.

The LXX continued to add superscriptions after the Hebrew Psalter's text type had become frozen. Rolf Jacobson writes, "Of the 150 poems in the Psalter, only 34 lack a superscription. In the LXX, which is generally expansionistic in the superscriptions, only 17 psalms lack a superscription."[12] However one interprets the evidence, the contents of the poems

9. LXX properly refers to an original Pentateuchal translation but has come to refer to the whole collection of Greek translations of the Hebrew Old Testament. I use the common sense of the term here for the sake of simplicity as a shorthand term for various Old Greek translations.

10. Jennifer M Dines, *The Septuagint*, ed. Michael A Knibb (London: T&T Clark, 2004), 19.

11. Οὗτος ὁ ψαλμὸς ἰδιόγραφος εἰς Δαυιδ καὶ ἔξωθεν τοῦ ἀριθμοῦ· ὅτε ἐμονομάχησεν τῷ Γολιαδ. Peter Gentry introduced me to this idea that Ps 151 itself claims to be outside the number of the canonical Psalms in a LXX seminar in the spring of 2015.

12. DeClaissé-Walford, Jacobson, and Tanner, *Psalms*, 11.

in the LXX and the MT closely align, even if the LXX adds more superscriptions to the MT.[13]

Desert Scrolls

Additional historical evidence appears in texts from Qumran that were found in the middle of the twentieth-century. They provide further physical evidence that contributes to an understanding of the Psalter's canonization. At Qumran, thirty-seven manuscripts were unearthed as well as three others farther south.[14] While the Psalm superscriptions basically agree with those in the MT,[15] Qumran texts vary from the MT in their order and content. For example, 11QPs[a] contains about fifty compositions, presents a different order for the Psalter's fifth book, and includes poems that do not appear in the MT Psalter. In light of psalmic evidence in Qumran, Flint concludes that the MT Psalter is not normative but represents one edition among others.[16] Talmon Shemeryahu offers another interpretation of the data. He concludes that 11QPs[a] constitutes "a collection of liturgical compositions which the sect used for its sacred service."[17] Even if Flint's interpretation is accurate, this would mean only that 11QPs[a] constitutes a Psalter edition of an insular sect in Judea. The MT may still be the normative Hebrew Psalter, and 11QPs[a] could represent merely a sectarian Psalter. Furthermore, Qumran scrolls (like 11QPs[a]) that differ from the MT may simply be liturgical texts and not proper editions of the Psalter.[18]

---

13. For a helpful overview of LXX superscriptions and their meaning, see Albert Pietersma, "Septuagintal Exegesis and the Superscriptions of the Greek Psalter," in *The Book of Psalms: Composition and Reception*, ed. Peter W. Flint and Patrick D. Miller Jr. (Boston: Brill, 2005), 443–75.

14. Peter W. Flint, "Dead Sea Scrolls, Psalms," in *The Lexham Bible Dictionary*, ed. John D. Barry (Bellingham, WA: Lexham, 2012), s.v. "The Psalms Scrolls and Their Features."

15. Flint, "Dead Sea Scrolls, Psalms," s.v. "The Psalms Scrolls and Their Features."

16. Flint, "Dead Sea Scrolls, Psalms," s.v. "Major Disagreements with the Masoretic Psalter and Issues That Arise." In contrast, Peter Gentry argues that there was a standard proto-MT text. See Peter J. Gentry, "The Text of the Old Testament," *Journal of the Evangelical Theological Society* 52, no. 1 (2009): 19–45.

17. Talmon Shemaryahu, "'Pisqah Be'emṣa' Pasuq and 11 QPsa,'" *Textus* 5 (1966): 12, http://www.hum.huji.ac.il/upload/_FILE_1371645130.pdf.

18. Roger T. Beckwith, "The Early History of the Psalter," *Tyndale Bulletin* 46, no. 1 (1995): 22.

Two (or perhaps more) editions of a Psalter in the first century do not undermine the canonical assumptions of this study. This study assumes (1) that prophets wrote individual psalms along with their superscriptions and (2) that editors later shaped individual psalms into book-compositions. Since the Qumran sect does not represent a community in which prophetic persons existed (their eschatological prophecies, for example, did not come to pass),[19] their Psalter edition may witness to the prophetic text but does not supplant it.[20]

New Testament

Further evidence emerges from the New Testament because it testifies to a canonical order and to the validity of psalm superscriptions for interpretation. For example, Jesus asks certain religious leaders a question concerning Psalm 110: who is the Messiah's father? They answer that David is the father of the Messiah (Matt 22:42). Jesus replies, "How does David, then, by the Spirit call him 'Lord' saying: 'The Lord says to my Lord: "Sit at my right hand until I place your enemies under your feet."' If David, then, calls him 'Lord,' how is he [the Messiah] his [David's] son?" (Matt 22:43–45). Jesus and his interlocutors believe that David authored Psalm 110, as the psalm superscription indicates.

Not only does the New Testament confirm the validity of psalm superscriptions, but it also knows of a canonical order. In Acts 13:33, Paul quotes the second Psalm: "because God has fulfilled this [promise] to their children by raising Jesus as it is written also in the second psalm: 'You are my son. Today I have begotten you.'" Paul specifies that his quotation comes from the second psalm, which suggests that he knows of an ordered collection of Psalms.

Collectively, the early history of the Psalter testifies to the interpretive significance of its superscriptions and the importance of its canonical shape. Inductive studies explore the resulting canonical shape of the Psalter, and this study assumes their basic findings.[21] But the question remains: Why prioritize the MT of the Psalter over 11QPs[a] and the LXX?

19. No physical evidence exists that John the Baptist was an Essene or part of the Qumran community. Perhaps he associated with desert communities, but association does not mean that he identified with these desert groups.

20. The Psalter, composed and shaped by prophets, does not equal the MT, although the MT witnesses to it.

21. For example, see Howard, *Structure of Psalms 93–100*; Mitchell, *Message of the Psalter*; Wilson, *Editing of the Hebrew Psalter*.

The MT represents a stable text-type that testifies to inspired documents. Its caretakers kept it stable as it passed through the centuries, and the MT was preserved among a community who valued the prophetic word. Unlike Qumran, which had its own body of prophetic literature, some of which proved false, the MT's caretakers looked back at the written, prophetic word, none of which has proved false.[22] The LXX generally confirms the MT albeit with exceptions, and the LXX also existed among faithful communities.[23] The LXX is, however, translated from a Hebrew text. So even though the LXX and the MT represent faithful witnesses to the inspired texts, the MT is a better witness because it was transmitted in the same language as the original, inspired documents.

CANONICAL SCHOLARSHIP

Canonical approaches to the Bible seek meaning not only at the level of a single verse or chapter in Scripture but at the level of a book or collection of books. Applied to Psalm 108, a canonical approach opens new interpretive angles for understanding Psalm 108 by seeing it not merely as an individual psalm but as one psalm in a collection of psalms that together communicate an idea. A canonical approach shows how Psalm 108 contributes to its canonical context, namely, the Psalter as a whole. To illustrate how this approach contributes in such a way, a brief survey of recent canonical scholarship follows.

Brevard Childs pioneered a canonical method or approach to the Bible in the late twentieth century.[24] His major contributions to scholarship include (1) defining the canon of Scripture as a context for interpretation, (2) proposing a historical explanation for the process of canonization, and (3) submitting that the canon is theological by nature.

Childs's 1979 work, *Introduction to the Old Testament as Scripture*, illustrates these contributions. In this work, Childs presents a new context for biblical interpretation: the biblical canon. His is an "attempt to hear

---

22. I hold this position as a presupposition based upon the preponderance of evidence that the Hebrew Old Testament corresponds to reality, although I grant that some futuristic prophecies are disputed or have not yet occurred. This is thus a working hypothesis.

23. LXX Jer, for instance, differs significantly from MT Jeremiah.

24. For a helpful overview of Childs's approach, see Joel Barker, "Brevard S. Childs and the Canonical Approach," in *Prevailing Methods after 1980*, vol. 2 of *Pillars in the History of Biblical Interpretation*, ed. Stanley E. Porter and Sean A. Adams, Biblical Studies Series 2 (Eugene, OR: Pickwick, 2016), 359–79.

the biblical text in the terms compatible with the collection and transmission of the literature as scripture."[25] Unsatisfied with the then current approaches to the Bible, Childs proposed a complete rethinking of the relationship between critical and theological interpretation of the Old Testament.[26]

Practically, this rethinking meant that the final form of the canon became the context for studying the Bible: "The formation of the canon was not a late extrinsic validation of a corpus of writings, but involved a series of decisions deeply affecting the shape of the books."[27] In other words, ancient Israelites shaped the biblical canon into a form that functions as Scripture, and they also shaped it into a text that would instruct future generations: "The ordering of the tradition for this new function involved a profoundly hermeneutical activity, the effects of which are now built into the structure of the canonical text."[28] For Childs, the historical process of the canon embedded a scriptural function into the Old Testament's final form.

The historical process of the canon also involves a theological agenda. Childs disagrees with James Sanders, for example, who held that Israel formed the canon "in Israel's search for identity," a proposal that shifts the canonical process from theology to anthropology.[29] Instead, Childs perceives the canonical process as theological, as Israel's testimony about God.[30]

In summary, Childs saw the canonical process as a historical and theological enterprise. Historically, Israel formed her canon so that it would function as Scripture, to be a guide to future generations. Theologically, Israel recorded her experience of God in Scripture for future generations. Biblical interpreters must therefore read a passage of Scripture as part of a larger whole, as part of the canon; further, the goal of interpretation is to uncover what the text says of God and his relationship to his people.

James Sanders disagrees. Sanders argues for a canonical criticism, one that embraces earlier critical studies (as Childs affirms), but adds, as an object of study, the community who formed the canon. Unlike

25. Childs, *Introduction to the Old Testament as Scripture*, 16.

26. Childs, *Introduction to the Old Testament as Scripture*, 15.

27. Childs, *Introduction to the Old Testament as Scripture*, 59.

28. Childs, *Introduction to the Old Testament as Scripture*, 60.

29. Childs, *Introduction to the Old Testament as Scripture*, 59.

30. Childs, *Introduction to the Old Testament as Scripture*, 59.

Childs, who studies the final form of the canon as a theological document, Sanders perceives various strands of tradition in the canon. These strands date back to the Exile and extend to around the first century of this era. Part of Sanders's canonical criticism, then, is the attempt to uncover the communities behind these pluriform traditions that are evinced in the present form of the canon. Hence, the community or communities behind traditional layers in the canonical text become the object of study. By defining the traditional layers that these communities embedded into the canon, one can see a mirror of that community in the Scripture.

Sanders illustrates these points in *Torah and Canon*, in which he isolates canonical criticism's contribution to the disciplines of biblical criticism as giving attention *"to the origins and function of canon."*[31] By function, Sanders seems to mean the function that the community gives to the canon;[32] the canon's nature is a "mirror for the identity of the believing community."[33]

In *Canon and Community*, Sanders offers a guide to canonical criticism. While the precise nature of Sanders's critical method seems elusive, he provides a serviceable definition of his proposal that illustrates how he uses critical methods, how he aims to discern different tradition layers within the canon, and how he focuses on the communities who shaped the canons:

> Canonical criticism traces the history of the function of those authoritative traditions which ended up in one of the canons. In order to do so it uses all the valid and pertinent tools of biblical criticism, especially tradition criticism, but focuses on the believing communities at every stage along the way rather than only on the individual discreet geniuses, such as original thinkers, editors, redactors, and the like, whose hands may be evident in the process.[34]

Sanders's canonical criticism provides a sharp focus on the communities of faith that shaped canons of Scripture, although his project comes

31. James A. Sanders, *Torah and Canon* (Philadelphia: Fortress, 1972), xv.

32. Sanders, *Torah and Canon*, ix–xx.

33. Sanders, *Torah and Canon*, xv.

34. James A. Sanders, *Canon and Community: A Guide to Canonical Criticism* (Philadelphia: Fortress, 1984), 37.

with all the liabilities of historical criticism. Liabilities include the subjective nature of discerning traditional layers in the Bible and the use of limited historical data to identify religious communities in ancient Israel who would shape canons of Scripture. Further, while Sanders focuses on the canon and community, he fails to deal adequately with the meaning of the final form of the text. The canon becomes the mirror of hypothetical communities rather than a testimony about God. Childs's critique summarizes the problem:

> For Sanders the heart of the canonical process lay in Israel's search for identity. In my judgment, this approach turns the canonical process on its head by couching a basically theological move in anthropological terms. It thus replaces a theocentric understanding of divine revelation with an existential history.[35]

Childs's approach provides a better vantage point for seeing how a psalm contributes to the meaning of the Psalter, which is a particular goal of this book. Sanders's canonical criticism may help to identify social-historical data about the persons who may have compiled the Psalter. But it will not help one interpret the text as it has been transmitted in the Hebrew canon, as this book intends to do.

A student of Childs, Gerald Wilson, provided a way forward for Psalter study by using a disciplined canonical approach. In *The Editing of the Hebrew Psalter*, Wilson studies the constituent elements that compose the canonical Psalter, and he concludes that the Psalter communicates a purposeful message by means of its canonical structure. Up to that point, Psalter scholarship had generally focused on small portions of Scripture to determine historical sources or traditions that spawned that particular portion. The object of such study was the history behind the final form of the text rather than the text itself. Into this atmosphere and following the trajectory of Childs, Wilson posits a paradigm shifting set of arguments:

> First, I contend there is evidence within MT 150 itself of an editorial movement to bind the whole together. Second, I submit that the unity achieved by this process is not merely a convenient combination of disparate items into an "accidental" formal

35. Childs, *Introduction to the Old Testament as Scripture*, 59.

arrangement, but represents the end result of purposeful, editorial organization.[36]

The purposeful editorial organization of the Psalter can most easily be discerned by studying the seams within the Psalter.[37] For example, Psalm 72:20 reads, "The prayers of David, the son of Jesse, are completed,"[38] an explicit editorial comment. Other signs of editorial shaping must be discerned through implicit evidence of editorial shaping. For example, each of the five books of the Psalter end with a doxology (Pss 41:13, 72:18–19, 89:52, 106:48, 146–150).

Wilson finds clear editorial signs in three areas of the Psalter: (1) Psalm 1 as an introduction to the Psalter, (2) the division of the Psalter into five books, and (3) the concluding Hallel (Pss 146–150).[39] After isolating and defining editorial elements within the Psalter, Wilson specifies the function of the Psalter's editorial shaping. Psalm 1 provides the hermeneutical key to read the Psalter: the Psalter in its final form is something to be read and not performed.[40] The five-book structure details the Davidic monarchy and the failure of the Davidic covenant, while Book IV answers this failure by replacing David with YHWH as king.[41] Book V answers the plea of the exilic community, introducing Davidic psalms as a model of dependence on YHWH.[42] Finally, Psalms 145 and 146 connect David and YHWH together, and in those psalms YHWH's rule fulfills the Davidic responsibility of kingship.[43] Psalms 146–150 as a doxology appear to function, then, as a celebration of YHWH's reign.[44]

Following Wilson, the Society of Biblical Literature soon began discussing canonical readings of the Psalter in its sections. Based on these SBL discussions, Sheffield Academic Press published *Shape and Shaping of the Psalter*.[45] Its editor, J. Clinton McCann, builds on Wilson's argument that Books IV and V answer the problem posed in Books I–III. But

36. Wilson, *Editing of the Hebrew Psalter*, 4.
37. Wilson, *Editing of the Hebrew Psalter*, 5.
38. כָּלּוּ תְפִלּוֹת דָּוִד בֶּן־יִשָׁי.
39. Wilson, *Editing of the Hebrew Psalter*, 204.
40. Wilson, *Editing of the Hebrew Psalter*, 207.
41. Wilson, *Editing of the Hebrew Psalter*, 207–8, 213, 215.
42. Wilson, *Editing of the Hebrew Psalter*, 227.
43. Wilson, *Editing of the Hebrew Psalter*, 226–27.
44. Wilson, *Editing of the Hebrew Psalter*, 227.
45. McCann, *The Shape and Shaping of the Psalter*.

he adds that Books I–III have begun to answer, "the problem posed by the exile."[46] McCann's method involves not only looking at the last psalm of each book (Wilson's seams) but also at the initial psalms of each book (so, Pss. 1–2, 42–44, and 73–74).[47] He concludes by stating that the editorial purpose of the Psalter "was to address the problem posed by exile and dispersion, namely, the apparent failure of the traditional Davidic/zion covenant theology."[48]

David M. Howard also wrote a chapter in *Shape and Shaping of the Psalter*,[49] in which he demonstrates how Psalms 90–94 connect together, suggesting that Psalms 95–100 and 101–106 function the same way.[50] Book IV, then, may comprise three groups of psalms that relate to one another.[51] Notably, Howard proposes a rigorous methodology for discerning links between psalms, allowing researchers to identify psalm-groups within the canonical Psalter.

Adding to the scholarship that supports a canonical approach, David Mitchell published *The Message of the Psalter*. In it, Mitchell "maintains that the Hebrew Psalter was designed by its redactors as a purposefully ordered arrangement of lyrics with an eschatological message."[52] One way that he verifies his thesis is by comparing Zechariah 9–14's visions of the messiah and the future[53] with the Psalter's depiction of the messiah and eschatological exile.

While the book is well-written, Mitchell's conclusions sometimes seem improbable. For example, he argues that the Psalter mimics the five-fold structure of the Pentateuch in overly specific ways. Book I uses morning and evening themes and is foundational to the rest of the Psalter, Book II of the Psalter represents the exodus, Book III is Levitical due to Asaph and Korah's influence, Book IV represents the time in the desert as in Numbers, and Book V brings Israel together to worship in Jerusalem as Deuteronomy details.[54] Even if one is not persuaded by the

---

46. McCann, "Books I–III," 95.
47. McCann, "Books I–III," 95.
48. McCann, "Books I–III," 104.
49. Howard later expands on his reading of Pss 93–100 psalms in Howard, *Structure of Psalms 93–100*.
50. Howard, "Contextual Reading of Psalms 90–94," 123.
51. Howard, "A Contextual Reading of Psalms 90–94," 123.
52. Mitchell, *Message of the Psalter*, 15.
53. Mitchell, *Message of the Psalter*, 199.
54. Mitchell, *Message of the Psalter*, 301.

totality of Mitchell's argument, his basic thesis that the Psalter points in an eschatological direction exists as a hallmark in contemporary canonical study of the Psalter.

Jamie Grant's *The King as Exemplar* further contributes to the canonical study of the Psalter. His work integrates an intertextual reading between Deuteronomy 17 and the Psalter for the purpose of clarifying the canonical structure of the Psalms: "the placement of kingship psalms alongside torah psalms was a deliberate editorial act through which the Psalter's redactors intended to reflect the theology of the Deuteronomic Law of the King in the Book of Psalms."[55] The connection between kingship and piety also reveals an eschatological perspective in the Psalter because post-exilic persons would have seen the Davidic king as a "restored Davidic king."[56]

Rolf Rendtorff, a student of Gerhard von Rad, wrote *The Canonical Hebrew Bible*, using a similar approach to Childs.[57] Rendtorff's particular genius is to clearly articulate a canonical approach, having the benefit of years of canonical scholarship that Brevard Childs was not privy to in his early publications. The first sentence of Rendtorff's work reads, "The Old Testament is a theological book."[58] One has to consider only the last 150 years of biblical scholarship and its historical focus to realize the significance of this statement. Rendtorff, professor at the University of Heidelberg, defines the nature of the Old Testament as theological rather than historical.

Yet Rendtorff does not disregard historical-critical study of the Bible. He simply asks different questions: "[T]he first and primary task of a theologically motivated exegesis is the exposition of the existing text."[59] In contrast, literary-critical approaches examine the earlier stages of the text before it became what it is today. The final form dissipates from view.[60] Rendtorff is committed, in contrast, to reading the Bible in its final, canonical form for its theological meaning.

Rendtorff respects historical-critical scholarship and admits that tensions exist within the canon but warns against separating the text

55. Grant, *King as Exemplar*, 2.

56. Grant, *King as Exemplar*, 3.

57. Rolf Rendtorff, *The Canonical Hebrew Bible: A Theology of the Old Testament*, trans. David E. Orton, TBSS (Leiderdorp: Deo, 2005).

58. Rendtorff, *Canonical Hebrew Bible*, 1.

59. Rendtorff, *Canonical Hebrew Bible*, 720.

60. Rendtorff, *Canonical Hebrew Bible*, 720.

into problem-free originals:[61] "rather, we should endeavor to interpret the tensions within the text. Only thus can historical-critical exegesis reach its true goal, the understanding of the texts."[62] In other words, one can discern tensions in the text, presumably from layers of tradition within the text. But whoever compiled the final form of the text kept those tensions for a theological purpose.[63]

Rendtorff also makes advances in canonical Psalter scholarship. Reading the Psalms as part of the canon embeds a messianic reading into the Psalter, with the (so-called) royal psalms playing a particular role in this canonical function. For example, although in Book III Psalm 89 recounts the nearness of the monarch's demise, Psalms 1 and 2 have already clarified the destiny of the monarchy by adding an additional layer of meaning to the entire Psalter. In Psalm 2, God's king is called the messiah, and God appoints him from Zion. In Psalm 1, the righteous one associates closely with the king. From Psalm 3 on, this king becomes a suffering righteous person: "So here the kingship is interpreted anew from the post-exilic perspective in a 'messianic' sense."[64]

The insights that Psalms 1 and 2 introduce the entire Psalter and that the king in Psalm 2 represents the righteous man in Psalm 1 contribute to a robust canonical reading of the Psalter. Rendtorff comments on the king and the righteous man, saying:

> The "Anointed One" of God (2.2), the king whom God has appointed on Mount Zion (v. 6) and who himself speaks (v. 7), is none other than David, who from Ps 3 on appears as the "author" of the Psalms. Thus David himself is presented as the righteous man who leads his life in accordance with the Torah (cf. 1 Kgs 2.1-4; 3.14 etc).[65]

Having just spoken of Psalm 1, Rendtorff is clearly arguing that king David models righteousness throughout the Psalter like the blessed man of Psalm 1. Hence, the demise of the monarchy represents only part of the trajectory of the righteous, suffering messiah within the Psalter.

---

61. Rendtorff, *Canonical Hebrew Bible*, 3.

62. Rendtorff, *Canonical Hebrew Bible*, 3.

63. John Sailhamer exemplifies this method in *The Meaning of the Pentateuch: Revelation, Composition and Interpretation* (Downers Grove, IL: InterVarsity Press, 2009).

64. Rendtorff, *Canonical Hebrew Bible*, 739.

65. Rendtorff, *Canonical Hebrew Bible*, 320.

In *Psalms 1–2: Gateway to the Psalter*, Robert Cole does not see the king of Psalm 2 as an example of the righteous man from Psalm 1. Rather, he identifies the righteous man of Psalm 1 with the king in Psalm 2.[66] Similar to Grant, Cole uses an intertextual approach in his canonical conclusions.[67] His major contribution is to identify and clarify how Psalms 1 and 2 function as the gateway to the Psalter.

In 2014 Nancy L. deClaissé-Walford edited *The Shape and Shaping of the Book of Psalms*, a multi-author work which mainly originates from 2011 sections on the shaping and shaping of the Hebrew Psalter at the Society of Biblical Literature meeting. Significantly, this work focuses on Psalms scholarship in the wake of Gerald Wilson's *The Editing of the Hebrew Psalter*. The volume demonstrates that Psalms scholarship now focuses on canonical approaches to the Psalter, which Wilson popularized in 1985.

Brevard Childs introduced modern scholarship to the idea of a canonical approach to the Scripture, and Gerald Wilson applied this model to the Psalms. The subsequent history of canonical Psalter research is a footnote to Childs and Wilson. This book enters the canonical discussion and seeks to contribute to it by showing how Psalm 108 fits into the eschatological trajectory of Book V of the Psalter. The book also takes into account the unique inner-biblical nature of Psalm 108 within the canonical Psalter in ways similar to Grant and Cole. Hence, a survey of recent research into biblical citation methods follows.

BIBLICAL CITATION METHODS

Psalm 108 includes parts of Psalms 57 and 60, meaning that Psalm 108 cites earlier Scripture to communicate its message. "Intertextuality" and "inner-biblical exegesis" are terms that describe how one text cites another. "Intertextuality" is generally found in discussions of how the New Testament uses the Old Testament and originates in modern literary theory.[68] "Inner-biblical exegesis" refers to any biblical author citing a biblical text and integrating it with an author-centered interpretation. The latter term, "inner-biblical exegesis," more closely describes this book's method of studying how a later psalm cites an earlier psalm.

---

66. Cole, *Psalms 1–2*, 80–87.

67. Cole, *Psalms 1–2*, 58–59.

68. I will discuss the origin and use of intertextuality below.

Even as intertextuality does not adequately describe Psalm 108's use of earlier Psalms, so also inner-biblical exegesis does not quite describe Psalm 108's unique situation. Psalm 108 does not use earlier Scripture as a way to make sense of the present, as Jeremiah might make use of Deuteronomy, citing the Torah as part of a larger argument. Almost exclusively, Psalm 108 quotes and paraphrases Psalms 57 and 60. Therefore, Psalm 108 does not simply cite the two earlier psalms to contribute to its larger argument or body of writing; Psalm 108 is—in its entirety—Psalms 57 and 60.

Inner-biblical exegesis and intertextuality, nevertheless, provide helpful tools to understand the unique situation of Psalm 108. These disciplines supply new ways of conceiving of how Psalm 108 cites earlier Scripture and provide helpful vocabulary for describing inner-biblical citations. Consequently, briefly recounting the history of research in these fields will demonstrate how this book seeks to engage the scholarly discussion.

Inner-biblical exegesis

In *Biblical Interpretation in Ancient Israel*, Michael Fishbane broke new ground in Old Testament studies by explaining how biblical authors used earlier tradition to grow or clarify the tradition. In simpler terms, Fishbane explains how a later author integrates the writings of an earlier author into his or her argument. For example, Fishbane provides the language and theory to understand how Isaiah adapts the writings of Moses for Isaiah's prophetic word to Israel.

Key to Fishbane's argument is the distinction between *traditum* and *traditio*. *Traditum* represents the content of tradition, while *traditio* refers to the process of transmission.[69] For example, the Torah may represent the *traditum* for the author of Psalm 119, who uses what he considers to be Scripture (the Pentateuch) and integrates it into his psalm (*traditio*). When someone can identify both the *traditum* and the *traditio*, he or she has discovered an example of inner-biblical exegesis.[70] *Traditio* (e.g., Ps 119) either clarifies or adds independent ideas to the *traditum* (e.g., Torah).[71]

---

69. Michael A Fishbane, *Biblical Interpretation in Ancient Israel* (New York: Oxford University Press, 1985), 6.

70. Fishbane, *Biblical Interpretation in Ancient Israel*, 12.

71. Fishbane, *Biblical Interpretation in Ancient Israel*, 13–14.

Fishbane further points out that Israelites looked back to their *traditum* to revitalize their faith.[72] For instance, the editor(s) of the Psalter may have used Deuteronomy 17's kingship code to shape the Psalter, adding significant clarity and expanding the idea of what it means to be the king of Israel. The Psalter may portray Israel's kings as failing to fulfill God's promises, suggesting that an eschatological king will come to fulfill these promises (cf. Pss 2 and 110). Based on this reading, the Psalter clarifies the Torah's promises of kingship (Deut 17:14–20; Gen 49:10; etc.), adding a clear eschatological dimension to them (e.g., Pss 2 and 110).

Inner-biblical exegesis, thus, began in the Old Testament itself. Fishbane perceives four types of inner-biblical exegesis: scribal, legal, haggadic, and mantological.[73] By studying these types and seeking to understand a text's *Sitz im Leben*, researchers can discern "the mental matrix within which inner-biblical exegesis operated and from which early Jewish exegesis emerged."[74] This "mental matrix" clarifies how biblical authors read their Scripture and how they wrote new Scripture. The mental matrix also provides an especially helpful concept for interpreting the Old Testament. Readers must ask how a biblical author conceived of his *traditum* or Scripture and how this author interpreted it in his context. By doing so, readers gain a tool that will help them understand the author's communicative intent.

Fishbane rightly asserts that biblical authors engage in inner-biblical exegesis, and he provides usable vocabulary to describe how later authors cite earlier authors. At the same time, his vocabulary is far from comprehensive, and his method seems to focus on defining inner-biblical exegesis rather than exploring the biblical and theological meaning that an author intends by citing an earlier text.[75] Therefore, Fishbane's

---

72. Fishbane, *Biblical Interpretation in Ancient Israel*, 18.

73. Scribal exegesis mostly refers to explanatory comments in the biblical text (cf. Josh 18:13; Esth 3:7). Legal exegesis reinterprets or extends existing legal texts (2 Chr 35:13 with Deut 16:7 and Exod 12:8). Haggadic exegesis draws out latent ideas in earlier texts and applies them to the present and usually is marked by lexemes or themes shared between the two texts. Mantological exegesis interprets oracles and ominous material. These definitions follow the guidance provided by Russell Meek, "Intertextuality, Inner-Biblical Exegesis, and Inner-Biblical Allusion: The Ethics of a Methodology," *Biblica* 95, no. 2 (2014): 285–87.

74. Fishbane, *Biblical Interpretation in Ancient Israel*, 17–18.

75. This insight in large part comes from digital correspondence with Abner Chou.

inner-biblical exegesis provides helpful but limited aid to understanding the theological intent of Psalm 108's citation of earlier psalmic material.

Intertextuality

Inner-biblical exegesis has become less popular than intertextuality to describe how one biblical author cites another text. By contrast, intertextuality describes how two or more texts interact together regardless of their authorially-intended meaning or their diachronic trajectory.[76] Intertextuality's focus on the reader rather than the authorial intention has, however, not stopped scholars from using it to understand the authorial intent of the Bible. "Intertextuality originated," writes Stanley Porter, "as a philosophically bolstered theory of language relations, distinguished from simpler concepts such as influence. It has rarely, however, been picked up in this way in NT studies."[77] In fact, NT studies or biblical studies sometimes use the term "intertextuality" in much the same way that Fishbane defines inner-biblical exegesis.[78]

This misappropriation of intertextuality entails that some authors who use intertextuality comport well with the approach of this book, while other authors who use intertextuality do not fit into this book's author-centered approach. Nevertheless, this latter group contributes to studies of how later authors cite earlier authors for at least four reasons. First, intertextual studies clarify terminology to describe how one author cites a text (e.g., direct citation, allusion, echo), and this accurate terminology allows for a clearer discussion of how an author references earlier material.

76. Benjamin Sommer writes, "Intertextuality is concerned with the reader or with the text as a thing independent of its author. … The study of intertextuality is synchronic." Benjamin D. Sommer, "Exegesis, Allusion and Intertextuality in the Hebrew Bible: A Response to Lyle Eslinger," *VT* 46 (1996): 487.

77. Stanley E. Porter, *Sacred Tradition in the New Testament: Tracing Old Testament Themes in the Gospels and Epistles* (Grand Rapids: Baker Academic, 2016), 12.

78. Porter, *Sacred Tradition in the New Testament*, 12. Michael Holmes observes how current intertextual studies often use the term differently than it was originally intended to be used: "On a more theoretical level, there is the matter of what seems to be one of the major sources of confusion associated with the term: conceived as a synchronic concept, 'intertextuality' is frequently employed in a diachronic way that stands in sharp tension with its original vision." Michael W. Holmes, "Intertextual Death: Socrates, Jesus, and Polycarp of Smyrna," in *Intertextuality in the Second Century*, ed. D. Jeffrey Bingham and Clayton N. Jefford, The Bible in Ancient Christianity 11 (Leiden: Brill, 2016), 58.

Second, intertextual studies often uncover the author's intent even though the method does not focus on it. For example, Richard Hays's recent work on the Gospels aims to discover how NT authors read the OT (authorial intent) although he does not argue that NT authors interpret OT authors according to their authorial intent. Rather, he asserts that NT authors read the OT in a figural way.[79] Hays, in this sense, aims to uncover the intent of NT authors but not of OT authors. Nevertheless, he often uncovers the intent of OT authors because NT authors generally cite OT authors according to their authorial intent.

Third, intertextual studies outline methodologies to understand how to identify a relationship between two texts when one text cites the other.

Fourth, intertextual studies also provide examples of how to draw theological meaning from textual connections.

In light of all four reasons, this book builds on certain aspects of intertextuality (citation terminology, etc.) but differs from the original vision of intertextuality, which is synchronic and not moored to authorial intent.[80] Specifically, this book engages with the scholarly discussion of intertextuality to identify how Psalm 108 cites Psalms 57 and 60 to communicate theological meaning.

Probably the most influential book in recent years on the phenomenon of intertextuality is *Echoes of Scripture in the Letters of Paul* by Richard Hays. It has become a standard manual for the biblical discipline of intertextuality. In this text, Hays defines intertextuality as "the imbedding of fragments of an earlier text within a later one."[81] He also identifies Paul as one who "saw himself as a prophetic figure, carrying forward the proclamation of God's word as Israel's prophets and sages had always done, in a way that reactivated past revelation under new

---

79. Richard B. Hays, *Echoes of Scripture in the Gospels* (Waco, TX: Baylor University Press, 2016), 2–4.

80. Julia Kristeva coined the term "intertextuality" in 1969 and speaks of the notion of intertextuality in this way: "Any text is constructed as a mosaic of quotations; any text is the absorption and transformation of another. The notion of *intertextuality* replaces that of intersubjectivity, and poetic language is read as at least *double*" (italics original). Julia Kristeva, "Word, Dialogue, and Novel," in *Desire in Language: A Semiotic Approach to Literature and Art* (New York: Columbia University Press, 1980), 66.

81. Richard B. Hays, *Echoes of Scripture in the Letters of Paul* (New Haven, CT: Yale University Press, 1989), 14. Hays's definition leans toward a diachronic definition of intertextuality, which may be why some readers have viewed it this way.

conditions."[82] Hays thus builds on Fishbane's work of inner-biblical exegesis in the field of biblical studies.

In his work, Hays focuses on indirect ways of citation, such as allusion or echoes in Scripture. For Hays, an allusion constitutes an obvious intertextual connection, while an echo is a subtler intertextual connection.[83] According to Hays, both author and reader must share a common body of knowledge to make an allusion possible.[84]

Hays mistakes, however, the effect of recognizing an allusion for the author's intended use of an allusion. Porter, in contrast, states that an "allusion can take place even if the reader does not grasp the allusion, because it is authorial intent that defines the presence of an allusion."[85] Agreeing with such a critique, Hays notes in a later writing that "It is difficult to separate the concept of allusion from notions of authorial intentionality."[86] A speaker must intend an allusion for an allusion to take place. The reader or hearer may not pick up on the allusion, and that same reader may need to re-read the text until the allusion becomes apparent.

An echo is a subtle intertextual reference, according to Hays, and to test the presence of an echo in a given text the following criteria are used: availability, volume, recurrence, thematic coherence, historical plausibility, history of interpretation, and satisfaction.[87] Only the first five criteria actually refer to elements found within the text while the last two criteria point to features that lie outside of the text.

The obvious contribution of Hays's work to the scholarly discussion is his straight-forward definitions of terms and the outline of his methodology. Although he is a pioneer in the application of intertextuality to biblical studies, Hays presents arguments with flaws. His definitions of allusion and echo are vague and non-specific. His method is a mixture of objective and subjective elements that require greater specificity. For example, the criterion of satisfaction is, "Does the proposed reading make sense?" or it asks, "whether the proposed reading offers a good account of the experience of a contemporary community of competent

---

82. Hays, *Echoes of Scripture in the Letters of Paul*, 14.
83. Hays, *Echoes of Scripture in the Letters of Paul*, 29.
84. Hays, *Echoes of Scripture in the Letters of Paul*, 29.
85. Porter, *Sacred Tradition in the New Testament*, 43.
86. Hays, *Echoes of Scripture in the Gospels*, 10.
87. Hays, *Echoes of Scripture in the Letters of Paul*, 29–32.

readers."[88] Hays makes an obvious point—an intertextual connection must make sense—and an unhelpful point—an intertextual connection must make sense to the "experience of a contemporary community of competent readers." The statement is unhelpful because an author could echo an earlier text whether a community recognizes it as such. Surprisingly, Hays calls satisfaction "the most important test."[89]

Christopher Stanley's *Paul and the Language of Scripture* represents another advance in the methodology of intertextual studies. As Porter notes, Stanley's work uniquely deals with how one determines a citation from other sorts of references.[90] Studying Paul's citation of the Old Testament, Stanley locates Paul's *Vorlage* as the LXX or a Hebraizing revision of an Old Greek text or another translation.[91] However, Stanley claims that Paul diverges from his *Vorlage* for interpretational reasons, using Scripture to push his own ideas on his audience, ideas that are not necessarily found in the Old Testament text that he cites.[92] Stanley's work thus helps to define citations, but many would disagree with the position that Paul did not, in fact, always cite his texts in context.

Hays provides an update to his intertextual study of Scripture in *The Conversion of the Imagination: Paul as Interpreter of Israel's Scripture.* The book is a collection of essays that aim to "discover a way of reading that summons the reader to an epistemological transformation, a *conversion of the imagination.*"[93] At least one effect of this conversion is to read Scripture with a hermeneutic of trust, leading him to claim: "The real work of interpretation is to *hear* the text."[94] It is to engage with Paul's imaginative world without the hermeneutic of suspicion that seeks to critique but not hear the text.[95] Hay's emphasis on listening to the text and entering into the world of the writer clarifies what it means to read a text intertextually. Typical critical methodologies may contribute to

88. Hays, *Echoes of Scripture in the Letters of Paul*, 31–32.

89. Hays, *Echoes of Scripture in the Letters of Paul*, 31.

90. Porter, *Sacred Tradition in the New Testament*, 7.

91. Christopher D. Stanley, *Paul and the Language of Scripture: Citation Technique in the Pauline Epistles and Contemporary Literature*, Society for New Testament Studies Monograph Series 69 (Cambridge: Cambridge University Press, 1992), 67.

92. Hays, *Echoes of Scripture in the Letters of Paul*, 259, 263–64.

93. Richard B. Hays, *The Conversion of the Imagination: Paul as Interpreter of Israel's Scripture* (Grand Rapids: Eerdmans, 2005), x.

94. Hays, *The Conversion of the Imagination: Paul as Interpreter of Israel's Scripture*, 198.

95. Hays, *The Conversion of the Imagination: Paul as Interpreter of Israel's Scripture*, x.

understanding an intertext, but they fundamentally approach the text with an erroneous worldview, an erroneous hermeneutic.

Steve Moyise attempts to provide a handbook on Paul's use of the Old Testament in *Paul and Scripture: Studying the New Testament Use of the Old Testament*. Moyise's introduction seems to indicate that he will study Paul's use of the Old Testament, but he does not specify what sorts of uses he will study nor what constitutes a use. Moyise has clearly studied only Paul's explicit quotations, although it is unclear what Moyise means by explicit quotations.[96] For example, Moyise claims that Philippians contains no citations of Scripture, but as Porter states, "five words from Job 13:16 LXX are found in exactly the same order and arrangement in Phil. 1:19."[97] Specifically, Job 13:16 contains the clause, τοῦτό μοι ἀποβήσεται εἰς σωτηρίαν, which matches exactly the phrase τοῦτό μοι ἀποβήσεται εἰς σωτηρίαν in Philippians 1:19. If this does not represent an explicit quotation, what does?

Three other works furnish a contemporary perspective on the state of scholarly discussion of intertextuality. First, the multi-author monograph, *Intertextuality in the Second Century*, appeared in 2016.[98] This work posits that post-apostolic Christianity emphasized receiving and interpreting traditions in their context. This shows that intertextuality is not an isolated biblical phenomenon but is something that is part of early Christian literature. Humans live and act on the basis of tradition, received and interpreted afresh in every generation.[99]

Additionally, in *Echoes of Scripture in the Gospels*, Richard Hays provides an analysis of intertextuality in the Gospels as his earlier work did for Paul. Hays builds on his own methodology as he defines categories of intertextual reference, which he calls quotation, allusion, and echo. These terms represent a spectrum of intertextual reference moving from direct to indirect references.

For Hays, quotations generally have a citation formula or "verbatim reproduction of an extended chain of words, often a sentence or more,

---

96. Steve Moyise, *Paul and Scripture: Studying the New Testament Use of the Old Testament* (Grand Rapids: Baker Academic, 2010), 111.

97. Porter, *Sacred Tradition in the New Testament*, 19.

98. Bingham andJefford, *Intertextuality in the Second Century*.

99. Alasdair MacIntyre has shown, for example, how the loss of a moral tradition created moral confusion in the Western world. See Alasdair MacIntyre, *After Virtue*, 3rd ed. (Notre Dame, IN: University of Notre Dame Press, 2007).

from the source text."[100] "An 'allusion,'" writes Hays, "usually imbeds several words from the precursor text, or it at least in some way explicitly mentions notable characters or events that signal the reader to make the intertextual connection."[101] Significantly, Hays reverses his earlier conclusion that allusions happen only when both writer and reader recognize them in his earlier work. Instead, Hays associates allusion with authorial intention.[102] Echoes are not as distinct as allusions and advance meaning beyond the surface sense of the text to those who can hear them; an echo might be a word or a phrase that reminds one of an earlier text.[103]

Stanley Porter also expands the scholarly discussion of intertextuality in *Sacred Tradition in the New Testament: Tracing Old Testament Themes in the Gospels and Epistles*. In this text, he advances the methodological discussion in a precise direction and advocates for reading earlier traditions in later texts, rather than focusing on quotations and allusions as Hays and others have done. Porter rightly criticizes the state of intertextual studies for its sloppy definitions; however, his tradition-focused approach does not appear to be a *better* approach but a complementary one to that of Hays and others.

Porter suggests three categories of reference: quotation, indirect citation, and echo.[104] A quotation may be formulaic ("as it is written") or simply a direct quote of at least three words.[105] Indirect citations include paraphrase and allusion. Paraphrase is "an intentional and specific invoking of a definable passage, even if it is made in other words and in another form."[106] An allusion involves "the indirect invoking of a person, place, literary work, or the like, designed to bring the external person, place, literary work, or similar entity into the contemporary material."[107] Finally, an echo "may be consciously intentional or unintentional, involving not paraphrase of a specific passage nor allusion to a person,

100. Hays, *Echoes of Scripture in the Gospels*, 10.
101. Hays, *Echoes of Scripture in the Gospels*, 10.
102. Hays, *Echoes of Scripture in the Gospels*, 10.
103. Hays, *Echoes of Scripture in the Gospels*, 10.
104. Porter, *Sacred Tradition in the New Testament*, 34.
105. Porter, *Sacred Tradition in the New Testament*, 34–35.
106. Porter, *Sacred Tradition in the New Testament*, 36.
107. Porter, *Sacred Tradition in the New Testament*, 39.

place, literary work, etc., but by means of thematically related language invoking some more general notion or concept."[108]

Porter has successfully clarified the citation language that Fishbane and Hays pioneered in their respective works. The history of inner-biblical and intertextual research has been one of muddled definitions and methodology that sought to understand how later authors reference earlier texts or, in the case of intertextuality, how one text evokes another text. While Porter and, to some degree, Hays have clarified the discussion, this book seeks to provide further clarification for how parallel psalms cite one another (e.g., how Psalm 108 cites Psalms 57 and 60).

Summary

This book engages with the discussion of intertextuality as it relates to definitions and meaning rather than to intertextuality as a whole. In contrast to intertextuality as it was originally defined, and in closer alignment with inner-biblical exegesis, this book maintains an emphasis on authorial intent and historical diachrony.

This work primarily interacts with the field of inner-biblical exegesis by identifying the unique ways that Psalm 108 cites earlier material. However, it bypasses questions of redactional layers within the Psalter because the editor's or editors' redaction of the canonical form of the Psalter is the only layer that a person can confidently discern in the text. Readers must therefore interpret and discuss the final form of the canon or engage in historical speculation.[109]

From this foundation, this book engages the fields of intertextuality and inner-biblical exegesis in at least two ways. First, recent discussions on intertextuality have provided adequate definitions to describe how Psalm 108 cites earlier psalmic material, but such definitions need to be applied in a consistent manner to the psalm. This has yet to be done, and this book aims to carefully define how Psalm 108 cites Psalms 57 and 60. Second, this work will elucidate the intended theological meaning behind the citations in Psalm 108 and not merely define how Psalm 108 cites earlier material. This sort of in-depth study has yet to be done in a comprehensive manner.

---

108. Porter, *Sacred Tradition in the New Testament*, 45–46.

109. I do not mean the phrase "historical speculation" to be pejorative. I simply see the pursuit of discerning redactional layers in the Psalter as a nearly impossible task. The hand of the editor(s) is too good, which makes it difficult to accurately define a traditional layer in the Psalter.

CONCLUSION

Psalm 108's history of interpretation demonstrates the need for a dedicated study of Psalm 108 within its canonical setting as well as the need to engage with canonical and citation scholarship to clarify the psalm's meaning. The sketches of recent canonical and citation research situate this book within these two fields and show how this study will engage current canonical and citation scholarship.

4

Translation and Exegesis of Psalm 108

This chapter translates and exegetes Psalm 108. Afterwards, it locates Psalm 108 within the redemptive-historical story of the Psalter. Psalms 104–106 narrate Israel's history, and Psalm 106 ends with a call for rescue (Ps 106:47). Psalm 107 speaks of the regathering of Israel to the land with eschatological language. Psalm 108 carries forward the story of eschatological redemption.

TRANSLATION OF PSALM 108

1. A song, a *mizmor*[1] by David.
2. My heart is steadfast, O God.
   I will sing and praise,[2] even my glory.[3]

1. A *mizmor* is "a song with instrumental accompaniment," according to W. F. Cobb, *The Book of Psalms: With Introduction and Notes* (London: Methuen, 1905), x.

2. The praise envisioned here and in Ps 108:4b probably includes playing music with a stringed instrument. The root of the verb is זמר, and it can mean praising God with an instrument. *HALOT*, 274. Further, זמר is related to the noun *mizmor*, which is the genre of Ps 108. As noted above, a *mizmor* is a song "with instrumental accompaniment." Ps 108:3 confirms this reading because of the mention of "harp" and "lyre."

3. Louis Jacquet, Frank van der Velden, and Erich Zenger interpret "glory" as a title for God rather than as a term describing the psalmist. See Jacquet, *Les Psaumes et le Coeur*, 181; Van der Velden, *Psalm 109*, 146n21; Hossfeld and Erich Zenger, *Commentary on Psalms 101–150*, 114. While this is a possible way to read Ps 108:2, the discussion below and in ch. 4 will ultimately reject it. The simplest explanation is that the psalmist calls his tongue "my glory." John Wesley, for example, interprets the phrase as meaning "my tongue." John Wesley, *Wesley's Notes on the Bible* (Grand Rapids: Francis Asbury, 1987), 296. I have retained a literal translation of the phrase here because of the difficulty of translation. A smoother translation might be "I will sing and praise with my glory."

3. Awake, O harp and lyre!
   I will awaken the dawn![4]

4. I will laud you among the peoples, YHWH,
   and I will praise you among the nations.[5]

5. For your faithfulness is great above[6] the heavens,
   and your truthfulness[7] comes to the clouds.

6. Rise[8] above the heavens, O God,

---

4. J. W. Rogerson and J. W. McKay assert that "dawn" is a mythological term. For them, Dawn is a "winged goddess" (Ps 139:9) "with a womb" (Ps 110:3) and "beautiful eyelids" (Job 3:9) and is "the mother of the Day Star, Venus" (Isa 14:12). J. W. Rogerson and J. W. McKay, *Psalms 101–150*, Cambridge Bible Commentary (New York: Cambridge University Press, 1977), 57. Given the monotheistic convictions of Israel, it seems unlikely that Psalm 108 refers to a winged goddess by the use of the word "dawn." Rather, the word "dawn" here refers to the early parts of the morning. See *DCH*, 8:326.

5. The MT reads בַּל־אֻמִּים ("not nations"), but *BHS* notes that many manuscripts and editions read בִּלְאֻמִּים ("among the nations"). The above translation agrees with the alternative reading in the *BHS* because Ps 108:4a ("I will praise you among the peoples") expects a similar, parallel statement in Ps 108:5b. It would be peculiar for David to say that he will praise God to the "not nations." The LXX further confirms this reading by translating the phrase with ἐν ἔθνεσιν. Jacques Tourney calls a בַּל־אֻמִּים "a deprecating spelling" (*une graphie dépréciative*) meant to convey "not nations." Raymond Jacques Tournay, "Psaumes 57, 60 et 108: Analyse et Interprétation," *Revue Biblique* 96, no. 1 (1989): 25.

6. The phrase מֵעַל is a "heaped-up" preposition according to Mitchell Dahood, *Psalms III: 101–150* (Garden City, NY: Doubleday, 1970), 94. Another term to describe מֵעַל is "compound preposition." Paul Joüon, *A Grammar of Biblical Hebrew*, trans. T. Muraoka (Rome: Pontifical Biblical Institute, 1996), 461, Logos. Heaped-up prepositions place two prepositions side-by-side. In this case, the preposition מִן is connected to עַל, creating מֵעַל.

7. The noun אֱמֶת can also mean "trustworthiness" and "constancy." *HALOT*, 69. Translating אֱמֶת with "your truth" or "your truthfulness" creates a contrast with its near synonym חֶסֶד in Ps 108:5a and also fits the context of Ps 108. In Ps 108:8–10, David recounts God's earlier promise and holds God accountable to be truthful and faithful to fulfill it. The LXX translates אֲמִתֶּךָ in Ps 108:5b with ἡ ἀλήθειά σου ("your truth"). The Clementine Vulgate uses *veritas tua*.

8. W. E. Barnes detects an echo to the exodus because the psalmist requests that God would rise like he had at the Red Sea. Barnes, *Psalms*, 2:525. The language of "right hand" in Ps 108:7 may allude to Exod 15:6 and 12 in which God's right hand is said to save Israel. However, Ps 108:7 may simply be drawing on a common motif of salvation, namely, the right hand of God, and not necessarily alluding directly to the exodus. Furthermore, in Ps 108:6, God rises above the heavens, which is different than when God parted the sea and raised the waves. This makes Barnes's argument that Ps 108:6 echoes the exodus unlikely.

and let your glory rise[9] above the whole earth,

7. In order that your beloved ones may be rescued,
save with your right hand[10] and answer me!

8. God spoke in his sanctuary:[11]
"I will exult and divide Shechem!
I will measure out the Valley of Succoth.

9. Gilead is mine. Manasseh is mine. And Ephraim is my helmet.[12]
Judah is my scepter.

10. Moab is my wash-basin.[13]
I will cast my shoe on Edom.
I will exult over Philistia."

11. Who will bring me to the fortified city?
Who will lead[14] me to Edom?

12. Has God rejected us?
You do not go out, O God, with our armies.

13. Give us help from the enemy;
The salvation of man is vain.

---

9. The verb "rise" does not occur in Ps 108:6b but is implied. Psalm 108:6a uses the imperative verb רוּמָה, which is understood to apply also to Ps 108:6b. In Ps 108:6b, however, "rise" is in the third person because "your glory" is its subject.

10. The phrase יְמִינְךָ is an "adverbial accusative" according to Erich Zenger. See Hossfeld and Zenger, *Commentary on Psalms 101–150*, 114. Hence, the above translates the phrase as "with your right hand."

11. The phrase בְּקָדְשׁוֹ could equally be rendered "in his holiness." As the discussion below and as ch. 4 will argue, the phrase probably means "in his sanctuary."

12. The text literally reads, "Ephraim is the stronghold of my head" (מָעוֹז רֹאשִׁי).

13. *HALOT* glosses the phrase סִיר רַחְצִי as "wash-basin" in *HALOT*, 221.

14. Nancy deClaissé-Walford reads the verb נָחַנִי as an imperfect and explains "the missing initial *yôd* as a case of haplography with the previous word." DeClaissé-Walford, Jacobson, and Tanner, *Book of Psalms*, 822n8. This argument to explain the verb is unnecessary. Hebrew poetry often changes the aspect of a verb for poetic beauty. There is no reason to assume that the perfect verb נָחַנִי cannot refer to the future and be translated as "will guide me." Additionally, John Goldingay notes, "the qatal itself can be used in doubtful questions (see *TTH* 19)." John Goldingay, *Psalms 90–150*, Baker Commentary on the Old Testament Wisdom and Psalms (Grand Rapids: Baker Academic, 2008), 263.

14. With God, we will do valiantly,
but[15] he will tread down our enemy.

EXEGESIS OF PSALM 108

Psalm 108 is divided into two halves, which are separated by material from Psalms 57 and 60.[16] Psalm 108:2–6 corresponds to Psalm 57:8–12, and Psalm 108:7–14 corresponds to Psalm 60:7–14. Consequently, Psalm 108 separates into one half that concerns David's praise for God among all people (108:2–6) and another half that speaks of God's salvation of Israel and establishment of his rule (108:7–14).

The first half of Psalm 108 (108:2–6) contains an inclusio, signaled by the term כָּבוֹד (108:2, 6). Psalm 108:2–4 describes David's intent to worship God, forming another inclusio with the term זמר (108:2, 4).[17]

The psalm's first half, therefore, separates into two sub-groups: 108:2–4 and 108:5–6. The second half of Psalm 108 presents the idea of salvation, enclosing that second half in something of a thematic *inclusio* (108:7, 13).[18]

Other explanations of the structure exist, but they either present a structure based primarily upon thematic features[19] or rely too heavily on form-critical features.[20] The former explanation is too subjective and may undervalue the explicit linguistic features of Psalm 108. The latter explanation works only if one can demonstrate that the author of Psalm 108 intended to structure his psalm according to form-critical standards, which seems improbable. Instead, readers should analyze

15. The *vav* + pronoun construction (וְהוּא) signals a contrast. Bruce Waltke and Murphy O'Connor explain, "Interclausal *waw* before a non-verb constituent has a disjunctive role." *IBHS*, 650 (39.2.3a). Hence, the translation "but he." The point is that God will help Israel's armies, but it is truly God who will tread down the enemies.

16. Concerning Ps 60, Wilson notes "The comparison of these three psalms (57; 60; 108) demonstrates how psalms or psalmic segments could be recombined and reused to speak to different settings and times. The use in Psalm 108 of 60:5–12 also helps indicate structural divisions within our psalm." Gerald H. Wilson, *Psalms*, vol. 1, NIV Application Commentary (Grand Rapids: Zondervan, 2002), loc. 18152, Kindle. The opposite is also true. How Ps 108 cites Pss 57 and 60 helps determine the structural divisions of Ps 108 itself.

17. Vesco, *Le Psautier de David*, 2:1039.

18. Vesco, *Le Psautier de David*, 2:1039.

19. DeClaissé-Walford, Jacobson, and Tanner, *Psalms*, 821.

20. Hossfeld and Zenger, *Commentary on Psalms 101–150*, 116–17.

Psalm 108's structure by noticing the psalm's explicit linguistic features (e.g., key-word repetition) and its two-part division due to its unique citation of Psalms 57 and 60.

Superscription

According to the superscription, Psalm 108 is a שִׁיר מִזְמוֹר לְדָוִד. The word שִׁיר is a generic word for "song," but the word מִזְמוֹר refers to "a song with instrumental accompaniment."[21] Furthermore, the terms שִׁיר and מִזְמוֹר define the genre of the psalm. In psalm superscriptions, psalm genres are marked by singular, common nouns without a definite article.[22] Both שִׁיר and מִזְמוֹר satisfy this criteria. As a genre, מִזְמוֹר is common in the Psalter, appearing 52 times in the Psalter by itself, and, in 5 cases, מִזְמוֹר appears with שִׁיר to signify a psalm's genre.[23] In Daniel Bourguet's study of the psalm superscriptions, he found that, when מִזְמוֹר and שִׁיר appear together, as they do here, they relate appositionally and are in the absolute state.[24]

The phrase לְדָוִד identifies the author of Psalm 108, namely, David. Egbert Ballhorn notes that שִׁיר מִזְמוֹר followed by a *lamed* plus a name occurs with Korah (Pss 44:1; 88:1) and Asaph (Ps 83:1), but this is the first time that this particular construction appears with David.[25] Psalm 109 is also a מִזְמוֹר written by David. After considering the superscription of Psalm 109, Ballhorn concludes that Psalm 108 is a new composition meant to fit within its canonical context.[26] Likewise, Psalm 110 is also a מִזְמוֹר written by David. This further shows that Psalm 108 is intentionally placed before Psalms 109 and 110.[27]

The superscription thus defines the genre of Psalm 108 as a "song, a *mizmor*" as well as identifying the author: David. David wrote Psalm 108 to be a song that was accompanied by stringed instruments. Canonically,

21. Cobb, *Book of Psalms*, x.

22. Daniel Bourguet, "La Structure des Titres des Psaumes," *Revue d'Histoire et de Philosophie Religieuses* 61, no. 2 (1981): 112.

23. Bourguet, "Structure des Titres des Psaumes," 115.

24. Bourguet, "Structure des Titres des Psaumes," 115.

25. Ballhorn, *Zum Telos des Psalters*, 148.

26. Ballhorn, *Zum Telos des Psalters*, 148.

27. Martin Leuenberger also argues that the shared genre and authorship of Pss 108–110 demonstrate that these three psalms are a compositional unity. Leuenberger, *Konzeptionen des Königtums Gottes*, 286.

the genre and authorship of Psalm 108 unite Psalms 108–110 into a group. All three psalms are *mizmorim* by David.

Psalm 108:2–6

In Psalm 108:2, David affirms his steadfastness before singing praises to God. When David says "my heart is steadfast," he means my heart is ready.[28] The niphal verb נָכוֹן can express the idea of readiness.[29] In context, David would be affirming his readiness to "sing and praise with my glory" (Ps 108:2b). In contrast, the same line in Psalm 57:8 speaks of David's steady soul, and נָכוֹן probably conveys the idea of "firmness."[30]

The phrase "even my glory" (אַף־כְּבוֹדִי) refers to the psalmist's tongue, not his soul[31] or God.[32] The phrase "my glory" refers to the psalmist's tongue because David claims that he will sing to God: "I will sing and praise, even my glory." Glory is, therefore, probably a metonymy for "tongue,"[33] and David means that he will glorify God with his tongue through singing.[34] The אַף adds emphasis ("even") to what follows: "even my glory."[35] The LXX renders the phrase *ἐν τῇ δόξῃ μου*, perhaps translating אַף with *ἐν*.[36]

28. Botha, "Psalm 108," 586.

29. *HALOT*, 464.

30. Jacquet, *Les Psaumes et le Coeur*, 179. Both the double repetition of "my heart is firm" (נָכוֹן לִבִּי אֱלֹהִים נָכוֹן לִבִּי) and the total context of Ps 57 lead to this conclusion. In Ps 57, David is in dire straits and confesses the firmness of his faith in God. In Ps 108, David may once again need God's rescue. But the psalm's tone is much more positive and triumphant. The portions of Pss 57 and 60 that David selects to form Ps 108 create a psalm with a hopeful, positive tone. Grogan, *Psalms*, 182.

31. Rashi, *Rashi's Commentary on Psalms*, trans. Mayer I. Gruber, Brill Reference Library of Judaism 18 (Boston: Brill, 2004), 637.

32. Jacquet, *Les Psaumes et le Coeur*, 181; Hossfeld and Zenger, *Commentary on Psalms 101–150*, 114. In ch. 4, I detail my arguments for this position extensively.

33. John Gill, *An Exposition of the Old Testament, vol. 4* (1810; repr., Paris, AR: Baptist Standard Bearer, 2005), 175.

34. David prays that God's glory would rise above the earth in Ps 108:6. It is reasonable to assume, therefore, that David's praying with his glory (tongue) signifies that he will verbally glorify God, especially since he does just that in Ps 108:4–6.

35. Hossfeld and Zenger, *Commentary on Psalms 101–150*, 115.

36. Nancy deClaissé-Walford states that the LXX translates אַף with *ἐν*. DeClaissé-Walford, Jacobson, and Tanner, *Psalms*, 822n6. But it is not certain that this is what the LXX translators are doing. They may simply have added *ἐν* to ensure that the Greek text was readable. If so, they either did not translate אַף or they translated from a text that did not contain אַף.

In Psalm 108:3, David personifies his instruments when he says, "Awake, O harp and lyre!" He then proclaims that he will praise God with his instruments in the early part of the morning: "I will awaken the dawn!"[37] His praise for God is not restricted to a private audience. Rather, David will praise YHWH "among the peoples" and "among the nations" (Ps 108:4). God is not a local deity nor is his power restrained. Instead, David confesses that YHWH's faithfulness "is great above the heavens" and his truthfulness "comes to the clouds" (Ps 108:5). Finally, David calls on God to rise above the heavens and to let his glory fill the earth (Ps 108:6).[38]

Psalm 108:7–14

The term "glory" in Psalm 108:6 functions as an *inclusio* with "my glory" in Psalm 108:2.[39] In Psalm 108, the glory of God is not an undefined entity. Rather, the glory of God is the concrete theophany of YHWH in salvation as Psalm 108:7 verifies.[40] David says, "In order that your beloved ones may be rescued, save with your right hand and answer me!" (Ps 108:7). After praying that God's glory would span the earth, David ties God's answer ("answer me!) to the rescue of his beloved ones.[41] Psalm 108:6 ends the citation of Psalm 57:8–12, and Psalm 108:7 begins the citation of Psalm 60:7–14. David, therefore, skillfully ties what was Psalm 60:7 to what was Psalm 57:8–12.

---

37. Rashi claims that David awoke at midnight, citing a rabbinic tradition in which a north wind would blow into a lyre sitting above David's bed. In this sense, David would awaken the dawn. Rashi, *Psalms*, 637. This seems to be an overly literal understanding of what David means. Likely, David means that he will praise God in the early hours of the morning. Theodoret argues that the dawn refers to the incarnation. Theodoret of Cyrus, *Commentary on the Psalms: Psalms 73–150*, trans. Robert C. Hill (Washington, DC: Catholic University of America Press, 2001), 198 (§2). Isa 58:8 may provide biblical evidence for taking "dawn" as the messiah: "Then shall your light break forth like the dawn, and your healing shall spring up speedily; your righteousness shall go before you; the glory of the LORD shall be your rear guard" (ESV).

38. Joachim Becker argues that Ps 108:6 refers to the world-spanning revelation of God's glory (Isa 35:2; 40:5; 59:19; 60:2; 66:18; Pss 97:6; 102:16). Becker, *Israel deutet seine Psalmen*, 66. Following Becker, Steven Cook defines God's exaltation as an eschatological revelation of God's glory. Cook, "Apocalypticism and the Psalter," 92.

39. Vesco, *Le Psautier de David*, 2:1039.

40. Becker, *Israel deutet seine Psalmen*, 67.

41. According to Zenger, Ps 108:7 uses the first person pronoun "me" to underscore that the king is speaking. In Ps 60:7, the text reads "answer us." Hossfeld and Zenger, *Commentary on Psalms 101–150*, 116.

In Psalm 108:8–10, David recounts an earlier promise of God. He introduces the promise with "God spoke in his sanctuary." The word sanctuary (קֹדֶשׁ) could also mean "holiness."[42] However, the term sanctuary or heavenly sanctuary makes better contextual sense in this passage.[43] In Psalm 108:6, David prays that God would rise above the heavens, and it is not unreasonable to argue that Psalm 108:6 could elucidate the meaning of קֹדֶשׁ in Psalm 108:8. David perhaps envisions God as speaking from heaven or from above the heavens. God also speaks from heaven in Psalm 2:6 (cf. 2:4). Moreover, the language of sanctuary fits with the Zion and temple themes that are present in Psalm 110.[44]

God promises victory over the nations surrounding Israel. The oracular promise names nine entities over which God will claim victory. The nine entities can be divided into three sets of three. There are three places (Shechem, Succoth, and Gilead), three tribes (Manasseh, Ephraim, and Judah), and three enemies (Moab, Edom, and Philistia).[45] Erich Zenger teases out the different ways that God claims authority over these nine entities. He redistributes the inhabitants of Shechem and Succoth, cares for Gilead and Manasseh, uses Ephraim and Judah to aid in his regal duty, subjugates Moab and Edom, and exults over Philistia.[46]

According to Vesco, the entities named in Psalm 108:8–10 follow a geographical movement that begins in Israel and then moves from east to west.[47] Botha and Zenger track the movement from north to south.[48] Konrad Schaefer seems to track the movement from the west to the east:

> Shechem with a large part of Manasseh west of the Jordan is claimed as well as Succoth together with Gilead east of the Jordan. Northern Ephraim will serve as a military helmet and southern Judah as scepter. The oracle confirms Israel's rights over three

---

42. *HALOT*, 1076.

43. Becker calls it the "heavenly temple of Yahweh" (*himmlische Heiligtum Jahwes*). Becker, *Israel deutet seine Psalmen*, 67; Botha, "Psalm 108," 577; Hossfeld and Zenger, *Commentary on Psalms 101–150*, 114.

44. Hossfeld and Zenger, *Commentary on Psalms 101–150*, 114.

45. Benjamin J. Segal, *A New Psalm: The Psalms as Literature* (New York: Gefen, 2013), 523.

46. Hossfeld and Zenger, *Commentary on Psalms 101–150*, 121.

47. Vesco, *Le Psautier de David*, 2:1039.

48. Botha, "Psalm 108," 581–82; Hossfeld and Zenger, *Commentary on Psalms 101–150*, 120.

> longstanding enemies, as the divine warrior claims neighboring Moab in the south-east, Edom in the south and coastal Philistia.[49]

Schaefer thus appears to track the movement from the west (chehem) to the east (Succoth and Gilead) and then from the north to the south.

Why do Vesco, Botha, Zenger, and Schaefer appear to track the movement of the entities differently? Vesco defines Succoth and Gilead as part of Israel, and so he begins tracking the movement in Moab (east). Botha likely starts with Ephraim (north) and moves downward. Zenger defines Succoth and Shechem as the north (not west and east).[50] Schaefer simply comments on the geographical location of the places as they appear in the passage without intentionally tracking their movement in a line. No matter the starting point, however, it is clear that God systematically names regions surrounding Israel and claims victory over them.

Botha argues that Shechem and Succoth bring to mind the patriarchal period, suggesting the fulfillment of the Abrahamic land promise.[51] In Genesis 12:6–7, God promises the land of Shechem to Abraham (Abram). Jacob dwelled in Shechem and Succoth (Gen 33:17–18),[52] and he had earlier dwelled in Gilead (Gen 31:21).[53] Further, Psalm 108's canonical context alludes to the fulfillment of another promise made in Genesis. Psalm 110:1 and 6 allude to Genesis 3:15,[54] indicating a fulfillment of the promise to crush the serpent's head in Genesis 3. It seems likely, therefore, that the place names Shechem, Succoth, and Gilead allude to the patriarchal period, bringing to mind God's promise that Israel would inherit the land. The context of Psalm 108 bears this observation out because the whole psalm concerns a new conquest of the land.

Moreover, the enemies described in Psalm 108:8–10 correspond to the hope of the Davidic kingdom.[55] Isaiah 11:13–14 recounts:

> The jealousy of Ephraim shall depart, and those who harass Judah shall be cut off; Ephraim shall not be jealous of Judah, and Judah shall not harass Ephraim. But they shall swoop down

49. Schaefer, *Psalms*, 269.

50. Hossfeld and Zenger, *Commentary on Psalms 101–150*, 120.

51. Botha, "Psalm 108," 582.

52. Hossfeld and Zenger, *Commentary on Psalms 101–150*, 120.

53. Segal, *A New Psalm*, 523.

54. James Hamilton, "The Skull Crushing Seed of the Woman: Inner-Biblical Interpretation of Genesis 3:15," *SBJT* 10, no. 2 (2006): 37.

55. Hossfeld and Zenger, *Commentary on Psalms 101–150*, 120.

> on the shoulder of the Philistines in the west, and together they shall plunder the people of the east. They shall put out their hand against Edom and Moab, and the Ammonites shall obey them. (ESV)

Ephraim and Judah work together to defeat the Philistines, Edom, Moab, and the Ammonites. In Psalm 108, Ephraim (the helmet) and Judah (the scepter) exult over Philistia and subjugate Edom and Moab.[56] Through the tribe of Judah, David and the Messiah come (Gen 49:10; Num 24:17-19.[57] Ephraim probably represents the northern kingdom of Israel, and their reunion is part of the eschatological coming together of the kingdom (see Ezek 37:19). The conquest that Psalm 108 describes, therefore, points to the future fulfillment of the Davidic kingdom with Judah—through whom the Messiah would come—ruling. Psalm 108 thus describes an eschatological victory.

Edom represents Israel's great eschatological enemy, and it is mentioned twice in Psalm 108 (108:10, 11). Leslie Allen writes, "As in Amos 9:12, Edom is the eschatological archenemy (cf. Ps 137:7)."[58] Edom stood by as Judah was plundered and exiled (Obad 10–14). In the kingdom, however, the survivors of the exile will rule over Edom (Obad 21). The double mention of Edom in Psalm 108 underscores the animosity towards Edom and its unique status as Israel's "eschatological archenemy."[59]

Notably, both Edom and Moab are not annihilated, but they join the kingdom of God as servants. Moab becomes Israel's wash-basin, and Edom fetches God's shoe like a slave.[60] Some argue that hurling a shoe at Edom signifies ownership, citing Ruth 4:7 as evidence for this ancient custom.[61] While God certainly claims ownership of Edom, he also press-

---

56. Moab, Edom, and Philistia are also mentioned in Exod 15:14–15. DeClaissé-Walford, Jacobson, and Tanner, *Psalms*, 824.

57. Raymond Jacques Tournay, *Seeing and Hearing God with the Psalms: The Prophetic Liturgy of the Second Temple in Jerusalem*, trans. J. Edward Crowley, JSOTSup 118 (Sheffield: Sheffield Academic, 1991), 179.

58. Allen, *Psalms 101–150*, 79.

59. Goldingay states that "there is no particular reason to interpret Edom as an eschatological enemy." Goldingay, *Psalms 90–150*, 264. But given Amos 9:12, Obad, and the placement of Ps 108 in the fifth Book of the Psalter, there are ample reasons to interpret Edom eschatologically.

60. Alexander, *Psalms*), 2:70; Rogerson and McKay, *Psalms 101–150*, 58.

61. Tournay, *Seeing and Hearing*, 179; Richard J. Clifford, *Psalms 73–150*, AOTC (Nashville: Abingdon, 2003), 170; deClaissé-Walford, Jacobson, and Tanner, *Psalms*, 824.

es Edom into service. Casting a shoe at Edom, therefore, probably should be interpreted in the same manner as God calling Moab his wash-basin. Both nations serve God. Just as Moab becomes God's wash-basin, so also is Edom his slave. The phrase "I will exult over Philistia" in Psalm 108:10 is an "expression of triumph over a conquered enemy."[62]

Psalm 108:11 continues God's speech but is not part of the oracular promise (Ps 108:8–10). David records God asking two questions: "Who will bring me to the fortified city" and "Who will lead me to Edom?" The questions are rhetorical. God's glory rises above the earth, and he claims it as his own. He needs no guide. The subtext behind the rhetorical questions is that no one can bring God to a fortified city nor lead him to Edom. God is over all.

The fortified city may be Bozrah, which is located in Edom (Gen 36:33).[63] Rogerson and McKay suggest the city of Petra (Obad 3).[64] Defining a specific location for the generic noun מִבְצָר is a tenuous venture. It may not even be the intent of the psalm to define a specific geographical location. Botha, for example, notes how Psalm 108:11 uses מִבְצָר instead of מָצוֹר, as Psalm 60:11 uses,[65] which he suggests creates a wordplay with Psalm 108:13: "Give us help from the enemy (מִצָּר)."[66] It is possible that the psalm uses מִבְצָר simply to create this wordplay with מִצָּר. But Botha's argument may be only partially correct. Read within its canonical context, the "fortified city" of Psalm 108:11 may refer to the city for which the redeemed of God sought in Psalm 107 (Ps 107:4, 7, and 36).[67] If so, the rhetorical question in Psalm 108:11 implies that God is able to lead his people to a fortified city, a place safe from the enemy. This clarifies why Psalm 108 switches מָצוֹר (Ps 60:11) for מִבְצָר in Psalm 108:11, namely, because of the wordplay in Psalm 108:13 and because of the connection to Psalm 107.[68] God will lead his people to מִבְצָר, which protects them from the enemy (מִצָּר).

---

62. Alexander, *Psalms*, 3:91.

63. Segal, *A New Psalm*, 523.

64. Rogerson and McKay, *Psalms 101–150*, 58–59.

65. According to Tournay, מָצוֹר is a play on words with Bosra (i.e., Botsrah), the capital of Idumaea. Tournay, *Seeing and Hearing*, 179.

66. Botha, "Psalm 108," 588.

67. Vesco, *Le Psautier de David*, 2:1037.

68. The editor(s) may have made this switch to tie Ps 108 closer to Ps 107. If the change is original to David, then the editor(s) would have intended this connection to be made between Ps 107 and Ps 108. In ch. 5, I suggest a hermeneutical framework

In Psalm 108:12, the voice of the community joins with David in prayer. The prayer of David becomes the prayer of the people of God. In the beginning of the psalm, the prayer seems to be the prayer of an individual, but it soon takes on universal significance. In Psalm 108:7, David's prayer already includes the community ("beloved ones").[69] Psalm 108:5–6 expands the scope of the psalm to include the entire world. Moreover, the oracle in Psalm 108:8–10 concerns the nations surrounding Israel. In this psalm, David's individual prayer to God thus includes God's people, the nations, and the entire world. The psalm speaks in cosmic terms.[70]

In Psalm 108:2, David readies his heart and praises God (see Ps 108:3–4). He confesses God's faithfulness (Ps 108:5) and trusts in God's promise of victory (Ps 108:8–10). It seems unlikely, therefore, that David believes that God has "rejected us" (Ps 108:12). Rather, David leans into God's faithfulness.[71] He asks whether God has rejected his people in order to persuade God to act on what he has promised. God had promised victory over Israel's enemies (Ps 108:8–10), but David complains that God does not go out with Israel's armies.

Only with God's help will David lead his people to victory for the "salvation of man is vain" (108:13).[72] The term "vain" (שָׁוְא) resonates with biblical wisdom literature (Job 7:3; 11:11; 15:31; 31:5, 35:13; Prov 30:8). This resonance may be significant because Psalm 107 ends with a call to be wise: "Whoever is wise, let him attend to these things; let them consider the steadfast love of the LORD" (Ps 107:43 ESV). Following after Psalm 107, Psalm 108 may continue the message of Psalm 107.

Moreover, the transition from the singular in Psalm 107:43a ("him") to the plural in Psalm 107:43b ("them") may carry messianic implications. Nancy DeClaissé-Walford argues, "By placing fifteen psalms of David in

---

to understand how David's intent and the editor's intent can work together without David's intent being lost.

69. W. Dennis Tucker notes that the shift to the plural in Ps 108:7 indicates the communal nature of the psalm in W. Dennis Tucker Jr., *Constructing and Deconstructing Power in Psalms 107–150* (Atlanta: SBL, 2014), 70.

70. Tucker, *Constructing and Deconstructing Power*, 69.

71. Goldingay comments, "[T]he function of the rhetorical question is to press the matter into God's own thinking, to drive God to think about it and to dare to take responsibility for the answer." Goldingay, *Psalms 90–150*, 270. Goldingay uses overly provocative language to make his point. David does not give God new information or "dare" him to act. David, instead, calls on God to fulfill his promise.

72. Clifford economically describes Ps 108:13–14 with "Human help is worthless." Clifford, *Psalms 73–150*, 170.

Book Five and, specifically, Psalms 108, 109, and 110 directly after Psalm 107, the shapers of the Psalter suggest that the answer to the question, 'Who is the wise one?' of Psalm 107:43 is David, the ideal king of ancient Israel."[73] According to her, when David swears fealty to YHWH in Psalm 108:13–14, the "postexilic community" would afterward imitate David's example.[74] On this reading, the "him" in Psalm 107:43a would be the messiah. It also seems possible to identify the "them" who "consider the steadfast love of the LORD" in Psalm 107:43b as the post-exilic community. Psalm 108:13–14 would thus intentionally carry forward the message of Psalm 107 by highlighting the "wise" man who is the messiah.

Psalm 108 ends with a statement of trust in God who will conquer Israel's foes. When God faithfully fulfills his promise to reconquer the land (Ps 108:8–10), then Israel's armies will do valiantly (Ps 108:14a). Ultimately, however, God "will tread down our enemy" (Ps 108:14b).[75] In these verses, David speaks in the first person plural. According to Vesco, this means that David functions as "the spokesperson of Israel" (*comme porte parole d'Israël*).[76] As king, David represents his people. He uses the royal "we," showing his solidarity with the community of faith. David's wise confession of trust in God overlaps with the voice of the community.

Conclusion

In Psalm 108, David asks God to reveal his eschatological glory and to assert his sovereignty over the world. In so doing, God will deliver the kingdom to David, and the people of God will dwell securely. Psalm 108 is not an example of "grotesque nationalism," as Terrien claims.[77] It is, instead, a song of trust in God who is faithful and who will fulfill his

---

73. Nancy L. deClaissé-Walford, *Reading from the Beginning: The Shaping of the Hebrew Psalter* (Macon, GA: Mercer University Press, 1997), 97. Wilson already argued that David is the wise man who heeds the words of Ps 107 in *Editing of the Hebrew Psalter*, 221.

74. DeClaissé-Walford, *Reading from the Beginning*, 93.

75. Rogerson and McKay see God here as a "warrior king." Rogerson and McKay, *Psalms 101–150*, 58. Cf. Clifford, *Psalms 73–150*, 169–70.

76. Vesco, *Le Psautier de David*, 2:1039. Grogan sees the roles of the king and individual uniting, so that the king is the "royal representative of the people, on whom the whole nation speaks in prayer and praise." Grogan, *Psalms*, 182.

77. Terrien, *Psalms*, 742.

promises to his people. God will lead David to absolute victory over his enemies and will establish the kingdom of God.

CANONICAL CONTEXT OF PSALM 108

The Psalter narrates the redemptive-historical story of Israel.[78] Books I–III of the Psalter relate to the kingdom era,[79] Book IV to the exile,[80] and Book V to the post-exilic period.[81] The location of Psalm 108 in Book V clarifies how the psalm contributes to the redemptive-historical story of the Psalter. Since Psalm 108 is in Book V, the psalm appears in a post-exilic context. Understanding that context is, therefore, vital to understanding Psalm 108.

Book V

In their introduction to Book V of the Psalter, Nancy deClaissé-Walford, Rolf Jacobson, and Beth Tanner characterize Book V as a celebration of life after returning from Babylon: "Book Five of the Psalter leads readers/

78. Nancy deClaissé-Walford writes,

> The Psalter is shaped traditionally into five books which narrate a history of ancient Israel. Books One and Two celebrate the reigns of David and Solomon; Book Three laments the dark days of oppression during the divided kingdoms and the Babylonian exile; and Books Four and Five look forward to and rejoice in Israel's restoration to the land and in the reign of YHWH as king. With the surety of the story of the Psalter (and the story in the rest of the Hebrew scriptures), the postexilic Isralite [sic] community could continue to exist as an identifiable entity in a world it no longer controlled.

DeClaissé-Walford, *Reading from the Beginning*, 5.

79. Wilson, *Editing of the Hebrew Psalter*, 207–8, 213.

80. Book IV at least points to a time in which David no longer ruled and the kingdom of Israel was in decline. For a helpful overview of Book IV, see Erich Zenger, "The God of Israel's Reign," 161–90.

81. Goulder, *Psalms of the Return*, 17. In their introduction, Hossfeld and Zenger describe Book V in this way: "whereas the exilic perspective had dominated the Fourth Book of Psalms, Psalm 107 and those that follow present the end of the exile and the beginning/already begun restoration of Zion/Israel—and do so in the form of a grand literary-fictional 'liturgy of thanksgiving' whose compositional arc extends to Psalm 136 and that, in terms of its origins, can be located within the sections made up of Psalms 107; 108–110; 111–112; 113–118; 119; 120–134; 135–136." Hossfeld and Zenger, *Commentary on Psalms 101–150*, 2. The language of "literary-fictional" is unfortunate. Book V of the Psalter does narrate events that did not happen in history, but this is not because Book V is fictional. Rather, Book V is eschatological. The events it describes go beyond Israel's historical past.

hearers from the despair of exile in Babylon to the celebration of a new life in the land of Israel with God as sovereign and the torah as the guide for life."[82] After their return to the land, the people of God needed to learn how to live in their new situation. According to these authors, this new situation included the failure of the Davidic monarchy and Israel's subjugation to major world powers.[83] "Thus," they explain, "the Psalter is a story of survival in the changed and changing world that confronted the postexilic Israelite community of faith."[84]

DeClaissé-Walford, Jacobson, and Tanner understand the Psalter's story historically. God's people returned to the land and dealt with the new reality there. According to these authors, Book V teaches the community of believers how to live in light of their new historical situation.

In a similar way, Tucker studies Book V of the Psalter in light of imperial dominance over Israel. He sees "an anti-imperial tendency in the Psalter."[85] Thus, Psalm 108 is part of a story of hostility toward the nations.[86] Within this context, Psalm 108 highlights the hostility of the nations that surround Israel.[87]

Understanding the broader historical context of the Psalter helps to elucidate its meaning. However, deClaissé-Walford, Jacobson, Tanner, and Tucker overemphasize the history outside of the text and underemphasize the redemptive-historical narrative of Book V.[88] In contrast, Robert Wallace speaks of the Psalter as a story, and he defines the

82. DeClaissé-Walford, Jacobson, and Tanner, *Psalms*, 811.

83. DeClaissé-Walford, Jacobson, and Tanner, *Psalms*, 811.

84. DeClaissé-Walford, Jacobson, and Tanner, *Psalms*, 811.

85. Tucker, *Constructing and Deconstructing Power*, 16. See also Dennis Tucker Jr., "Empires and Enemies in Book V of the Psalter," in *The Composition of the Book of Psalms*, ed. Erich Zenger, Bibliotheca Ephemeridum Theologicarum Lovaniensium 238 (Leuven, Belgium: Uitgeverij Peeters, 2010), 723–31.

86. Tucker, *Constructing and Deconstructing Power*, 68.

87. Tucker, *Constructing and Deconstructing Power*, 68. For more on the idea of the enemy in Book V, see W. Dennis Tucker Jr., "The Role of the Foe in Book 5: Reflections on the Final Composition of the Psalter," in *The Shape and Shaping of the Book of Psalms: The Current State of Scholarship*, ed. Nancy L. deClaissé-Walford (Atlanta: SBL, 2014), 179–91.

88. I am not creating an opposition between history and canon. As Geerhardus Vos states, "The Psalter is wide awake to the significance of history as leading up to the eschatological act of God." Geerhardus Vos, "Eschatology of the Psalter," *The Princeton Theological Review* 18 (1920): 13, https://commons.ptsem.edu/id/princetontheolog1811arms-dmd002. Rather, I am arguing that the history that the Psalter explicitly narrates leads to a clear understanding of the Psalter's meaning.

canonical shape of the Psalter as the setting to understand Book IV of the Psalter:

> The canonical shape of the Psalter provides a hermeneutical setting in which one can productively read Book IV. While according to traditional form-critical categories the Psalter is not classified as "narrative," a narrative impulse exists within the Psalter, and Book IV is a part of that story.[89]

Book V continues this narrative impulse as it narrates the story of the Psalter.[90] Wallace's approach more closely follows the history narrated within the Psalter than deClaissé-Walford, Jacobson, Tanner, and Tucker do. By tracing the story that the opening of Book V tells, readers can understand the redemptive-historical narrative found within the Psalter. While the exilic situation under Persian dominance provides historical information that can furnish an understanding of the possible motivation behind the compilation of Book V, the primary interpretive emphasis should lie on the canonical story being told in Book V.

Located at the beginning of Book V, Psalm 108 exists within an eschatological context because Psalms 107–110 present God's eschatological redemption of Israel and the establishment of his kingdom. This eschatological accent does not suddenly appear in Book V but follows naturally from Book IV. Psalms 106 and 107 retell Israel's history and set up the expectation for an eschatological redemption. In Psalm 106, Israel suffers in exile.[91] When Psalm 107 recounts Israel's return from exile (cf. Pss 107:1–3; 106:47), it casts Israel's hope in eschatological terms. The return signals a restoration to paradise (Ps 107:35). Furthermore, when Psalm 107 highlights Israel's redemption from exile (Ps 107:3),[92] it uses language reminiscent of a new exodus (e.g., Ps 107:4, 7). Psalm 108 continues this eschatological trajectory. In this psalm, God's glory extends across the globe and Israel has absolute victory over the nations that surround her (Ps 108:5–6, 8–10). In Psalm 110, God along with the king

89. Wallace, *Narrative Effect of Book IV*, 1.

90. Wallace, *Narrative Effect of Book IV*, 84.

91. Zenger specifies that Israel's dire situation is due to the collapse of Alexander's empire. Zenger, "The God of Israel's Reign," 187. Undoubtedly, the fall of Alexander's empire would have affected Israelites. However, the redemptive-historical story that the Psalter tells locates Pss 105 and 106 within the period of Babylonian captivity.

92. For Wilson, Book V is the answer to the plea of the exilic community to be gathered from *diaspora*. Wilson, *Editing of the Hebrew Psalter*, 227.

will claim absolute victory over the nations (Ps 110:5–7).[93] In these ways, the introductory psalms in Book V are eschatological.

The following discussion will provide further details concerning the canonical and eschatological context of Psalm 108. It will demonstrate that Psalms 104, 105, 106 naturally lead up to Psalms 107 and 108 and that these psalms narrate an eschatological story.

Psalms 104, 105, and 106

The choice to limit Psalm 108's preceding context to Psalms 104–107 is not arbitrary because certain qualities of Psalms 104–107 give credence to the notion that Psalms 104–107 should be intentionally read as the near canonical context to Psalm 108.[94] First, Psalms 104–106 narrate Israel's history from creation to covenant and then to exile. Additionally, Psalms 104, 105, and 106 form a narrative conclusion to Book IV. Psalm 106, in particular, concludes Book IV with a call for rescue from exile as God had rescued Israel in the past (cf. Ps 106:47). Psalm 107 answers the cry of Psalm 106:47 to save Israel from exile. As a unit, Psalms 104–107 narrate a sequence of events that lead to Psalm 108. Psalm 108, along with Psalms 109 and 110, gives shape to that rescue.

By noting the ways in which Psalms 104–106 join through the use of word-links, thematic links, and contextual cues, readers may better appreciate the story being told. This discussion continues, therefore, with an outline showing how these psalms relate to one another and lead into Psalms 107 and 108, giving weight to their thematic progression.

Psalm 104 celebrates God's power to create and his divine providence.[95] Psalms 103 and 104 share a catch phrase, serving to transition from one psalm to the next. Specifically, the first verse of Psalm 104 repeats the phrase that ends Psalm 103:

---

93. According to David Mitchell, Ps 110 is eschatological, and it elucidates the eschatological time table of surrounding psalms. In his program, Ps 107 celebrates the ingathering of the latter-day exile, Ps 108 might be the "Messiah's petition and sword song," and Psalm 109 may portray a "pre-battle ritual curse." Mitchell, *Message of the Psalter*, 266. Mitchell rightly detects the eschatological nature of Pss 107–110, although this book will not follow his suggestions for the specific meaning of these psalms.

94. In an obvious sense, Pss 1–107 supply the preceding context for Ps 108. But for the sake of practicality, Pss 104–107 will provide a near context.

95. Mitchell says that Ps 104 celebrates "Yhwh's creator benefits to his creatures." Mitchell, *Message of the Psalter*, 293.

103:22 בָּרֲכִי נַפְשִׁי אֶת־יְהוָה

104:1 בָּרֲכִי נַפְשִׁי אֶת־יְהוָה

The repetition transitions Psalm 103 to Psalm 104. Also of note is that Psalm 104's lack of superscription possibly aligns it with Psalm 103, which carries a superscription identifying David as its author.[96] Psalm 103 highlights God's salvation and Psalm 104, as noted, focuses on God's creation.[97]

Although Psalms 103 and 104 share similarities and Psalm 104 lacks a superscription, there is canonical warrant for reading Psalms 104–106 together and apart from Psalm 103. For instance, Psalm 103's shared language with Psalm 104 may simply serve to transition from Psalm 103 to Psalm 104. Moreover, there is no rule stating that Psalm 104 cannot both share similarities or even pair with Psalm 103 and yet be part of another group of psalms.[98] Another point of consideration is that Psalm 104's historical focus (creation) thematically fits with the focus of Psalms 105 and 106. Psalm 105 recounts Israel's history, and Psalm 106 ends with Israel in exile. Also, this study claims that Psalm 103 organically flows into Psalm 104 because the editors of the Psalter have skillfully tied psalms together across the Psalter. Therefore, readers should expect Psalms 103 and 104 to share thematic and linguistic similarities. Finally, while reading Psalms 103–106 as a unit is formally valid, Psalms 104–106 narrate the story of Israel from creation to exile and, consequently, form a narrative backdrop to Psalm 107. This backdrop allows Psalm 107 to begin a trajectory of eschatological salvation to which Psalm 108 also contributes. For these reasons, this study is justified in presenting a conjoined reading of Psalms 104–106.[99]

---

96. Beat Weber, *Werkbuch Psalmen II: Die Psalmen 73 Bis 150* (Stuttgart: W. Kohlhammer GmbH, 2003), 184.

97. Weber sees Pss 103 and 104 as twin psalms. For Weber, Ps 103 concerns salvation and Ps 104 speaks of creation. The psalms thus highlight *Heil und Schöpfung*. Weber, *Werkbuch Psalmen II*, 192. In contrast, Mitchell (*Message of the Psalter*, 293) argues that Ps 104 highlights a different theme than Ps 103, namely, God's benefits being given to his creatures.

98. As Rolf Rendtorff notes, "This psalm is closely linked connected with other hymns that precede and follow it" in Rolf Rendtorff, *Canonical Hebrew Bible*, 332.

99. Formally, Pss 103–106 seem to constitute a group. Thematically, however, Pss 104–106 appear to narrate the world's history from creation to exile. I have limited my discussion to Pss 104–106 primarily for the sake of simplicity, although I also think it is justified due to their narrative continuity.

Psalm 104:1–4 presents God in his majesty before lauding his power to create and his providence (104:5–35). Psalms 104 and 103 share common words at their borders. Such words include "to bless" (Ps 103:1, 2, 20, 21, 22; Ps 104:1, 35) and "soul" (Ps 103:1, 2, 22; Ps 104:1, 35). Their repetition smoothly transitions one psalm to the next.[100] As the beginning of a narrative sequence, Psalm 104 speaks of God's creation and providence. Following the account of God's creation, Psalms 105 and 106 recount Israel's history.[101] Psalm 105 begins with Abraham and ends with the exodus. Psalm 106 reflects on Israel's past sins and ends with Israel in exile.[102] Like Psalms 104 and 105, Psalms 105 and 106 smoothly transition from one to the next. For example, Psalm 105's ending sounds like Psalm 106's beginning:

105:45 בַּעֲבוּר יִשְׁמְרוּ חֻקָּיו וְתוֹרֹתָיו יִנְצֹרוּ הַלְלוּ־יָהּ׃

106:1 הַלְלוּיָהּ הוֹדוּ לַיהוָה כִּי־טוֹב כִּי לְעוֹלָם חַסְדּוֹ

The phrase that ends Psalm 105 (הַלְלוּ־יָהּ) is the same phrase that begins Psalm 106: "praise Yah" or *halleluyah* (הַלְלוּ־יָהּ). In addition to this linking mechanism, Psalm 105:1 opens the psalm with the term הוֹדוּ, and the same word appears in the opening of Psalm 106:1 (הַלְלוּיָהּ | הוֹדוּ). The terms "remember" (105:5, 8, 42; 106:4, 7, 45),[103] "covenant" (105:8, 10; 106:45),[104] "wonder" (105:2, 5; 106:7, 22),[105] and "chosen" (105:6, 43; 106:5, 23)[106] contribute to a sense of cohesion among these psalms. These thematic, exegetical,

---

100. Catchphrases are not the best sign of editorial cohesion. See Wilson, *Editing of the Hebrew Psalter*, 196. Catchphrases, however, add to a sense of continuity as one psalm gives way another.

101. Rendtorff (*Canonical Hebrew Bible*, 333) comments, "Psalm 106 is, as it were, 'twinned' with Ps 105, since again it speaks of the same history between God and Israel."

102. Wallace (*Narrative Effect of Book IV*, 80) writes, "Psalm 105 emphasizes God's faithfulness to the covenant to Abraham by mighty works. Nothing compromises God's actions in Ps 105. Psalm 106, however, tells of an Israel that failed to remember YHWH's mighty works in its continual sinning. The first psalm calls for trust, the second psalm for repentance."

103. The verb "remember" or זכר appears uncommonly in Book IV of the Psalter (Pss 98:3; 103:18; 105:5, 8, 42; 106:4, 7, 45).

104. All but one occurrence in Book IV appears in these two psalms (Pss 103:18; 105:8, 10; 106:45)

105. In Book IV, four out of six occurrences appear in these two psalms (Pss 96:3; 98:1; 105:2, 5; 106:7, 22)

106. The term only occurs in these two psalms in Book IV (Pss 105:6, 43; 106:5, 23)

and contextual cues solidify the relationship between the two psalms. Clearly, these psalms should be read together.

Psalm 105 encourages readers to seek God's face and rejoice by remembering how God rescued Israel from Egypt.[107] God did so by honoring his covenant to Abraham (105:6, 9–10, 42) and bestowing the land upon Israel for their obedience (105:45). However, they were not always obedient. In Psalm 106, the psalmist recounts Israel's continual sin and God's repetitive rescue of Israel.[108] God remembers his covenant (106:45) and always has. Therefore, the psalmist cries on behalf of the exilic community: "Save us, YHWH our God, and gather us from the nations to praise your holy name and to laud your praises" (106:47).

Psalms 105 and 106 have the canonical effect of embedding a narrative into the end of Book IV. The psalms record God's history of redemption, and they expect him to redeem Israel again on the basis of his covenantal faithfulness (cf. Ps 106:1, 7, and 45).[109] Significantly, the term חֶסֶד appears 127 times within the entire Psalter, and sixty of those occurrences are in Book V of the Psalter, which begins immediately after Psalm 106 (i.e., Pss 107–150).[110] Nearly half of the uses of חֶסֶד appear in the Psalter's final book, perhaps answering the call of Psalm 106: God is always faithful (חֶסֶד) to rescue his chosen people.

Psalm 107

A number of thematic connections bind Psalms 106 and 107. The beginning of Psalm 107:1 alludes to the end of Psalm 106, just as Psalm 106 alludes to Psalm 105. The language of "praise" and חֶסֶד resound in the entrance to Psalm 107 and the exit from Psalm 106:

---

107. According to Mitchell, "The desert theme and the related exodus theme reoccur in Psalm 105, which celebrates God's gift of a land to Israel and the deeds of power by which he gave it." Mitchell, *Message of the Psalter*, 294.

108. Nancy deClaissé-Walford describes Ps 106 as a psalm which highlights YHWH's salvation of Israel despite their failure. See deClaissé-Walford, *Reading from the Beginning*, 90.

109. Zenger argues that Psalms 105–106 present Israel's history as a "covenant history." Zenger, "The God of Israel's Reign," 186.

110. Michael Snearly argues that חֶסֶד is a major theme in Book V of the Psalter. See Snearly, *Return of the King*, 105.

107:1	הדו לַיהוָה כִּי־טוֹב כִּי לְעוֹלָם חַסְדּוֹ
106:47c	לְהֹדוֹת לְשֵׁם קָדְשֶׁךָ
106:45	וַיִּזְכֹּר לָהֶם בְּרִיתוֹ וַיִּנָּחֵם כְּרֹב חֲסָדוֹ

The phrase הדו לַיהוָה in Psalm 107:1 corresponds to לְהֹדוֹת לְשֵׁם קָדְשֶׁךָ in Psalm 106:47, and חַסְדּוֹ in Psalm 107:1 matches חֲסָדוֹ in Psalm 106:45.

The particular shape of God's *hesed* to Israel, which results in her praise of him, comes into focus as Psalm 107 repeatedly alludes to the end of Psalm 106. Psalm 107 seemingly answers specific requests from Psalm 106:

107:2a	יֹאמְרוּ גְּאוּלֵי יְהוָה
106:46b	לִפְנֵי כָּל־שׁוֹבֵיהֶם
107:3a	וּמֵאֲרָצוֹת קִבְּצָם
106:47b	וְקַבְּצֵנוּ מִן־הַגּוֹיִם
107:6a	וַיִּצְעֲקוּ אֶל־יְהוָה בַּצַּר לָהֶם
106:44a	וַיַּרְא בַּצַּר לָהֶם

In Psalm 106:46 God has compassion on Israel before her captors, but in Psalm 107:2 the redeemed of YHWH speak. The call for God to gather Israel from the nations in Psalm 106:47 finds an answer in Psalm 107:3 when God has gathered Israel from the nations. Finally, Psalm 107:6 looks back to Israel's call to God in distress, which alludes to Psalm 106:44 when God sees Israel in her distress. Considered together, Psalm 107 appears to provide the redemption that Psalm 106 seeks, using language specifically fitted to answer Psalm 106.

The shape of salvation in Psalm 107 is typological. God's rescue of Israel, chronicled in Psalms 106 and 107, recalls how God has saved in the past and will save again in the future. As God commanded Adam and Eve to be fruitful and multiply and made Israel be fruitful and multiply in the past (Gen 1:26–28; Exod 1:20), so also he continues to do (Ps 107:38 with Ps 105:24). Likewise, as God saved in the first exodus (Ps 106:9), he continues to do (Ps 107:33).

Psalm 107 portrays the redeemed of YHWH speaking from the perspective of the future. As such, Psalm 107 is a future-prophetic psalm.[111] It speaks of a redemption that goes beyond the historical circumstances of Israel.[112] For example, the return from exile is described in universal terms in Psalm 107:3. Additionally, Psalm 107:35–38 describes the land in eschatological terms, evoking images of a new Eden. This description does not correspond to the accounts of the return in Ezra and Nehemiah, both of which describe the return in rather muted terms (cf. Ezra 2:64; Neh 7:66). A full return of exiles from across the world had not occurred in the way that Psalm 107:3 describes. Therefore, Psalm 107 is likely referring to a time in the future when the redeemed of YHWH recount God's great salvation.

This type of reference is not uncommon in the Old Testament. Isaiah 53 is written from a futuristic point of view.[113] James Hamilton points to Exodus 15 and Isaiah 40 as further examples of this phenomena.[114] In Exodus 15, Israel sings a song about a future salvation although the song is framed as if Israel's salvation had already happened (cf. Exod 15:13). Isaiah 40:1–2 also speaks about an act of redemption that is clearly set in the future.

In Psalm 107, the theme of the exodus is developed by the use of the rare term יְשִׁימוֹן ("wilderness"), which occurs only four times in the Psalter and six times in the entire Bible (Isa 43:19–20; Pss 68:8; 78:40;

111. James Hamilton, "Psalm 107: Thank the Lord for His Steadfast Love" (Sermon presented at the Kenwood Baptist Church, Louisville, KY, July 23, 2017), https://kenwoodbaptistchurch.com/sermons/thank-the-lord-for-his-steadfast-love/.

112. Against Clifford (*Psalms 73–150*, 167) who comments, "Psalm 107 ends with Israel giving thanks for deliverance in Canaan." Tucker (*Constructing and Deconstructing Power*, 59) more accurately describes Ps 107 as God's faithful redemption and gathering of his people. But Tucker likewise reads Ps 107 historically and not eschatologically.

113. Brevard Childs writes of Isa 53:2, "The description is clearly retrospective in nature, and looks back on an experience in the past that continues to evoke painful reflection." Brevard S. Childs, *Isaiah: A Commentary*, Old Testament Library (Louisville, KY: Westminster John Knox, 2001), s.v. "Isaiah 53:2–3.". The same phenomenon occurs in the New Testament when Zechariah prays, "Blessed be the Lord God of Israel, for he has visited and redeemed his people" (Luke 1:68). At this time, God had not yet completed the redemption of his people nor visited. Mary would bear Jesus about six months later (see Luke 1:36).

114. Hamilton, "Thank the Lord."

106:14; 107:4).[115] Significantly, this term appears in both Psalms 106 and 107. In Psalm 106:14, the wilderness refers to Israel's sojourn in the wilderness during the exodus. In Psalm 107:4, the wilderness appears to be a metaphorical wilderness where the Israelites sojourned during the exile.[116] Psalms 106 and 107 recount two rescues from the wilderness: one rescue during the original wanderings of the exodus and the other rescue during the exilic wanderings in the wilderness. This pattern of wandering and rescue creates the expectation that the shape of God's salvation will look like it has in the past. If Psalm 107 speaks about God's redemption from the perspective of the future, then it confirms that God will save Israel as he has in the past.

Therefore, the typological logic of Psalms 105 and 106 brings with it an expectation that God will save Israel as he always has. Significantly, then, Psalms 108–110 and 138–145 focus on David, Psalms 111–117 and 120–134 relate to the exodus, and Psalm 119 highlights the Torah, all of which perhaps give shape to Israel's future salvation.

Link-words also tie Psalm 107 to Psalm 106. For example, Psalm 106 uses the term ידה (106:1, 47), a word heavily populated among Psalms 105–109 and especially used in Psalm 107 (Pss 105:1; 106:1, 47; 107:1, 8, 15, 21, 31; 108:4; 109:30). Psalm 107 begins and ends with the term חֶסֶד (107:1, 43), a word Psalm 106 also uses (106:1, 7, 45). The theme of rescuing someone in distress (בַּצַּר) also appears in both psalms (Pss 106:44; 107:6, 13, 19, 28).[117]

Psalms 105 and 106 concretely recount Israel's history, including Israel's wilderness wanderings. Psalm 107 identifies the wilderness as a place where some wandered during the exile before God redeemed them. The exilic language serves to frame Psalm 107's salvation in typological language. Additionally, Psalms 105–106 show that God blesses by multiplying, saves as he did in the exodus, rescues those in distress, and leads those who wander in the wilderness as he has done historically in

115. Pss 68, 78, and 106 tie the term יְשִׁימוֹן to the exodus and Israel's wandering in the wilderness. Isa 43:19–20 speaks of an eschatological transformation of the wilderness and uses language that brings to mind a new exodus (cf. Isa 43:16 with 43:19). Ps 107 seems to use יְשִׁימוֹן in an eschatological sense as in Isa 43.

116. In Isa 35, the wilderness (מִדְבָּר) is viewed in eschatological terms. The eschatological wilderness theme is also developed in Isa 43:19–20 in which the term יְשִׁימוֹן appears. Ps 107:4 may also speak of the wilderness in an eschatological way.

117. This phrase appears 14 times in the Psalter and 5 times here (Pss 4:2; 18:7; 31:8; 46:2; 66:14; 81:8; 91:15; 106:44; 107:6, 13, 19, 28; 112:8; 120:1). In Book V, בַּצַּר only occurs two other times, making the phrase a significant linking word in Book V.

the life of Israel. Psalm 107 speaks of how God will redeem his people and is spoken from the perspective of the future. Psalm 108's preceding context narrates God's acts of salvation and chronicles a pattern of typological fulfillment.

Psalm 108

Psalm 108 further narrates the events surrounding God's coming kingdom. This future kingdom of God involves David and the subjection of Israel's enemies. David's kingdom will revive, and the post-exilic community will once again enjoy prosperity and success. A number of connections between Psalms 107 and 108 bind these psalms together.[118] painting a picture of God's rescue of Israel and victory over her enemies. The most important connection is the sequence of events that Psalms 107 and 108 portray. Psalm 107 chronicles the return of Israel. Then, Psalm 108 speaks of the conquest and the establishment of the kingdom.[119]

The relationship between the two psalms is too obvious to be mere coincidence. The evidence suggests that an editor(s) placed Psalm 107 before Psalm 108 intentionally and that the editor(s) meant for Psalms 107 and 108 to be read in sequence. If such a proposition is granted, then Psalm 107's relationship to Psalm 108 parallels the relationship of Psalm 106 to Psalm 107, and Psalm 108 narrates the next stage of the story. Psalm 107 portrays God's future redemption of Israel as a past event. Psalm 108 then reveals the establishment of God's kingdom through a

---

118. The following paragraph paraphrases and clarifies Jean-Luc Vesco's observations in Vesco, Le Psautier de David, 2:1037. Both psalms praise God and his love (107:1, 8, 15, 21, 31, 43; 108:4, 5) and record Israelites praising God among people (107:32; 108:4). Both psalms also highlight God's exaltation (107:25–26; 108:6) and speak of ascending to or above heaven (107:26; 108:5–6). Further, they point to God's deliverance or redemption of Israel (Psalm 107:2; 108:7) and focus on the land (107:35; 108:6). In Ps 108, God's right hand saves (108:7; cf. Ps 107:13, 19) and, in Ps 107, it perhaps clashes with the adversary's hand (107:2; cf. Ps 108:13–14). In both psalms, God is a guide to others (108:11; 107:30). When God goes out with Israel's armies (Ps 108:12; cf. Ps 107:14, 28), he fights the adversary (Ps 108:14; Ps 107:2) and adversity (Ps 108:13; Ps 107:6, 13, 19, 28). In both psalms, God also does wonders for or rescues humankind (108:13; Ps 107:8, 15, 21, 31). Moreover, the two psalms share similar vocabulary like heart (107:12; 108:2), strength (107:26; 108:2), and city (107:4, 7, 36; 108:11). The preceding discussion highlights numerous thematic parallels between Pss 107 and 108. The thematic parallels sufficiently demonstrate a close relationship between the two psalms.

119. I am indebted to James Hamilton for how I describe the sequence of Pss 107–110. He communicated to me his ideas through electronic communication.

new conquest over the nations. Psalms 109 and 110 further elucidate the details of God's universal victory.

Reconsidering the Superscription

According to the superscription, David wrote Psalm 108. As the preceding discussion has shown, however, Psalm 108 exists as part of a redemptive-historical story, and it portrays the future kingdom of God. As the author, David participates in the eschatological events that Psalm 108 portrays. But if Psalm 108 describes the re-conquest of the land after the exile, then it points to a time after David is dead. Mitchell explains, "After the extinction of the kingdom psalms referring to the king or *mashiah* would have been understood as referring only to the anticipated future deliverer."[120] King David is the future deliverer.

With David long dead and the kingdom a distant memory, Psalm 108 reignites hope for the future David and kingdom. In this psalm, David casts his past experience into the future. Put another way, Psalm 108 typologically cites Psalms 57 and 60 to speak about the future. The editor(s) inserted Psalm 108 into Book V of the Psalter within an eschatological context (Pss 107–110) because Psalm 108 speaks about a future Davidic king. The superscription defines David as the author in order to speak of the eschatological king, the new David.

Summary

When we see the word-links, thematic-links, and exegetical cues that connect Psalm 105 to Psalm 106, Psalm 106 to Psalm 107, and Psalm 107 to Psalm 108, a picture emerges of the message they narrate. Psalms 105 and 106 conclude Book IV by recounting Israel's history and relaying an expectation that God will again rescue Israel, in much the same way he has in the past. God's future salvation will thus happen along typological lines. Psalm 107 answers the call for rescue, which is found in Psalm 106. It remains for Psalm 108 to provide further specificity to what God's rescue of Israel means or will mean. Psalm 108 portrays a time when God will rule over all nations, and, since David authored the psalm according to the superscription, Psalm 108 suggests that he plays a role in this reign of God. Psalm 108 thus introduces the idea of God's eschatological reign, which Psalms 109 and 110 further develop.

---

120. Mitchell, *Message of the Psalter*, 87.

CONCLUSION

Psalm 108 concerns the future. David prays that God would reveal his glory across the earth, and this concretely happens when God claims victory over the nations. Since he is the author, Psalm 108 portrays David as the speaker. According to the timeline of the Psalter's redemptive-historical story, Psalm 108 exists in a post-exilic period. David is dead, and therefore David's voice is seen to be the voice of the coming Davidic king. Further, the community of faith joins the prayer of David, so that God's victory over the nations is not only for the king but for the people as well. Psalm 108 is about the king and kingdom.

5

Psalm 108 with Psalms 57 and 60

When we analyze the differences between Psalm 108 and Psalms 57 and 60, a clearer picture emerges of the eschatological message that Psalm 108 communicates.[1] This chapter, therefore, compares Psalm 108 with Psalms 57 and 60 to clarify the meaning of Psalm 108 within its canonical setting. It also explores the interplay between the author of Psalm 108 and the editor(s) of the Psalter to gain a sharper understanding of Psalm 108 within its canonical context.[2] This interplay includes the au-

1. As outlined in ch. 1, the present argument assumes the research of Gerald Wilson and others who have argued that the Psalter is a canonical composition (Wilson, *Editing of the Hebrew Psalter*). In light of the Psalter's canonical composition, the chapter reads Ps 108 within its canonical context (*Sitz im Literatur*). The argument also assumes a basic position of David Mitchell, namely, that Davidic psalms have an eschatological purpose. Mitchell, *Message of the Psalter*. After the demise of the kingdom, psalms about the king anticipate a future king. Mitchell explains, "After the extinction of the kingdom psalms referring to the king or *mashiah* would have been understood as referring only to the anticipated future deliverer." Mitchell, *Message of the Psalter*, 87. As noted in ch. 1, a general redemptive-historical trajectory exists within the Psalter and Ps 108 exists within an eschatological location along that trajectory. Additionally, the chapter reads the Psalter as a theological document, meaning that its shapers formed it according to theological principles. Rolf Rendtorff states the matter plainly: "The Old Testament is a theological book." Rendtorff, *Canonical Hebrew Bible*, 1. It is not a stretch to say that since the Psalter is a theological book, its shapers were interested in theological matters.

2. I will suggest that the editor(s) of the Psalter shaped it to communicate theological meaning in ways that agree with the original authorial intent of each individual psalm. At the same time, the editor(s) may have extended or clarified the meaning already existing in those original psalms. For example, Ps 2 speaks of a messianic king. The editor(s) chose that psalm along with Ps 1 to function as an introduction to the rest of the Psalter. In so doing, the editor(s) presented the messianic king as central to the redemptive-historical storyline of the Psalter. This by no means contradicts Ps 2, but it certainly expands or clarifies how central the messiah is to the history of redemption.

thor[3] of Psalm 108 selectively citing Psalms 57 and 60 and thereby giving Psalm 108 an eschatological accent. It also involves the editor(s) of the Psalter deepening and extending the author's intended meaning by placing Psalm 108 within a sequence of eschatological psalms (Pss 107, 109–110).[4] One way to understand this interplay is to locate Psalm 108 within the redemptive-historical sequence of the Psalter.

REDEMPTIVE-HISTORICAL SEQUENCE

Psalm 108 appears in Book V of the Psalter, and Psalms 57 and 60 are in Book II of the Psalter. Their placement means that the editor(s) inserted Psalm 108 into the Psalter after Psalms 57 and 60. As a result, Psalm 108 can be read as citing Psalms 57 and 60 while differing from them in numerous and meaningful ways.[5]

---

3. This book does not require that David authored Ps 108 nor that the superscription is original to his hand. If these two premises seem impossible to readers, then it is only sufficient to believe that an editor put together the two earlier Davidic psalms (Pss 57 and 60) to highlight the eschatological nature of the coming Davidic king. In this case, a compiler put Ps 108 together, and the same compiler or a later editor placed Ps 108 into its canonical context. The editor would thus capitalize on the canonical placement of Ps 108 after Pss 57 and 60, which allows Ps 108 to be read as citing the two earlier psalms.

4. Ps 108 does not use traditional material for some unknown historical reason as, for example, Jean-Marie Auwers suggests : "L'existence de doublets (Ps 14 = 53 ; Ps 40, 14–18 = 70 ; Ps 108 = 57,8–12 + 60,7–14) ne se comprend bien que par la volonté des éditeurs de respecter les collections antérieurement constituées" ("The existence of doublets (Ps 14 = 53; Ps 40:14–18 = 70; Ps 108 = 57:8–12 and 60:7–14) can be understood only on the basis of the desire of the editors to respect earlier psalm collections"). Auwers, *La Composition Littéraire du Psautier*, 32. Moreover, Ps 108 is not merely a discrete psalm unconnected to its canonical context, as in Brueggemann and Bellinger, *Psalms* , 468–71. Instead, Ps 108 is an intentional composition thatan editor(s) placed into an eschatological *Sitz im Literatur*.

5. Egbert Ballhorn notes that, at the end of the Psalter, psalms begin to cite earlier psalms: "Ps 90 is an answer to Ps 89; Ps 96 is an adaptation of Ps 29; Ps 108 is a composite-psalm from Ps 57 and Ps 60; Ps 144 constitutes a creative re-reading of Ps 18; Ps 149 meaningfully incorporates Ps 2" ("Ps 90 ist eine Antwort auf Ps 89; Ps 96 ist eine Bearbeitung von Ps 29; Ps 108 ist ein Kompositpsalm aus Ps 57 und Ps 60; Ps 144 stellt eine kreative Relecture von Ps 18 dar; Ps 149 nimmt Ps 2 deutend auf"). Ballhorn further notes that the meaning of individual psalms is dependent upon their canonical location and that one must understand Books I–III to grasp Books IV–V of the Psalter. Ballhorn is concerned with how Books IV and V relate to Books I–III of the Psalter. His observations, however, agree with this book's argument that Ps 108 can be seen as citing Pss 57 and 60 due to its later canonical location. Ballhorn, Zum Telos des Psalters, 13.

Book II of the Psalter relates to the period of David's rule during the united kingdom of Judah and Israel within the redemptive-historical framework of the Psalter.[6] In contrast, Psalm 108 exists in Book V of the Psalter, and this book concerns post-exilic realities (e.g., Ps 137) and looks forward to the eschatological kingdom promised to David (e.g., Ps 110). The canonical location of these three psalms thus locates them within different parts of Israel's redemptive-historical story.

But Psalm 108 not only exists within a different canonical location than Psalms 57 and 60. It also differs from Psalms 57 and 60 in numerous ways. Paying attention to these differences clarifies the message that Psalm 108 conveys.[7] One major difference includes the non-historically specific superscription of Psalm 108 that contrasts with the historically specific superscriptions of Psalms 57 and 60.[8]

SUPERSCRIPTIONS

If Psalm 108 already existed when the editor(s) compiled the Psalter, then the editor(s) would have chosen an already existing psalm of David with a non-historically specific superscription that was appropriate for its new canonical context.[9] In contrast to the superscription of Psalm

6. Nancy L. deClaissé-Walford writes, "Books One and Two celebrate the reigns of David and Solomon." DeClaissé-Walford, *Reading from the Beginning*, 5.

7. In ch. 1 I argued that the Psalter was intended to be memorized, and thus the original readers of the Psalter would have been able to spot the differences between Ps 108 and Pss 57 and 60. Religious readers, like those who originally read the Psalter, memorize and meditate on texts. As Paul Griffiths explains after he studied four Buddhist texts, "The works are read (heard), reread, memorized, pondered upon, excerpted, commented upon, chewed over, smelled, and incorporated. This is what religious readers do; it is not what consumerist readers do."Griffiths, *Religious Reading*, 147. Griffiths (*Religious Reading*, 181) finds a similar reading practice among Christian communities in North Africa, "for Christians in Roman Africa, so also for Buddhists in classical India, learning a work was mostly a matter of ears, memory, and mouth." See also Wenham, *Psalms as Torah*, 41.

8. I assume that David penned the superscription of Ps 108. But if the editor(s) added the psalm's superscription, then Ps 108's superscription is consistent with Ps 108's authorial intent. The editor's addition of a non-historically specific superscription and placement into a new canonical context would serve to deepen and extend the meaning that the psalmist had intended the psalm to communicate. In the Psalter, David typologically speaks of a future king, and Ps 108's unique nature (its citation of earlier psalmic material) clarifies how a new David will participate in Israel's eschatological vindication. The vindication described in Ps 108 describes YHWH's conquest of the promised land.

9. Another plausible position is that the editors added a superscription to Psalm 108.

108, which contains no direct allusions to Israel's historical books, the superscriptions of Psalms 57 and 60 refer directly to 1 Samuel, tightly connecting these psalms to Israel's historical books. Due to this lack of historical specificity, the superscription of Psalm 108 invites readers to a deeper understanding of the identity of the Davidic king because, canonically, Psalm 108 exists further along the redemptive-historical storyline of the Psalter than do the two earlier Davidic psalms. The following paragraphs illustrate these points by discussing the superscriptions of Psalms 108, 57, and 60.

The Superscription of Psalm 108

Psalm 108's canonical genre is a שִׁיר מִזְמוֹר, or "a song, *a mizmor*."[10] Form-critical genres may accurately describe a psalm's content or may identify its *Sitz im Leben*, but they do not help a reader understand how a psalm explicitly identifies itself in its canonical location (*Sitz im Literatur*). The discussion that follows, consequently, highlights the canonical genres of the three psalms, which the superscriptions themselves define.

As a מִזְמוֹר, Psalm 108 may allude to Book I of the Psalter because many Davidic psalms define themselves as *mizmorim* in Book I (e.g., Pss 3–6). This connection may serve to cement the Davidic character of Psalm 108. But whatever the precise significance of Psalm 108's genre is, the psalm clearly aligns itself with David: he authors Psalm 108 according to the superscription.[11] As a שִׁיר מִזְמוֹר written by David, Psalm 108 situ-

10. The phrase שִׁיר מִזְמוֹר constitutes a word combination, which occurs together fourteen times in the Hebrew Bible and only in the Psalter (Pss 30:1; 48:1; 65:1; 66:1; 67:1; 68:1; 75:1; 76:1; 83:1; 87:1; 88:1; 92:1; 98:1; 108:1). This combination appears with David as the author four times (Pss 30:1; 65:1; 68:1; 108:1). The distribution of the combination with their various authors perhaps suggests that Ps 108 associates with earlier books, especially Books II and III where this combination primarily exists. The phrase שִׁיר מִזְמוֹר appears only once in Book I (Ps 30:1) and once in Book V (Ps 108:1). Ch. 3 discusses the meaning of this genre in greater detail.

11. The superscription identifies David as the author by the prepositional phrase, לְדָוִד. Daniel Estes disagrees. He argues that the phrase לְדָוִד is ambiguous. Estes, "Psalms," 142. Although the phrase לְדָוִד could mean "about David" or the like, it nevertheless should be read as an authorial designation. 2 Chr 29:30 certainly hints at this when it says: "And Hezekiah the king and the princes commanded the Levites to sing praises to the Lord with the words of David and of Asaph the seer. And they sang praises with gladness, and they bowed down and worshiped" (ESV). Likewise, the New Testament seems to confirm that phrases like לְדָוִד signify authorship (Luke 20:42; Acts 1:16; 2:25, 34). A counter-argument might be that David was associated with the whole Psalter and that the NT quotations thus do not provide evidence that NT authors associated phrases like לְדָוִד with authorship (cf. Acts 4:25). For example,

ates itself both as a Davidic psalm and as a psalm associated with earlier Psalter books that chronicle the story of king David. Psalm 108's Davidic grounding provides a key feature of Psalm 108's eschatological message: David plays a role in God's future reign.

David is the model king for the expected messiah who would rule with God (see Ps 2). Douglas Moo and Andrew Naselli explain:

> As the OT unfolds, Israel's Davidic king more clearly and specifically anticipates the messianic king. The "meaning" of the choice of David to be Israel's king deepens in light of further OT revelation; it goes beyond what David's contemporaries or even David himself recognized.[12]

The meaning of David's kingship deepens as the redemptive-historical storyline of the Bible progresses. The Psalter recounts Israel's history of redemption from the era of the kingdom (Books I–III) to the exilic and post-exilic eras (Books IV–V).[13] Psalm 108, therefore, canonically appears in a post-exilic setting (Book V), and, although David is dead, he will somehow be king when God conquers all of Israel's enemies and establishes his universal reign. A new David must arise after the pattern of the historical David, and Psalm 108 provides insight into the coming Davidic king.

---

after noting that 73 psalms are attributed to David in the Psalter, John Collins writes, "It is now generally accepted that these references were added by an editor long after the time of David, but they contributed to the tendency to see all the Psalms as Davidic." Collins, *Introduction to the Hebrew Bible*, 461. But even if this argument neutralizes the NT's evidence, 2 Chr 29:30, nevertheless, strongly suggests that biblical authors read phrases like לְדָוִד as identifying authorship. I would suggest that the Psalter invites readers to see phrases like לְדָוִד as author designations. If we read the Psalter as a canonical composition, then we should read לְדָוִד as an author designation because that will help us to understand the meaning of a psalm within the Psalter, within its *Sitz im Literatur*. I am indebted to James Hamilton who underscored to me the importance of 2 Chr 29:30.

12. Douglas J. Moo and Andrew David Naselli, "The Problem of the New Testament's Use of the Old Testament," in *The Enduring Authority of the Christian Scriptures*, ed. D. A. Carson (Grand Rapids: Eerdmans, 2016), 735.

13. For the seminal defense of this position, see Wilson, *Editing of the Hebrew Psalter*, 207–28. I disagree with Wilson on some of the particulars, especially his emphasis on the kingship of God without recourse to rule of the Davidic king alongside God (in Book V particularly). The Davidic king's reign is emphasized not only in Book V of the Psalter but also in Pss 1 and 2, which provide an introduction to the whole Psalter. For a cogent argument concerning Pss 1 and 2 as the introduction to the Psalter, see Cole, *Psalms 1–2*.

The Superscriptions of Psalms 57 and 60

The superscriptional genre of Psalm 108 differs from that of Psalms 57 and 60. Within their superscriptions, both psalms contain the term מִכְתָּם. The word מִכְתָּם is a singular, common noun without a definite article, satisfying the criteria for a genre designation in the Psalter.[14] These psalms are thus part of the genre of *miktamim*. The meaning of the term מִכְתָּם is unclear, although the LXX associates the term מִכְתָּם with an inscription in stone (εἰς στηλογραφίαν). William Holladay explains, "The Greek Septuagint translates the term as '(a poem) to be inscribed on a stele,' but whether this is a clue to its original meaning is uncertain."[15]

There are only six psalms whose superscriptions define their genres as *miktamim*: Psalms 16 and 56–60. With the exception of Psalm 16, each of these psalms provide detailed historical information in their superscription. Given this historical focus, it seems possible that a מִכְתָּם refers to historical events that were inscribed.[16] A מִכְתָּם may thus be a psalm that highlights historical events, events that have been or are worthy of being inscribed in stone. Whatever the precise meaning of מִכְתָּם, *miktam* psalms often appear within historically conditioned superscriptions (e.g., Pss 56–60).

According to Nancy deClaissé-Walford, Rolf A. Jacobson, and Beth Laneel Tanner, Psalms 57 and 60 constitute "two of the thirteen psalms in the Psalter whose superscriptions recall specific historical events in the life of David."[17] Certainly both Psalms 57 and 60 provide extensive historical information. The superscription of Psalm 57 reads, "To the choirmaster: according to Do Not Destroy. A Miktam of David, when he fled from Saul, in the cave" (ESV), while the superscription of Psalm 60 says, "To the choirmaster: according to Shushan Eduth. A Miktam of David; for instruction; when he strove with Aram-naharaim and with Aram-zobah, and when Joab on his return struck down twelve thousand

14. Bourguet, "La Structure des Titress," 12. Given Bourguet's study on superscriptions, it seems unlikely that מִכְתָּם is merely an unidentified "musical or liturgical term" as the ESV note on the superscription suggests.

15. William L. Holladay, *The Psalms through Three Thousand Years: Prayerbook of a Cloud of Witnesses* (Minneapolis: Fortress, 1993), 73. Samuel Terrien speculates that the term מִכְתָּם derives from Akkadian, suggesting that מִכְתָּם means "to cover" or "secret prayer" or "to hide." Terrien, *Psalms*, 29.

16. Willem VanGemeren speaks of a מִכְתָּם in this way. VanGemeren, *Psalms*, 66.

17. DeClaissé-Walford, Jacobson, and BTanner, *Book of Psalms*, 821.

of Edom in the Valley of Salt" (ESV).[18] By way of contrast, Psalm 108's superscription simply records, "A song, a *mizmor*. By David." Unlike Psalm 108, Psalms 57 and 60 supply ample information about the historical setting of the psalms.

The Meaning of the Superscriptions

One might expect Psalm 108 to share the same genre as Psalms 57 and 60 because it is made up of Psalms 57:8–12 and 60:7–14, yet it does not. Psalm 108 is its own psalm; its sum is more than its parts (Pss 57 and 60).[19] The reason why Psalm 108 differs in superscriptional genre from Psalms 57 and 60 becomes clear when one considers how the superscriptions clarify the meaning of these psalms.

In the case of Psalms 57 and 60, their superscriptions supply a historical backdrop to David's life and provide interpretive keys to understand the meaning of the psalms.[20] For example, the superscription of Psalm 57 controls how one can interpret Psalm 57. It reads, "To the leader: 'You must not destroy.' A *miktam* by David when he fled from the face of Saul in the cave." As a *miktam*, Psalm 57 canonically relates to Psalms 58 and 59, both of which are *miktamim*, share the "You must not destroy" phrase in their superscription, and are attributed to David.[21]

As to a historical, canonical setting, Psalm 57 refers to the events chronicled in 1 Samuel 24 and 26. 1 Samuel 24 records Saul relieving himself in a cave, while David secretly cuts off a piece of his clothing. David could have slain Saul, but he did not and even regrets cutting off a corner of Saul's robe: "YHWH forbids me from doing this thing to my lord, to the messiah of YHWH, to lay my hand against him, because he is YHWH's messiah" (1 Sam 24:6). A similar account happens in 1 Samuel

18. The ESV presents the superscriptions with small caps, which I have not replicated here.

19. Joachim Becker argues the same but for diachronic reasons. He argues that Ps 108 is an exilic or post-exilic composition and thus should be read as a unit. See Becker, *Israel deutet seine Psalmen*, 66.

20. Robert E. Wallace explains, "The superscriptions should find a significant place within the interpretation. When the text makes an association to a historical setting or with an individual, a canonical reader of the psalms needs to wrestle with the implications of that association." Wallace, *Narrative Effect of Book IV*, 87. The superscriptions thus create an interpretive setting for the reader.

21. One function of the superscriptions is to unite groups of psalms. As Rendtorff (*Canonical Hebrew Bible*, 318) explains, "The clearest indications of psalms belonging together are the superscriptions."

26:9 when David once again spares Saul's life, exclaiming: "Do not destroy him, for who can send his hand against the messiah of YHWH and be guiltless?" The phrase "do not destroy" in 1 Samuel 26:9 matches the "do not destroy" in the superscriptions of Psalms 57, 58, and 59.[22] This quotation ("do not destroy") and the historical, canonical background in 1 Samuel allow the superscription to guide how one reads this group of psalms.[23]

The superscription clarifies what David means when he calls for God to judge his enemies: "Rise up to punish all the nations. Never show grace to all those who treacherously do evil. Selah" (Ps 59:6). While David calls God to judge the nations without grace, the psalm's superscription, "Do not destroy," signals that David should not act on his macabre request, just as he spared Saul's life in 1 Samuel 24 and 26. The message of the superscription does not, however, rule out the possibility that God would bring Saul's life to an end. Curiously, Psalm 59's superscription also pinpoints the events of Psalm 59 to 1 Samuel 19, "when Saul sent [men] to watch the house of David in order to kill him" (59:1). Either the men Saul sent were Gentiles or David declares them to be such in Psalm 59:6 because they acted in such a way as to invalidate their identity as Israelites. The logic here may be similar to Peter's and John's in Acts 4:25–27 when they cite Psalm 2 as condemning both Jews and Gentiles, though Psalm 2 appears to reference only Gentiles as those who "plot in vain" (Acts 4:25 // Ps 2:1). In any case, the superscriptions of Psalms 57, 58, and 59 control how one reads the body of those psalms in significant ways.

In Psalm 57, David cries for help but will not destroy Saul. In Psalm 58, David prays an imprecatory psalm against his enemies although the reader knows that, in the end, David will say, "Do not destroy" God's messiah. Psalm 59's superscription points to events from 1 Samuel 19 and 1 Samuel 26, and one can reasonably assume that its "Do not destroy" superscription affects how one should read the psalm. In contrast to these psalms and to Psalm 57 in particular, the superscription of Psalm 108 does not allude to a historical book such as 1 Samuel.

Psalm 108 does not begin a series of psalms that use the words "Do not destroy" in their superscriptions as Psalms 57, 58, and 59 do. Psalm 108 also does not contain language that might be construed as imprecatory.

---

22. The text of 1 Sam 26:9 reads אַל־תַּשְׁחִיתֵהוּ, and Ps 57:1 reads אַל־תַּשְׁחֵת.

23. For the argument in this paragraph, I am indebted to Anderson, "King David and the Psalms of Imprecation," 34–41.

In fact, Psalm 108 contains generally positive language about God's rule over the nations. It also exists in a sequence of psalms that detail verbal abuse against the psalmist by an enemy (Ps 109) and God's victory over enemies through his king (Ps 110). Psalm 108 should be read in a different light than Psalm 57.[24] Indeed, Psalm 108's differing superscription as well as its citation of earlier psalmic material lead to the conclusion that David's historical life will be recapitulated in the life of the future David.[25] Psalm 108 demands to be read as a unique contribution to the Psalter rather than simply a repetition of earlier material.

In contrast to the superscriptions of Psalms 57 and 60, the superscription of Psalm 108 lacks the same historical specificity. If the superscriptions of Psalms 57 and 60 guide readers to a historical backdrop in Israel's historical books, then one might reasonably ask how the superscription of Psalm 108 leads readers to understand the psalm. What complicates the question is that the body of Psalm 108 contains large portions of Psalms 57 and 60. Psalm 108 is made up of parts from Psalms 57 and 60 without the historical context to read them in such a historical light. Instead, the superscription simply reads, "A song, *a mizmor* by David."

Two contextual cues clarify the meaning behind this simple superscription. First, Psalm 108 follows Psalm 107, which has set out a pattern of eschatological fulfillment. Second, Psalm 108 prefaces the Davidic trilogy of Psalms 108–110, which further continues the eschatological pattern begun in Psalm 107. Arguably, therefore, the editor(s) of the Psalter placed Psalm 108 in its current canonical context to recall Psalms 57 and 60, to deepen their meaning through Psalm 108's quotation and paraphrase of these earlier psalms, and to contribute to the eschatological message found within Psalms 107–110. Furthermore, if David penned the superscription for Psalm 108, then the editor(s) has clarified David's original intent for writing Psalm 108 and expanded its meaning by placing it in its current canonical location along a redemptive-historical trajectory. In other words, Psalms 57 and 60 appear in Book II of the Psalter, which narrates David's reign, while Psalm 108 appears in Book V of the

24. And also from Ps 60, whose superscription provides detailed historical information about the psalm.

25. After noting the Davidic authorship of Ps 108, Beat Weber explains the expression of Davidic authorship in the post-exilic era becomes associated with a new Davidic king (*eines neuen davidischen Königs*). Weber, *Werkbuch Psalmen II*, 213–14.

Psalter, which details post-exilic hope for a coming kingdom.[26] Psalms 57 and 60 speak of David's travails and victory over his enemies, which typologically point to the Davidic messiah's victory over the world, a victory that Psalm 108 narrates.

The superscription of Psalm 108 embeds an eschatological accent to the psalm because it contrasts with the historical focus of the superscriptions in Psalms 57 and 60 and because it appears within an eschatological canonical context. By conspicuously divesting itself of its historical moorings and by tying itself to the Davidic king, the superscription of Psalm 108 guides readers to see the psalm in an eschatological way.

HOW PSALM 108 CITES PSALMS 57 AND 60

A close reading of Psalm 108 demonstrates an eschatological accent to the psalm.[27] Moreover, Psalm 107 sets the stage for an eschatological reading of Psalm 108, which describes the next event in the eschatological story: a new conquest of the land and the establishment of the kingdom through a new David.[28] The discussion that follows highlights how Psalm 108 cites Psalms 57 and 60 to clarify how Psalm 108 communicates this eschatological message. Since Psalm 108:1 is the superscription of Psalm 108:2, the following analyzes Psalm 108:2–14.

Composition

Psalm 108 cites two large portions of Psalms 57 and 60 (Pss 57:8–12 and 60:7–14) and alters the portions of the two psalms that it cites. Psalm 108's selection of these portions is significant but so is the non-selection of the parts of Psalms 57 and 60 that Psalm 108 does not include. Benjamin Segal comments, "The thrust of Psalm 108 might first be appreciated by noting those aspects of the other psalms that it did not borrow."[29]

---

26. Leslie Allen comments, "In the Davidic group Pss 108–10, the first psalm via the voice of David functions as an eschatological hymn featuring Israel's future salvation from its enemies (vv. 13–14 [12–13])." Allen, *Psalms 101–150*, 79.

27. See ch. 3.

28. Frank-Lothar Hossfeld and Erich Zenger speak of an expansion of the kingdom in Ps 108. SeeHossfeld and Zenger, *Commentary on Psalms 101–150*, 2.

29. Segal, *A New Psalm*, 523.

Two key questions will elucidate the purpose behind the composition of Psalm 108: (1) Why was Psalm 108 written? and (2) Why did its author select certain portions of Psalms 57 and 60? David, the attributed author, could have simply written a new psalm. The editor(s) of the Psalter could have included a different Davidic psalm than Psalm 108. A number of proposals seek to answer one or both of these questions.

Robert Bellermin proposes that a compiler composed Psalm 108 to ensure that the Psalter did not have 149 psalms but the even number of 150![30] Bellermin's assertion overlooks that Solomon alone wrote 1,005 songs (1 Kgs 4:32). Additionally, 11QPs[a] also indicates that David wrote 4,050 psalms.[31] The large number of psalms authored by both kings gave the compiler many psalmic options. The compiler did not need to create a new psalm based on only existing canonical material to get 150 psalms in the Psalter, nor should one presume that Psalm 108's composition "depend[s] on the banal preoccupation of a scribe in search of arithmetical perfection."[32]

Louis Jacquet responds to Bellermin's proposal with his own: Psalm 108 was written for liturgical reasons. According to Jacquet, the liturgical intention of Psalm 108 approximates the purpose of the Psalms of Ascents, which he sees as a second-temple emphasis encouraging pilgrims in the restoration to trust in YHWH to overcome the discouragements and the defections of some Israelites.[33] "A liturgist," writes Jacquet, "wished in the same spirit to protect his fellow religious persons against defeatism before foreign threats by reviving the faith of all in their heavenly protector."[34] To some degree, Jacquet accurately points out the intended effect that Psalm 108 was to have on its audience. Nevertheless, he fails

30. Cited in Jacquet, *Les Psaumes et le Coeur*, 178.

31. DeClaissé-Walford writes, "A prose insert in the Dead Sea Psalms Scroll 11QPs[a] states that David composed some 4,050 psalms and songs." DeClaissé-Walford, *Reading from the Beginning*, 32. Robert Bellermin would not have had access to the DSS because he wrote in the seventeenth century.

32. My translation of "Car, le réemploi des Fragments précités paraît, non point dépendre d'une banale préoccupation de scribe en mal de perfection arithmétique, mais relever d'une intention 'liturgique' précise." Jacquet, *Les Psaumes et le Coeur*, 178.

33. Jacquet, *Les Psaumes et le Coeur*, 178.

34. My translation of "Un liturgiste aura voulu, dans le même esprit, *prémunir ses coreligionnaires contre le défaitisme* devant les menaces étrangères, en ranimant la Foi de tous en leur céleste Protecteur" (italics original). Jacquet, *Les Psaumes et le Coeur*, 179.

to account for Psalm 108's literary context, that is, how it fits into its new canonical setting in Book V of Psalter. As earlier demonstrated, Psalm 108 has too many connections to preceding psalms for its appearance in Book V of the Psalter to be a mere coincidence.

In contrast to Jacquet's proposed liturgical purpose for Psalm 108, James Mays proposes a specific historical reason for why Psalm 108 exists. Mays suggests that Psalm 108's mention of Edom provides the post-exilic closure to an unhappy rivalry with this nation: "Verse 10 is probably the clue to the interest and purpose of the psalm. It may reflect the unresolved conflict of the post-exilic community with Edom, whose treachery contributed to the fall of Jerusalem."[35] Mays has no doubt tapped into a valid function of Psalm 108, as Obadiah clearly highlights Edom's treachery against the post-exilic community (e.g., Obad 11). However, Psalm 108 applies to every subsequent generation until God brings about his rule because of the particular ways in which the psalm dissociates with the past to associate, instead, with the future (i.e., eschatology). Additionally, Edom as a traditional enemy eventually becomes something of an eschatological enemy who would be defeated during Israel's restoration (see Joel 3:19; Obad 15–21). Thus, although Mays rightly pinpoints a vital aspect of Psalm 108's function as well as a reason for its composition, he underplays its eschatological nature.[36]

William Holladay offers another historical explanation for Psalm 108's existence. In his view, the Psalter joined various sub-collections together into a whole. Psalms 57 and 60 were in one sub-collection and Psalm 108 was in another: "The existence of such a duplication suggests that the same psalm material had been in two different subcollections that were later combined."[37] Holladay may be correct about the provenance of these three psalms, but he downplays the possibility of an editor(s) who intentionally and reasonably shaped the book of Psalms. Holladay's position has some explanatory power, but for a fuller picture of why Psalm 108 was composed, one must also pay attention to its canonical function and how it cites earlier material.

---

35. Mays, *Psalms*, 348.

36. I provide further evidence for Ps 108's eschatological sense below and in the following chapter.

37. Holladay, *Psalms through Three Thousand Yearss*, 70.

Being agnostic as to why Psalm 108 comprises earlier psalms is another option for understanding its composition. For example, Hans-Joachim Kraus metaphorically shrugs at the purpose of Psalm 108:

> It is difficult to understand what the significance is of the combination in Psalm 108 of two completely different pieces. Significant for the interpreter's situation is the opinion of H. Schmidt: "It cannot be ascertained whether the combination is purely external and accidental or whether it came about for a specific liturgical purpose." For that reason it is also difficult, indeed almost impossible, to shed light on the trend of the statement of the new composition.[38]

The weakness of this view is, again, that Psalm 108 has too many connections to its surrounding canonical context, connections that at least provide a plausible explanation for why it appears where it does in Book V of the Psalter. Kraus, following Schmidt, seems to have eyes for only liturgical or historical reasons for Psalm 108's existence. Like Jacquet, he fails to account for the literary nature and context of Psalm 108.

A better method for understanding Psalm 108 is to see its citation of Psalms 57 and 60 and its placement in the fifth book of the Psalter as strategic and intended on the part of the editor(s),[39] who was honoring the authorial intent of Psalm 108. The editor(s) would have needed only to select Psalm 108, noting that David himself had embedded eschatological notions within it.[40] The same editor(s) could have then placed Psalm 108 alongside Psalms 107 and 109–110 because these psalms fit into the redemptive-historical storyline of the Psalter. Moreover, with shared language, themes, and theology, these psalms combine to communicate eschatological notions of the king and the kingdom. The editor(s) would simply be organizing what is already present in the material before him.

However one understands the interplay between editor(s) and author, Psalm 108 clearly contains only the victorious portions of its source material (Pss 57 and 60), communicating an absolute victory and

38. Kraus, *Psalms 60–150*, 333.

39. According to J. A. Alexander, Ps 108 intentionally functions as a preface to Pss 109 and 110. Alexander, *Psalms*, 3:89–90.

40. David was a prophet who often spoke beyond his current circumstances (2 Sam 23:2). David, for example, penned Ps 110, but that psalm clearly speaks beyond his lifetime.

the rule of God. Since the superscription refers to David as the author of Psalm 108, David is the subject of the psalm. He participates in God's coming rule, even if only in an intercessory role (cf. Ps 108:7).

To display victorious material from Psalms 57 and 60, Psalm 108 passes over the dour sections of those earlier poems. For instance, Psalm 57:1–7 paints a bleak picture of David's life: "My soul is in the midst of lions" (57:5a). On the other hand, Psalm 57:8–12 celebrates the psalmist's trust in God whose glory pervades the globe (Ps 57:8–12 // Ps 108:2–6). Similar to the first seven verses of Psalm 57, Psalm 60:1–6 describes the sorrow that God's people have experienced although they find some solace in God's banner. Then, Psalm 60:7–14 details God's victory over the nations surrounding Israel (Ps 60:7–14 // Ps 108:7–14). Because Psalm 108's author selects only the victorious portions of Psalms 57 and 60, he paints a clear picture of the victory of God over the nations.[41]

In their commentary, Alphonse Maillot and André Lelièvre also see the omissions from Psalms 57 and 60 as transforming Psalm 108 into a new psalm of YHWH's victory: "The double omission of individual supplication at the beginning of Psalm 57 and of the collective lamentation at the beginning of Psalm 60 make Psalm 108 a magnificent song of thanksgiving to honor YHWH, the victor of nations."[42] Regardless of how one understands the form-critical genre change in Psalm 108, the psalm clearly cites portions of Psalm 57 and 60 to highlight God's victory over the nations.

Psalm 108's victorious tone also shows how God will establish the kingdom for Israel, following the redemption that Psalm 107 reports (cf. 107:1–3). Considering Psalm 108's canonical location (Book V of the Psalter) and its psalm group (Pss 108–110), as well as the simple fact that the victory described in Psalm 108 had not yet happened, lead one to conclude that Psalm 108 expands the meaning of Psalms 57 and 60 along

---

41. Robert Jamieson, A.R. Fausset, and David Brown similarly comment, "Its altogether triumphant tone may intimate that it was prepared by David, omitting the plaintive portions of other Psalms, as commemorative of God's favour in the victories of His people." Robert Jamieson, A. R. Fausset, and David Brown, *A Commentary, Critical and Explanatory, on the Old and New Testaments* (Grand Rapids: Zondervan, 1940), 379.

42. My translation of "La double omission de la supplication individuelle au début du Ps.57, et de la lamentation collective au début du Ps. 60, font du Ps. 108 un magnifique chant d'actions de grâces en l'honneur de YHWH, le vainqueur des nations." Alphonse Maillot and André Lelièvre, *Les Psaumes: Traduction Nouvelle et Commentaire, vol. 3* (Geneva: Labor et Fides, 1969), 63.

redemptive-historical lines. Psalms 57 and 60 speak of David's battles as king over Israel, and Psalm 108 cites them to communicate God's victory over the nations through a future Davidic figure.[43]

Augustine supports a similar argument in his Psalter commentary. He reasons that Psalm 108's citation of the latter verses of Psalms 57 and 60 and their divergent titles from Psalm 108 mean that Psalms 57 and 60 communicate a deeper, spiritual sense: "We could have no clearer indication that both the earlier psalms are oriented to a single end not in their superficial historical sense but in the depth of the prophecy they express."[44] The deeper, spiritual sense is that they speak about the messiah. Augustine reasons that since Psalm 108 speaks about the messiah and cites Psalms 57 and 60, these two psalms must also speak about the messiah.[45] Consequently, Psalms 57 and 60 and their portions quoted in Psalm 108 are messianic or spiritual in nature.

Augustine did not have the benefit of centuries of historical study to help him define how Psalms 57, 60, and 108 relate. However, he intuitively understood that Psalms 57 and 60 must to some degree speak about the one who is to come since Psalm 108 does so. Reversing his logic, one might say that Psalm 108 cites that earlier material because it fits into a messianic or eschatological message.

In summary, portions of Psalms 57 and 60 were intentionally selected for inclusion in Psalm 108 to communicate God's universal rule. Since this rule had yet to come to fruition, Psalm 108 speaks of a future day. The particular differences between Psalm 108 and Psalms 57 and 60 further clarify this future-orientated notion.

Psalm 108:2–6 and Psalm 57:8–12

In Psalm 108:2–6, David worships God and declares him to be exalted above the entire world. God's exaltation over the world points to his eschatological rule over it. Readers can more clearly understand how

43. According to Joachim Becker, Ps 108 pictures the victory over the nations in eschatological terms ("zu einem Bild der eschatologischen Auseinandersetzung mit den Völkern"). See Becker, *Israel deutet seine Psalmen*, 66–67. In the next chapter, I will expand on Ps 108's eschatological meaning in conversation with its canonical context.

44. Augustine, *Exposition of the Psalms*, trans. Maria Boulding, vol. 5 (New York: New City, 2003), 240 (§2).

45. Augustine, *Exposition of the Psalms*, 240 (§ 2).

Psalm 108 communicates this idea by seeing how Psalm 108 differs from its source material.[46]

Psalm 108:2

Psalm 108:2 alters Psalm 57:8–9 by omitting the twofold repetition of "my heart is established" from Psalm 57:8, including the clause only once. By omitting the second instance of "my heart is established," Psalm 108 draws readers away from David whose heart is steadfast and to God, the one whom David worships.

In addition, Psalm 108 either re-locates the phrase "my glory" from Psalm 57:9 to its prior verse—what would be 57:8—or simply adds the phrase plus אַף to Psalm 108:2.[47] Whatever the case, the structure of Psalm 108 is changed. Compare the following:

נָכוֹן לִבִּי אֱלֹהִים נָכוֹן לִבִּי אָשִׁירָה וַאֲזַמֵּרָה׃
עוּרָה כְבוֹדִי עוּרָה הַנֵּבֶל וְכִנּוֹר אָעִירָה שָּׁחַר׃

> My heart is established, O God, my heart is established. I will sing and praise. Awake, my glory! Awake, O harp and lyre. I will awaken the dawn. (Ps 57:8–9)

נָכוֹן לִבִּי אֱלֹהִים אָשִׁירָה וַאֲזַמְּרָה אַף־כְּבוֹדִי׃

> My heart is established, O God. I will sing and praise even with my glory. (Ps 108:2)

One might be tempted to interpret Psalm 108:2 like Psalm 57:9.[48] Psalm 108:2 cannot, however, be read in the same way as Psalm 57:9 is read wherein "my glory" appositionally relates to an imperative verb (עוּרָה).

---

46. Phil Botha writes, "It seems that the purpose of creating a new composition from two existing texts was to facilitate an 'anthological' recasting and re-reading of earlier texts which must have been known to the audience of Ps 108. In this way the earlier texts were 'commented' upon and their horizons expanded."Botha, "Psalm 108," 574–75. The following discussion shows how the earlier texts (Pss 57 and 60) were "'commented upon' and their horizons expanded." The particular changes that Ps 108 makes to its donor texts elucidate Ps 108's meaning in Book V of the Psalter.

47. If the latter, then David would have omitted the phrase "my glory" from Ps 57:9 and added the same phrase to Ps 108:2. James Hamilton suggested this possibility to me in a digital communication.

48. Gunkel refers readers back to his comments on Pss 57 and 60 in his commentary on the Psalms. Gunkel, *Psalmen*, 5th ed., 475.

In Psalm 108:2, "my glory" follows a first person cohortative verb (וַאֲזַמְּרָה) and is separated from the verb by the particle אַף. Furthermore, a noun never follows a first person cohortative verb appositionally in the Psalter.[49]

Another possibility is to translate אַף as "with" and כְּבוֹדִי as the object of the preposition.[50] The LXX, for example, seems to translate אַף as a preposition with the sense of "with," rendering the phrase as *ἐν τῇ δόξῃ μου*.[51] The problem with this perspective is that אַף never means "with" nor does it function as a preposition.[52]

A further possibility is that Psalm 108 makes "my glory" a vocative phrase (e.g., "Oh, my glory") following the verbs "sing" and "make melody" when the psalm alters Psalm 57; in Psalm 57:9 "my glory" is the appositional subject of the verb "awake." Arguing for this position, Erich Zenger notes that "my glory" in psalm 108 possibly alludes to Psalm 3:4 in which God is called "my glory."[53] According to Zenger, David calls for help and receives an answer from YHWH's holy mountain in both

49. I used Accordance Bible Software 10.4.5. to search for first person, singular, cohortative verbs in the Psalter and discovered no instances where a noun follows in apposition to such a verb. Using the search terms "[VERB first singular cohortative-Both]," Accordance found 120 hits in 96 verses (Pss. 2:7–8; 4:9; 7:18; 9:2–3, 15; 13:6; 17:15; 18:50; 22:23; 25:2; 26:6; 27:6; 31:2, 8, 18; 32:8; 34:2; 39:2, 5, 14; 40:6; 41:11; 42:5, 10; 43:4; 45:18; 50:7, 21; 51:15, 18; 54:8; 55:3, 7, 9, 18; 57:5, 8–9; 59:10, 18; 60:8; 61:5, 9; 66:16; 69:15, 31; 71:1, 22–23; 73:15, 17; 75:10; 77:2, 4, 7, 12–13; 78:2; 81:9; 85:9; 86:12; 89:2; 101:1–2; 104:33; 108:2–3, 8; 119:15, 17–18, 27, 34, 44–46, 48, 73, 88, 115, 117, 125, 134, 145–146; 122:8–9; 139:8–9; 144:9; 145:1–2, 5; 146:2).

50. It is technically possible to see "my glory" as the direct object of the verb. וַאֲזַמְּרָה אַף can function as part of a direct object as it does in Pss 16:6 and 89:6.

51. The LXX translators may also have been paraphrasing the text to make it readable in Greek. The ESV translates the phrase this way: "I will sing and make melody with all my being!" Apparently, it translates אַף as "all."

52. Neither *HALOT* nor *DCH* lists "with" as a possible meaning for אַף. See *HALOT*, 76 and *DCH*, 1:352–53.

53. Hossfeld and Zenger, *Commentary on Psalms 101–150*, 119. While she does not explicitly say so, deClaissé-Walford (deClaissé-Walford, Jacobson, and Tanner, *Psalms*, 822–23) seems to take this position. She (*Psalms*, 822) translates Ps 108:2b–c as, "*I will sing and make music / even more, my glory!*" (italics original). DeClaissé-Walford (*Psalms*, 823) later comments, "The psalm opens with an individual singer addressing God with words of confidence stating that the singer will *give thanks* and *make music* to God in celebration of God's *hesed*-ness and *faithfulness*" (italics original). By saying that the psalmist makes music "to God," she seems to confirm that "my glory" refers to God in Ps 108:2.

psalms; additionally, Psalm 3 is a morning psalm like Psalm 108—both psalms ask God to arise and rescue (see Ps 3:6, 8).[54]

Other observations may further verify Zenger's argument. For example, Psalm 3 appears after two untitled psalms (Pss 1 and 2) and begins a set of four Davidic *mizmorim* in Book I of the Psalter. Similarly, Psalm 108 opens a set of three Davidic *mizmorim* in Book V of the Psalter and follows an untitled psalm (Ps 107). If the editor(s) intentionally created the Davidic sequence of Psalms 108–110, this collection may also intentionally correspond to Psalms 3–6. Based on this reasoning, "my glory" in Psalm 108:2 perhaps refers to God like it does in Psalm 3:4. The phrase "my glory" may thus refer to God in contrast to Psalm 57:9 in which "my glory" refers to the psalmist.[55]

Grammatically, Zenger defines "my glory" as a vocative phrase: "'indeed, you, my glory' is now a vocative addressed to God, analogous to the vocative 'God' in v. 2a."[56] Unfortunately, he provides no exegetical detail explaining how he comes to this conclusion. Frank van der Velden, however, attempts to provide an exegetical explanation by underscoring the grammatical relationship between אַף and כְּבוֹדִי: "אף has here no other meaning than to note the appositional place of כבודי and thus to prevent the translation, 'I will sing my glory (namely, God).'"[57] Instead, he translates the verse as, "I will sing and I will play, 'You, my glory' " (*ich will singen und ich will spielen, Du meine Ehre*), which identifies the words that he sings.[58] In other words, the song that David will sing includes the phrase, "You, my glory."

The structure of Psalm 108 adds further credibility to this position. The new structure of Psalm 108 (due to its alteration of Psalm 57) creates a verse structure in which "my glory" and "God" appear at the end of their respective lines: "My heart is established, O God. I will sing and

54. Hossfeld and Zenger, *Commentary on Psalms 101–150*, 119.

55. Raymond Jacques Tournay is less confident that an interpretive decision can be made. He calls the phrase "ambiguous." He thinks "my glory" can refer to the psalmist (Ps 7.6c), YHWH (Ps 3.4b; Ps 62.8), or "even to the divine glory bestowed on the believer (Pss 8.6b; 73.24b)." Tournay, *Seeing and Hearing*, 182.

56. Hossfeld and Zenger, *Commentary on Psalms 101–150*, 115.

57. My translation of "אף hat hierbei keine andere Bedeutung als auf die appositionelle Stellung von כבודי hinzuweisen und so die Übersetzung 'ich will meine Ehre [nämlich Gott] besingen' zu verhindern." Van der Velden, *Psalm 109*, 146n21. In this sense, Van der Velden goes beyond Zenger in his specificity of the meaning of the phrase.

58. Van der Velden, *Psalm 109*, 146.

praise even my glory."[59] "God" and "glory" are parallel, suggesting that God could be identified as glory.

Phil Botha proposes an alternative parallel structure. He suggests that "my glory" parallels "my heart."[60] If Botha is correct, then reading "glory" as a name for God seems less likely. However, the structure of Psalm 108:2 connects "my glory" with "God," as both "my glory" and "God" appear at the end of their respective sentences: נָכוֹן לִבִּי אֱלֹהִים אָשִׁירָה וַאֲזַמְּרָה אַף־כְּבוֹדִי ("my heart is steadfast, *God*. I will sing and praise even *my glory*"). Botha's proposal is, thus, probably incorrect.

The first half of Psalm 108 (108:2–6) also is framed by the term "glory" (vv. 2 and 6).[61] In Psalm 108:6, God is clearly in view: "Let your glory rise above the whole land" (108:6b). One may reasonably conclude that "glory" in Psalm 108:2 also refers to God.[62]

Finally, calling God "glory" fits the contextual thrust of the rule of God (cf. Psalms 93–99) in Book IV and his rule over the universe (Ps 108:7–14; Ps 110:5–7) in Book V. Clearly, a number of contextual and grammatical arguments provide enough evidence to grant the possibility that "my glory" may refer to God in Psalm 108:2.[63]

Despite these reasons to read "my glory" as a vocative referring to God, reading "my glory" in this way is not the obvious way to read אַף־כְּבוֹדִי as many English translations of Psalm 108:2 testify.[64] The argument of Zenger may work theologically, but grammatically it seems

59. נָכוֹן לִבִּי אֱלֹהִים אָשִׁירָה וַאֲזַמְּרָה אַף־כְּבוֹדִי.

60. Botha, "Psalm 108e," 576.

61. Vesco, *Le Psautier de David*, 2:1039.

62. Ps 108 demonstrates that God's glory extends above all else, and he faithfully discharges his covenantal love to rescue his people since human intervention is useless: "The salvation of man is vain" (108:13b). Canonically, Ps 108 follows Ps 107's answer to Israel's call for rescue from Exile (Ps 106), and Ps 108 highlights God's unique sovereign ability to save when the hosts of men fail. Keeping in step with its various contexts, the phrase "my glory" in Ps 108:2 contextually makes sense as a reference to God, the one to whom the psalmist ascribes glory.

63. More precisely, the phrase "my glory" would have to be the object of both "sing" and "make melody"

64. NIV 1984, NIV 2011, KJV, NKJV, NET, and HCSB translate אף as "with" and כבודי as "all my soul" (NIV 1984, NIV 2011), as "my glory" (KJV, NKJV), as "my whole heart" (NET), or as "the whole of my being" (HCSB). The RSV does not translate the phrase כְּבוֹדִי as "my glory" but as "my soul," and the RSV does not translate אף: "I will sing and make melody! Awake, my soul!" The LXX retains the word "glory" and translates the word אף with ἐν: ψαλῶ ἐν τῇ δόξῃ μου.

improbable. There is, in fact, a simpler Hebrew grammatical category that can account for the phrase אַף־כְּבוֹדִי, namely, the category of an adverbial accusative.[65] David prays "with my glory," that is, his tongue.[66] Psalm 57:9 provides precedent for the psalmist calling himself "glory." Likewise, Psalm 16:9 associates "glory" with the psalmist.[67]

The best option, therefore, is to see אַף־כְּבוֹדִי as relating to וַאֲזַמְּרָה as an adverbial accusative.[68] "Glory" refers to the means by which David will sing and praise God; he will do it with his glory. The addition of אַף intensifies the phrase ("even"). The resulting translation would be, "I will sing and praise even with my glory." David would be saying that he will praise God even with his glory, his tongue.

Even if "my glory" does not directly refer to God but to the psalmist, the way in which Psalm 108 alters its donor text allows for the possibility that the "glory" of the psalmist in Psalm 108:2 anticipates the glory of God in Psalm 108:6. In this verse, David prays with his glory (i.e., his tongue) that God's glory would spread across the world. David sings with his glory before he sees the glory of God. The language of "glory" in Psalm 108 draws readers to see God as the glorious one whose glory exceeds even the border of heaven in the kingdom (see Ps 108:6). The significance of God's eschatological glory being in Israel's midst bespeaks a hopeful future.

For those who returned to Israel after the Exile, the new temple was disappointing in comparison to the temple of Solomon: "Who is left among you that saw this house in its former glory? How does it look to you now? Is it not in your sight as nothing?" (Hag 2:3 NRSV). The nation of Israel never re-emerged, and any ruler in Israel lived under the thumb of another regional super power.[69] Therefore, David sings "even

65. *IBHS*, 169 (10.2.2).

66. In ch. 3, I specify that glory refers to the psalmist's tongue. He sings with his tongue, his glory, because, with his tongue, he glorifies God.

67. The ESV points to Ps 16:9 when it translates "my glory" in Ps 57:8 [57:9 MT].

68. The CSB translates the phrase as "I will sing praises with the whole of my being" but provides an alternative translation within a footnote: "*praises, even my glory*" (italics original). The alternative rendering is ambiguous, but it seems to allow that "glory" could refer to God. It could also refer to the psalmist or it might even describe David's singing as his glory. The meaning of the phrase אָשִׁירָה וַאֲזַמְּרָה אַף־כְּבוֹדִי in Hebrew is difficult to pin down exactly.

69. Excepting a brief time in the second and first centuries, Israelites lived as vassals after the exile, beginning with the Persians and ending with the Romans. See deClaissé-Walford, *Reading from the Beginning*, 4.

with his glory" (Ps 108:2) to glorify God and locates God's glory above the heavens, where God rules over the whole earth (Ps 108:6). The nations will be under God's reign.

Psalm 108:4

Psalm 108:4 exchanges אֲדֹנָי in Psalm 57:10 for YHWH.[70] Psalm 57:10 reads, "I will give thanks to you among the peoples, *Adonai* (אֲדֹנָי). I will make music among the peoples," and Psalm 108:4 reads: "I will give thanks to you among the peoples, YHWH (יְהוָה). I will make music among the peoples."

Erich Zenger explains that Psalm 108's switch to YHWH ties it closely with Psalm 107, which uses the motif of giving thanks to YHWH (cf. Ps 107:8, 15, 21, 31).[71] In addition, the name YHWH also corresponds to the emphasis on faithfulness in Book V of the Psalter. YHWH is the name that God gave to his covenantal people (Exod 3:14; 6:2–9), and it is YHWH who will faithfully fulfill his covenantal obligations to Israel. Zenger also suggests that Psalm 108's change from *Adonai* to YHWH may have been made to avoid confusing the king with YHWH because the king is called *Adon* in Psalm 110:1.[72] Since Psalm 108 portrays a Davidic ruler, the switch from *Adonai* to YHWH perhaps avoids any confusion over the referent in Psalm 108:4; the point is to thank YHWH rather than an earthly ruler.

Psalm 108:5

Psalm 108:5 also rewords Psalm 57:11 so that God's faithfulness goes above the heavens (חַסְדֶּךָ וְעַד־שְׁחָקִים אֲמִתֶּךָ) and not merely up to the heavens as Psalm 57:11 indicates: חַסְדֶּךָ וְעַד־שְׁחָקִים אֲמִתֶּךָ God's faithfulness extends beyond the heavens, and his power is supreme. Hence, God will dominate all of Israel's enemies (Ps 108:7–14).

Hans-Joachim Kraus advocates following the text of Psalm 57 and thus reading Psalm 108 as "up to the heavens" instead of "above the

70. Botha helped me see the significance of this change. Botha, "Psalm 108," 578, 586–87.

71. Hossfeld and Zenger, *Commentary on Psalms 101–150*, 115.

72. I infer that this is what Zenger means, but his comments on the matter are somewhat unclear. Here is the relevant text: "On the other hand, the change may well have been made in view of Ps 110:1, because there the title 'Adon' is given to the (Davidic) king by the (cultic fictional) speaker, and here in Psalm 108 the fictional speaker is the king." Hossfeld and Zenger, *Commentary on Psalms*, 115–16. Botha makes a similar suggestion in "Psalm 108e," 586.

heavens."[73] This proposal may stem from his belief that a compiler simply chose two parts of Psalms 57 and 60 to form Psalm 108 for unspecified historical reasons. A change between Psalm 108 and Psalm 57, then, may simply represent a historical accident. If one grants that Psalm 108 is intentionally different from Psalm 57, there is at least one plausible explanation for the change in Psalm 108:5.

The editor(s) may have made this change or included an already altered Psalm 108 because Psalm 108 is closely tied to the message and hope of Psalm 107, which celebrates the faithfulness of God (Ps 107:1, 8, 15, 21, 31, 43).[74] Additionally, Psalm 107 and Psalm 108 also relate to one another because both portray a similar upward movement. In Psalm 107, sailors attempt to ascend to heaven yet descend to the depths in great distress (107:26). In Psalm 108, God not only ascends to heaven, but he is also exalted above the heavens to rescue his beloved (108:5–6).[75] The change to "above the heavens" from "up to the heavens" thus connects Psalm 108 to Psalm 107 as well as contributes to the idea of God's sovereign rule.

Psalm 108:7–14 and Psalm 60:7–14

Psalm 108:2–6 praises and exalts God. Psalm 108:7–14 further highlights God as exalted above the world. Specifically, God conquers Israel's enemies and establishes his eschatological kingdom. Psalm 108 modifies its source psalmic material to communicate God's victory in numerous ways.

Psalm 108:7

Psalm 60:7 calls for God to rescue his beloved, to save with his right hand, and to answer "us." In Psalm 108:7, the "us" transforms into "me." Psalm 108 now reads "save me." This change underscores the individual person rather than the collective group, which was perhaps the congregation of Israel in Psalm 60:7.

One explanation for this change is that it is a historical accident and that readers should retain "us" in Psalm 108.[76] Additionally, the *qere* read-

---

73. Kraus, *Psalms*, 333.

74. Vesco, *Le Psautier de David*, 2:1037.

75. Vesco, *Le Psautier de David*, 2:1037. Admittedly, this connection between the sailors in Ps 107 and the heavens in Ps 108 merely shows a similar movement and may be incidental.

76. Kraus does not explicitly provide a reason as to why he corrects Ps 108:7 to Ps 60:7, but it seems clear that he sees Ps 60:7 as the better text. See Kraus, *Psalms*, 333.

ing of Psalm 60:7 is ועננו, which the editor(s) of the Psalter may have read while inserting Psalm 108 into the collection. Two weaknesses mark this particular view. First, claiming that the editor(s) inserted Psalm 108 into its present location due to its canonical coherence with its surrounding context is more plausible than claiming that Psalm 108 appears in its current location because of some historical happenstance. Second, proposing that the *qere* reading of Psalm 60 influences Psalm 108 seems to undervalue the literary nature of the Psalter.[77] The editor(s) has carefully placed Psalm 108 and its surrounding psalms into their present canonical, literary context.[78]

Another plausible explanation of the pronoun change is that Psalm 108 refers to events late in Israel's history and that "me" refers to Hyrcanus.[79] The weakness of this view is that locating the historical dating of a psalm is a tenuous venture at best.

A more concrete way to locate the psalm's historical setting is to place it along the redemptive-historical trajectory of the Psalter's canonical storyline. If this approach is taken, Psalm 108's historical backdrop appears to be sometime after the exilic community had returned to Israel. Therefore, "me" does not refer to a contemporary Davidic ruler since no such person existed. Instead, "me" refers to the author of the psalm, who is—as indicated by the superscription—David.

David as the "me" figure whom God would rescue is also now identified as being saved by God's right hand: הוֹשִׁיעָה יְמִינְךָ וַעֲנֵנִי ("save with your right hand and rescue me").[80] In addition, the change in Psalm 108:7 from "us" to "me" ties David to Israel as a representative figure: "So that your beloved ones may be delivered, save with your right hand and answer me." The grammatical logic implies that God will first need to answer David's prayer before God saves his "beloved ones." David's prayer precedes the salvation of the beloved. This change thus emphasizes Israel's corporate solidarity with David because his salvation intertwines with

77. It is also unclear that the *qere* reading would have existed when the editor(s) put the Psalter together.

78. I have detailed many connections between Pss 104–106, 107, and 108 earlier in ch. 3. In ch. 5, this study will show how Ps 108 relates to Ps 109 and Ps 110.

79. Knauf, "Psalm LX und Psalm CVIII," 63–64.

80. Canonically, this ties David in Ps 108 closely with the royal figure of Ps 109:31 and the eschatological figure of Ps 110:1 and 5, for whom the idea of right hand plays an important role.

the salvation of Israel.[81] Geoffrey Grogan similarly concludes that the king functions as a royal representative of the people through the use of singular and plural terms in 108:7: "Thus are combined the king's roles as individual Israelite and as royal representative of the people, in whom the whole nation speaks in prayer and praise."[82] As chapter 5 will demonstrate, David's priestly function in Psalm 108 introduces the theme of a priest-like king, which Psalm 110 further develops (110:4).

Psalm 108:10 and 11

Psalm 108 follows God's restoration of Israel from the Exile (Ps 107) and the hopes surrounding a new kingdom. In Psalm 60, God details how he will conquer various nations surrounding Israel. Edom, a traditional enemy of Israel, presents a particularly interesting case. The superscription of Psalm 60 points to a time when David fought and conquered Edom (60:1–2; 2 Sam 8:213–14). Psalm 60:10 records God promising to defeat Edom, yet Psalm 60 recounts events that happened during David's lifetime and before the Exile and the return. Within its post-exilic (Book V) and eschatological-canonical setting (Pss 108–110), Psalm 108 reinvigorates a desire to conquer Edom by picturing a new conquest of Edom.[83]

Psalm 108 appropriately pictures the defeat of Edom because this nation dealt treacherously with Israel when foreigners conquered and sent Israel into exile (cf. Obad 10–16).[84] With these acts, Edom deepened its identity as Israel's traditional enemy, and according to Obadiah, God will judge Edom "on that day," the day of eschatological judgment (Obad 8). Interestingly, Psalm 60 and Psalm 108 promise a literal victory over Edom, but that victory happens at different times along the

81. "Kings represented Israel in the OT, so that what could be said about the king was true of the nation, and vice-versa." G. K. Beale, "The Cognitive Peripheral Vision of Biblical Authors," *Westminster Theological Journal* 76, no. 2 (2014): 277.

82. Grogan, *Psalms*, 182.

83. Vesco, *Le Psautier de David*, 2:1037–38. According to Tournay, *Seeing and Hearing*, 181, "Edom becomes the symbol of all the enemies of God and God's people, as will be the case in Rabbinic literature where Edom will designate Rome." Klaus Koenen suggests the possibility that Edom is a cipher and that Ps 109 identifies this cipher by its discussion of the enemy. Klaus Koenen, Jahwe wird kommen, zu herrschen über die Erde: Ps 90–110 als Komposition, Bonner Biblische Beiträge 101 (Weinheim, DE: Beltz Athenäum Verlag, 1995), 105

84. For a helpful survey of Esau and Edom in the Old Testament, see Bryan R. Dyer, "Esau in Romans and Hebrews," in Stanley E. Porter, *Sacred Tradition in the New Testament: Tracing Old Testament Themes in the Gospels and Epistles* (Grand Rapids: Baker Academic, 2016), 209–26.

redemptive-historical timeline of the Old Testament. In Psalm 60:9 and 10, Edom refers to the Edom that existed during David's reign. In Psalm 108, however, Edom refers to the Edom that will exist at a time of future vindication. Psalm 108, therefore, presents a renewed hope in a kingdom for the redeemed of YHWH (Ps 107:2), whose traditional enemies are defeated.[85]

Psalm 108:12

Psalm 108:12 (הֲלֹא־אֱלֹהִים) omits the second person pronoun אַתָּה, which is present in Psalm 60:12 (הֲלֹא־אַתָּה אֱלֹהִים). One explanation for the omission is that the psalmist in Psalm 60:12 asks God why he has not defended Israel, but in Psalm 108:12 the psalmist explains that humans cannot provide salvation (cf. 108:13). Phil Botha advocates this position:

> This may be significant, since the original version in Ps 60 seems to mean: "Is it not you, O God? You have rejected us," while it now reads: "Is it not God, you who have rejected us?" The first sounds like an accusation, while the second can be interpreted as providing a reason why military campaigns fail. The version in Ps 108 thus seems to provide a reason for the current state of affairs, rather than forming an accusation as part of a lament.[86]

If Botha is correct, the point of Psalm 108:12 would be that Israel has not received victory because human effort cannot bring about salvation. Only God can. In contrast, Psalm 60:12 asks why God has seemingly rejected Israel and not helped her defeat her enemies.

Botha's interpretation becomes more plausible when one considers how Psalm 108 restructures Psalm 60. In Psalm 60, God's rejection of Israel brackets the psalm (60:3 and 12). Psalm 60:3 states "God, you rejected us. You broke out against us. You are angry. Will you restore us?" After detailing the hardship of Israel and the need for God to rescue her, Psalm 60:12 says, "Have you not rejected us, O God? You do not go out, O

---

85. *Contra* Erhard S. Gerstenberger, *Psalms Part 2, and Lamentations*, FOTL 15 (Grand Rapids: Eerdmans, 2001), 256., who states, "Since we do recognize some historical roots of our communal complaint, and furthermore suspect a contemporary cultic stimulus for hating Edom in a specific exilic situation, there is no real need to make Psalm 108 an 'eschatological' text (thus Becker, 67)." Gerstenberger reads the Psalter form-critically and thus does not read Ps 108 along the redemptive-historical storyline of the Psalter. Even assuming Gerstenberger's position, since Ps 108 is an exilic psalm, Edom would still be Israel's eschatological enemy (cf. Obad 8).

86. Botha, "Psalm 108," 588.

God, with our armies." The language of rejection inserts a grim tone to the psalm, which still hopes that God will give Israel victory.

In Psalm 108, none of that grim tone exists. In fact, the entire psalm is overwhelmingly positive. Psalm 108 does not have a "rejection" *inclusio* similar to Psalm 60 because Psalm 108 includes only Psalm 60:12, not 60:3. When Psalm 108:12 says, "Have you rejected us, O God?," the nuance here might better fit the sense of this translation: "God has not rejected us, has he?" In the latter translation, one can observe a stronger sense of hope, especially since Psalm 108 appears within a canonical context of God's victory. For example, Psalm 107 answers the call for redemption from Psalm 106, and Psalm 108 continues to give shape to that redemption.

Even by adding these reasons to Botha's argument, the omission of the second person pronoun "you" (אַתָּה) and the restructuring of Psalm 60 in Psalm 108 are not enough to prove that Psalm 60:12 asks a question while Psalm 108:12 provides a reason explaining why Israel had not yet won a victory.

Regardless of the precise difference in meaning between Psalm 60:12 and Psalm 108:12, Psalm 108's structure and positive perspective on God's victory over the nations leads to a notion akin to Botha's reading of Psalm 108:12. Israel had yet to experience victory in Psalm 108:12 because God did not go out with them; without God, the salvation of man is futile (Ps 108:13). When God finally does go out to fight for Israel, victory will be absolute (cf. Ps 110:6).

Exegetical Conclusions

Studying how Psalm 108 cites Psalms 57 and 60 sheds light on the meaning of Psalm 108, underscoring how the psalm envisions God's reign over the earth with David as a king who intercedes for the people of God.

CONCLUSION

Psalm 108 naturally follows Psalms 104–107 and appears in Book V of the Psalter. Psalm 108 therefore follows Psalms 57 and 60 within the canonical Psalter. Moreover, the lack of a historically moored superscription in Psalm 108 screens out a historical backdrop within 1 or 2 Samuel. The superscription contrasts the historically specific superscriptions of Psalms 57 and 60, and it guides readers to locate the historical backdrop of Psalm 108 by its canonical context (Pss 104–106, 107, and 109–110), which, as noted, is a post-exilic and eschatological context. Moreover, the ways in which Psalm 108 differs from Psalms 57 and 60 highlight God's kingdom and king, which further clarifies the message of Psalm 108.

Significantly, David wrote Psalm 108, according to the superscription, which inserts the idea of a Davidic king into the psalm. Since David had died about five-hundred years earlier, the editor(s) likely inserted Psalm 108 (along with Pss 109 and 110) into its current canonical location to reignite a hope for a Davidic king and kingdom.

The new canonical context, the lack of historical specificity, and the conspicuous differences in Psalm 108 communicate eschatological notions. Psalm 108 hints at hopes not yet realized: God will bring about his kingdom for Israel through a great battle involving a Davidic king.

6

Psalms 108, 109, and 110

This chapter argues that Psalms 108–110 advance the eschatological trajectory set by Psalm 107. Psalm 108 prefaces Psalms 109 and 110 and introduces the notions of the Davidic king and of the kingdom to these psalms. Psalms 109 and 110 continue to develop these notions. In these psalms, God reigns through a Davidic and priestly ruler who suffers at the hand of enemies.

To substantiate these claims, this chapter begins by defining how the intent of the author of Psalm 108 and the intent of the editor(s) of the Psalter coincide in these psalms. It then provides an overview of Psalms 108, 109, and 110 to supply a baseline interpretation of these psalms. Afterward, it identifies and interprets thematic connections within these psalms. This chapter, therefore, clarifies the meaning of Psalm 108 by highlighting its relationship with Psalms 109 and 110.

AUTHORIAL AND EDITORIAL INTENTIONALITY

The concept of intentionality complicates the picture somewhat because one must ask who intends to communicate theological meaning in Psalms 108, 109, and 110. Is it the author of these psalms or the editor(s) who placed them in a sequence that communicates theological meaning? Canonical approaches to the Bible often overlook this issue of intentionality, although not exclusively so.[1]

This book argues that the editor(s) organized individual psalms around a general historical and thematic framework. However, how does the editor's (or editors') organization of individual psalms into groups (like Pss 108–110) relate to the author's intent of an individual psalm like Psalm 108? Without direct historical evidence, this question

1. For example, Christopher Seitz deals with the issue of intentionality in *Joel*, International Theological Commentary (New York: Bloomsbury T&T Clark, 2016), 63.

cannot be answered with certainty. Nevertheless, this chapter can provide a plausible explanation of how editorial intent and authorial intent may relate to one another.

A simple explanation for this relationship is that in Psalms 108–110 the editor(s) has respected the authorial intent of each psalm. As has been argued of Psalm 108 and will be argued of Psalms 109 and 110, each psalm by itself contributes to the eschatological notions of the king and the kingdom. The editor(s) recognized the eschatological content of these psalms and placed them side-by-side in Book V of the Psalter. Of course, by placing them in sequence in Book V, the editor(s) has added a new context in which to interpret these psalms. Readers now read Psalms 108–110 according to their *Sitz im Literatur*.[2]

Willed Types

The concepts of willed types and pregnant meanings clarify how an editor(s) might insert a psalm into a new *Sitz im Literatur* while respecting the authorial intent of individual psalms. A willed type involves speaking about one type of thing, while consciously or unconsciously including similar things within that one type of thing. Put another way, a willed type is a verbal communication that wills a certain type of thing and includes "all possible members belonging to that type" within the verbal utterance.[3]

The following example clarifies this abstract description of willed types. Someone might say "Today is a beautiful day" without specifically explaining what makes the day beautiful. Were one to ask the speaker if he or she thought the day was beautiful due to the sun or due to the warmth of the day, the speaker might reply "Yes," although he or she did not specifically think of either when saying "Today is a beautiful day." The sun and its warmth are both included in the speaker's statement that today is a beautiful day, although the speaker may not have consciously considered those features of beauty in his or her original utterance. Nevertheless, the features of sun and warmth are included within the speaker's willed type (i.e., what makes a day beautiful).

Similarly, Psalm 108:6 may refer to God's eschatological glory in theophany, and although David may not have explicitly thought that this

---

2. Auwers, *La Composition Littéraire du Psautier*, 176.

3. E. D. Hirsch, *Validity in Interpretation* (New Haven, CT: Yale University Press, 1967), 49.

theophany would parallel God's victory in Psalm 110, had someone asked him if such was the case, his answer may have been "Yes, these events are related."

If one grants that this scenario is plausible, the concept of a willed type provides an explanation for how an editor(s) can organize an author's psalms into a sequence according to theological principles while honoring the author's intent. For example, the editor(s) gathered psalms that share members within the type of an eschatological fulfillment. David willed to speak about future events in Psalms 108, 109, and 110. The later editor(s) collected these Davidic psalms, placing them side-by-side to communicate fuller meanings than the psalms would otherwise convey. In this way, the editor(s) would have honored David's intent because the new meanings are members of David's willed type.

Pregnant Meaning

The language of pregnant meaning provides another tool to clarify how an author might speak of a specific idea but intend a larger and more complex notion. For the purposes of this study, pregnant meaning refers to how biblical authors wrote without understanding the full import of their words. For example, Isaiah speaks of the mountain of YHWH in Isaiah 2 that would be established in the latter days (Isa 2:2), but the language that Isaiah uses is open to clarification. Perhaps Isaiah did not know the full picture of the events in the latter days, even if he had a sufficient picture of them. Later authors deepen the theological notion of the latter days (e.g., Dan 10:14). In so doing, later authors do not contradict earlier authors but clarify or deepen the meaning that the earlier author intended. Douglas Moo and Andrew Naselli explain:

> The human authors may have had inklings that their words were pregnant with meanings that they did not yet understand, but they would not have been in a position to see the entire context of their words. Some biblical books written before them may not have been available to them, and they were unaware of subsequent revelation.[4]

The concept of pregnant meaning helps to clarify how the editor(s) might have added new meaning to a psalm by placing it into a sequence

4. Moo and Naselli, "The Problem of the New Testament's Use of the Old Testament," 735.

of psalms. Notably, the editor(s) would have had access to a wider range of Scripture and could rely on a longer tradition of theological reflection on Scripture than David, allowing the editorial work to clarify the pregnant meaning in David's words in Psalms 108, 109, and 110. Placing these psalms in sequence, the editor(s) clarified his words. Accordingly, the meaning of each psalm should be considered in conversation with its neighboring psalms. Consequently, Psalms 108, 109, and 110 are intended by the editor(s) to be read as a unit, and this new reading strategy accords with the pregnant meaning of David's words in each psalm.

The theoretical concepts of willed types and pregnant meanings provide tools to explain how the editor(s) of the Psalter could create new meaning through arranging individual psalms into a sequence while respecting the psalmists' intent. It is within this framework that this study interprets Psalms 108–110. Even if the above explanation seems implausible, readers who believe the editor(s) did not respect authorial intent or doubt the cohesiveness of their message must consider the abundant evidence that binds these psalms into a unit communicating eschatological meaning.

A SKETCH OF PSALMS 108–110

The following paragraphs provide a basic overview of Psalms 108, 109, and 110. The purpose of this overview is to supply a baseline interpretation of these psalms to help readers understand the subsequent discussion of cohesive elements that are found within Psalms 108–110 and their meaning.

Psalm 108

As argued in Chapter 3, Psalm 108 splits into two parts: Psalm 108:1–7 and 108:8–14. The parts draw their material from portions of Psalms 57 and 60. The first half contains praise for God (108:1–5) and a prayer to God (108:6–7). The second half contains God's answer to David's prayer (108:8–11) as well as a community prayer (108:12–14).

Psalm 109

Psalm 109 splits into four parts: Psalm 109:1–5, 6–20, 21–29, and 30–31. Psalm 109:1–5 conveys David's complaint, and Psalm 109:6–20 describes David delivering a notable imprecation against his enemies. Psalm 109:21–29 returns to David's prayer, and Psalm 109:30–31 ends the psalm with a note of praise. The primary interpretive issue in Psalm 109 is how to understand the imprecation of Psalm 109:6–20. According to Goulder, "Psalm 109 is the most shocking psalm in the Psalter, the pure vitriol of distilled hatred."[5] C. S. Lewis agrees, for he has noted how the "spirit of hatred" appears in some psalms, but he identifies Psalm 109 as perhaps the worst example of this hatred.[6]

Imprecatory psalms have often been downplayed or outright rejected by scholars, as Kraus notes: "In more recent times a total rebuff of the 'unchristian' imprecatory psalms has triumphed."[7] To illustrate his point, Kraus cites R. Kittel, B. Duhm, and F. Baumgärtel because they lambast Psalm 109 as being unchristian.[8] These scholars assume that Psalm 109:6–20 records the speech of the psalmist, but Kraus proposes that Psalm 109:6–20 contains the words of the psalmist's opponents: "Verses 6ff. are pronouncements of the enemies."[9] In other words, Psalm 109:6–20 does not contain the psalmist's words; the psalmist was simply recording the imprecatory language of his opponents.

Jean-Luc Vesco outlines the exegetical evidence for the citation-hypothesis.[10] One form of evidence is that in Psalm 109:6–20 the addressee is spoken of in the singular. Hence, the enemy speaks of the psalmist (singular). Psalm 109:28 also claims that the enemies curse, but the psalmist trusts that God will bless him.[11] But as Vesco points out, Psalm 109:16 seems to describe the psalmist's situation rather than the enemy's situation.[12] The enemy has faithlessly pursued David who was poor and needy: "Since he [the enemy] did not remember to act faithfully, and he pursued the poor and needy [the psalmist] to kill the brokenhearted" (Ps 109:16). Later, Psalm 109:22 identifies the psalmist as "poor and needy," suggesting that he is the poor and needy person of Psalm 109:16.[13] Goulder records that some limit the enemies' quotation to Psalm 109:6–15.[14] However, as Vesco notes, Psalm 109:13 and 15 place the

5. Goulder, *Psalms of the Return*, 132.

6. C. S. Lewis, *Reflections on the Psalms* (New York: Mariner, 2012), 20.

7. Kraus, *Psalms 60–150*, 341.

8. Kraus, *Psalms 60–150*, 341–42.

9. Kraus, *Psalms 60–150*, 342.

10. Vesco, *Le Psautier de David*, 2:1045.

11. Hossfeld and Zenger, *Commentary on Psalms 101–150*, 130.

12. Vesco, *Le Psautier de David*, 2:1045.

13. Goulder, *The Psalms of the Return*, 137.

14. Goulder, *Psalms of the Return*, 137.

addressee in the plural form rather than the singular.[15] A plurality of addressees calls into question the entire citation-hypothesis because it is partly based on the psalmist's enemies accusing the psalmist (singular) in Psalm 109:6–19.

The citation-hypothesis is not convincing because it is seemingly driven to free the psalmist of blame for his imprecatory language. Additionally, the citation-hypothesis disagrees with the New Testament's interpretation of the psalm. In Acts 1, Peter refers to Psalm 109:6 as a prophecy about Judas (Acts 1:16, 20)[16] and so reads Psalm 109's imprecation as being about the enemy rather than being the words of the enemy. The dubious motivation behind the citation-hypothesis, the tenuous textual evidence, and the conflict the hypothesis causes with the New Testament's interpretation of Psalm 109 lead to the conclusion that Psalm 109:6–19 contains the psalmist's words.

At the theological level, readers must nevertheless grapple with Psalm 109's unrelenting imprecations. For my part, I find Augustine's explanation of Psalm 109's imprecations satisfying. As Augustine explains, the psalmist does not desire evil to happen but predicts it. The psalmist foretells that future retribution will come upon his enemies "in accordance with the justice of God."[17] Thus, God will judge the psalmist's enemies: "He [God] imposes punishment not because he enjoys someone else's misery, which would be to render evil for evil, but out of delight in justice, which is to render good for evil."[18] Augustine's interpretation highlights the prophetic nature of the psalmist, whom Augustine identifies as Christ. I disagree with Augustine's direct identification of the speaker as Christ. I come to the same conclusion, but I understand the speaker to be David, who prophetically and typologically speaks about the messiah. Prophetically, he outlines exactly what will happen to those who are faithless. Typologically, his experience finds fuller fulfillment in the experience of a future king.

However, one resolves the theological tension in Psalm 109, the psalm still records the psalmist using imprecatory language. Enemies surround the king, who identifies with his people by being poor and

15. Vesco, *Le Psautier de David*, 2:1045.

16. Peter also identifies David as the author of both Pss 69 and 109 in Acts 1:16.

17. Augustine, *Exposition of the Psalms*,5:245 (§7).

18. Augustine, *Exposition of the Psalms*, 5:245 (§7).

needy. His only hope is to entrust himself fully to YHWH who "stands at the right hand of the needy person" (Ps 109:31).

Psalm 110

Like Psalm 108, Psalm 110 splits into two parts. Psalm 110:1–3 contains an oracle of YHWH regarding the rule of a royal figure. Psalm 110:4–7 contains a second oracle of YHWH in which YHWH declares the psalm's subject to be a priest after the order of Melchizedek. Although the psalm's structure is simple and uncontroversial, its content is complex and controversial. In the following, I present a reasonable but basic interpretation of Psalm 110.[19] This book's purpose is to show how Psalm 108 introduces eschatological notions that Psalms 109 and 110 progressively clarify. I do not intend to work exhaustively through the peculiarities of Psalm 110 but to outline a tenable reading to help fulfill this purpose as well as to avoid unnecessary controversy.

Psalm 110:1 records YHWH speaking to אדני ("my lord"), who is a royal figure and not the psalm's author. Rather, the author is David, as the superscription notes. David speaks about a royal figure ("my lord") to whom YHWH promises a kingdom (Ps 110:2) and a holy people (Ps 110:3). YHWH swears that "you are a priest forever according to the order of Melchizedek" (Ps 110:4). The "you" of 110:4 is probably "my lord" from 110:1 since no obvious switch in addressee occurs between Psalm 110:1–3 and Psalm 110:4. On this reading, Psalm 110 contains two oracles of YHWH, both of which address a royal figure ("my lord"). Given Psalm 110:4, the oracles could also be interpreted as addressing a priestly figure who acts in a royal fashion.[20] Whatever is the case, the above sketch of Psalm 110's structure and content is not greatly affected.

In the discussion below, the terms "lord," "royal figure," or "king" refer to the person to whom YHWH speaks. Although the lord in Psalm 110 is not David, the royal figure appears to be a Davidic figure because he shares characteristics of an eschatological king, and the Old Testament generally describes Israel's future ruler as Davidic (e.g., Amos 9:11). In Psalm 110, David prophetically recounts two divine conversations

19. For two recent treatments of Ps 110, see Matthew Habib Emadi, "The Royal Priest: Psalm 110 in Biblical-Theological Perspective" (PhD diss., The Southern Baptist Theological Seminary, 2016) and Ian James Vaillancourt, "The Multifaceted Savior of Psalms 110 and 118: A Canonical Exegesis" (Sheffield: Sheffield Phoenix, 2019).

20. Goulder, *Psalms of the Return*, 145.

between YHWH and the eschatological king of Israel (110:1, 4) whom David believed would come through his royal line (cf. 2 Sam 7:16).

Conclusion

Psalms 108, 109, and 110 describe David, or a royal figure, in conflict with many enemies and trusting fully in God for deliverance. Building on this basic picture of Psalms 108–110, the following discussion identifies and interprets the cohesive elements in these three psalms, demonstrating how Psalm 108 introduces major themes into the collection.

THREE LEVELS OF READING

The following sections uncover how the editor(s) creates new meaning by queueing Psalms 108, 109, and 110 while also honoring and deepening the intended meaning of their author, David. Three levels of reading aid in discovering and interpreting cohesive elements in Psalms 108–110.

The first level of reading centers on superscriptions, whose repetition and placement bind psalms together and shape groups of psalms. The second level of reading pinpoints shared language and themes within adjacent psalms and psalm groups. Link-words may simply reflect common vocabulary among the psalms without intentionally binding the psalms together. Hence, link-words are considered only as possibly uniting psalm groups when their appearance is common within Psalms 108–110 and uncommon elsewhere in Book V. Shared themes are stronger evidence of unity than link-words because they demonstrate how theological ideas develop across Psalms 108–110, as seen in the argument below. The final level of reading combines the pieces to make sense of the psalms as a unit. Put in simple terms, this level narrates the story of Psalms 108–110. To conclude, the discussion claims that Psalms 108–110 contain an eschatological message, namely, that God and a priest-king will conquer Israel's enemies and establish a kingdom.

Superscriptions

Psalms 108–110's superscriptions identify these poems as *mizmorim*. English translations generally render the word מִזְמוֹר as "psalm," which is an appropriate translation.[21] Superscriptions often bind psalm groups by the repetition of link-words or, as in this case, genre. In particular,

21. *HALOT*, 566.

Book V uses genre repetitions to link psalms. For example, Psalms 120–134 link through their common superscriptions: they are "songs of ascent."

The superscriptions of Psalms 108–110 also identify David as the author of these three psalms by using the phrase לְדָוִד.[22] Authorship provides an avenue of unity, an avenue that the Psalter frequently uses. For example, Psalms 42–49, 84–85, and 87–88 are linked because they are all associated with the Sons of Korah.[23] Likewise, Psalms 50 and 73–83 unite around Asaph. In short, common authorship or subject-matter in superscriptions gathers psalms into groups.

Psalms 108–110 share a common genre and author, binding these psalms into a group. Additionally, Psalms 108–110 share similarities with Psalms 138–145, four of which are titled as *mizmorim* (Pss 139, 140, 141, 143) and all of which are authored by David. Thus, Psalms 108–110 and 138–145 have parallel features, linking them as related groups of psalms.

In addition to superscriptions and common authorship, shared language and themes also connect Psalms 108–110. The discussion that follows examines link-words.

Link-words

While less important than thematic connections, link-words nevertheless provide limited verification that Psalms 108–110 should be read in sequence and as communicating a unified message.

Link-words[24] include לֵב, or "heart," which primarily appears in three places in Book V: the beginning of Book V (107:12; 108:2; 109:22), Psalm 119 (119:2, 10–11, 32, 34, 36, 58, 69–70, 80, 111–112, 145, 161), and the second

---

22. The phrase לְדָוִד could mean that a psalm is written by David, is about David, or is Davidic. In a sense, all three can be true in one psalm. A psalm could be written by David about his own experiences, and yet contain editorial updates, making it Davidic. I prefer to see the phrase as signifying authorship (as I argued in ch. 3), while allowing for the possibility that an editor could have added a superscription to a psalm by David and also could have placed that psalm into a new context to extend its meaning (i.e., placed it into the canonical Psalter).

23. Michael Goulder associates Ps 89 with the Sons of Korah. He also considers Ps 86 (a Davidic psalm) to be an interpolation. See Michael D. Goulder, *The Psalms of the Sons of Korah*, JSOTSup 20 (Sheffield: JSOT, 1982), 2.

24. All link-word occurrences found by using Logos Bible Software 6 and/or Accordance version 11.1.4. I listed the terms that Pss 109 and 110 share with Ps 108 and appear less frequently elsewhere in Book V.

Davidic group (138:1; 140:3; 141:4; 143:4).[25] The weight of the term's twenty-six occurrences thus falls on the two Davidic groups (Psalm 108–110 and 138–145) and Psalm 119, which is associated with the king.[26] Psalms 107, 112, 125, and 147 are the only other psalms in Book V containing the term "heart," and its use in Psalm 107 may function to smoothly transition into Psalms 108–110.

Likewise, more than half of the twenty-seven occurrences of יָדָה, or "praise," occur in the Davidic bookends of Psalms 108–110 (108:4; 109:30) and 138–145 (138:1–2, 4; 139:14; 140:14; 142:8; 145:10) or in psalms adjacent to them (107:1, 8, 15, 21, 31; 111:1). The rest of the occurrences either appear in Psalms 118 and 119 (118:1, 19, 21, 28–29; 119:7, 62), which are psalms associated with the king, or elsewhere (122:4; 136:1–3, 26).

The term רום or "to be high" occurs eighteen times in Book V. Four of these are within or adjacent to the Davidic triptych (107:25, 32; 108:6; 110:7), and another three are within the last Davidic group (138:6; 140:9; 145:1), with the remaining uses somewhat near in proximity to the Davidic bookends (112:9; 113:4, 7; 118:16, 28; 131:1; 148:14).

The verb יָשַׁע or "to save, deliver" occurs twelve times, five of which are in the Davidic triptych or its preceding psalm (107:13, 19; 108:7; 109:26, 31). Two others are in the other Davidic group (138:7; 145:19), and the rest occur within the Egyptian Hallel psalms or Psalm 119 (116:6; 118:25; 119:94, 117, 146).

The term יָמִין or "right" occurs seventeen times, five of which appear in the Davidic triptych (108:7; 109:6, 31; 110:1; 110:5) while eight appear in the other Davidic group or in the psalm preceding it (137:5; 138:7; 139:10; 142:5; 144:8 [2x], 11[2x]). Remaining instances of its use are in Psalms 118 and 121 (118:15, 16 [2x]; 121:5).

The word קֹדֶשׁ or "holiness" occurs seven times. Two of these are in the Davidic triptych (108:8; 110:3), two are in the later Davidic group (138:2; 145:21), and the remaining three are elsewhere (114:2; 134:2; 150:1).

25. Pss 107:12; 108:2; 109:22; 112:7–8; 119:2, 10–11, 32, 34, 36, 58, 69–70, 80, 111–112, 145, 161; 125:4; 131:1; 138:1; 140:3; 141:4; 143:4; 147:3.

26. Pss 118 and 119 match Pss 1 and 2, both highlighting Torah and king. Ps 119 seems to deliberately link to Ps 1 with its use of terms and phrases like blessed, way of blamelessness, walking, and in the Torah of Yahweh. See Grant, *King as Exemplar*, 184. Significantly, Ps 1 closely relates to Ps 2, suggesting that the blessed man of Ps 1 may be the same as the king of Ps 2. In effect, the person who meditates day and night on the Torah in Ps 119 may be the king, a king who obeys the mandate of Deut 17:14–20. See Grant, *King as Exemplar*, 1–5.

The word ראשׁ or "head" occurs thirteen times, four of which are in the Davidic triptych (108:9; 109:25; 110:6, 7) and six of which appear in the later Davidic group (137:6; 139:17; 140:8, 10; 141:5[2x]), with the rest appearing elsewhere (118:22; 119:160; 133:2).

The verb יָצָא or "to bring out" occurs eleven times. In the Davidic triad, Psalm 107 (107:14, 28; 108:12; 109:7,) and the later Davidic collection (142:8; 143:11) it appears two times each. Elsewhere, יָצָא appears five times (114:1; 121:8; 135:7; 136:11; 146:4).

In summary, Psalms 109 and 110 share numerous words with Psalm 108. Shared vocabulary alone does not necessarily bind these psalms, but the abundance of shared vocabulary among the psalms suggests that these psalms are intended to be read together.

Thematic Elements

Superscriptional repetition and key-words demonstrate that Psalms 108, 109, and 110 contain shared elements. One could, nevertheless, argue that common vocabulary is due to chance or reasons that do not relate to intentionality. However, common thematic elements develop across the three psalms, demonstrating not only their formal unity but also their material unity. Their thematic development also works with the parallel superscriptions and link-words, uniting Psalms 108–110 into a group with a coherent message.

Right Hand

The theme of the right hand (or just the hand) appears frequently in Psalms 108–110. For example, in Psalm 108:7, the psalmist requests that God would bring salvation with his right hand. In addition, the psalmist desires an accuser to stand at the right hand of a wicked man in Psalm 109:6, and in Psalm 109:27, the psalmist wants God's hand to deliver and save (cf. 109:26). At the end of Psalm 109, God himself stands at the right hand of the needy one (Ps 109:31). Moreover in Psalm 110:1, YHWH commands David's lord (אדֹנִי, "my lord") to sit at YHWH's right hand until YHWH defeats the lord's enemies. Also, the Lord or אֲדֹנָי (not אדֹנִי from Ps 110:1) is at the right hand of the royal priest in Psalm 110:5 and אֲדֹנָי will bring judgment to the nations (110:6).[27]

27. As Vaillancourt notes, David's lord sits at the right hand of YHWH in Ps 110:1, but in Ps 110:5 *Adonai* (אֲדֹנָי) is at the right hand of David's lord. In Ps 110:5, *Adonai* fights for David's lord at his right hand "even as YHWH sends out the mighty ruler's

The word pair "right hand" next appears in Psalm 118:15–16 (3x), again occurring in the context of salvation and victory. The same word pair appears in the later Davidic group with some frequency (Pss 138:7; 139:10; 144:8 [2x], 11 [2x]).

In these psalms, "right hand" or "hand" is a metaphor for power, a power that can destroy enemies, subjugate nations, and bring salvation.[28] Additionally, "right hand" appears in royal or messianic contexts (cf. Ps 118:15–16). God's right hand, or sometimes the right hand of another person, signifies judgment and victory in battle (cf. Exod 15:6).[29] In Ancient Near Eastern ideology, God stands at the king's side, which closely associates the king with God.[30] The close link between the lord and God in Psalm 110:5 means that when the royal figure's ("my lord" from Ps 110:1) enemies attack him, they also attack God. Consequently, *Adonai* will destroy the lord's enemies in Psalm 110:5.[31]

The theme of the right hand develops across Psalms 108–110. Frank van der Velden writes, "The original royal-psalm, Psalm 110, then continues [the theme of] God's standing at the right hand of the poor (Ps 109:31) with the promise to the messianic king 'Sit at my right hand!' and thus fulfills the request of the psalmist from Psalm 108:7: 'Help with your right hand!' "[32] Indeed, in Psalm 108:7, the king asks that God would help with his right hand. Then, in answer to the king's request

---

staff of David's lord to rule in the midst of his enemies in verse 2." Vaillancourt, "Multifaceted Savior," 110.

28. For a helpful overview of the phrase "right hand," see Joel F. Drinkard Jr., "Right, Right Hand," in *The Anchor Bible Dictionary*, ed. David Noel Freedman (New York: Doubleday, 1992), 5:724.

29. Joel Drinkard notes, "To have Yahweh at one's right hand virtually assured victory, for it implied that Yahweh was supplying the might for the confrontation: 'The Lord is at your right hand; he will shatter kings on the day of his wrath' (Ps 110:5)." Drinkard also points to Exod 15:6 as an example of YHWH's victory with his right hand: "The right hand of Yahweh was that which delivered Israel, shattering the enemy (Exod 15:6)." Drinkard, "Right, Right Hand," 5:724.

30. Stefan H. Wälchli, *Gottes Zorn in den Psalmen: Eine Studie zur Rede vom Zorn Gottes in den Psalmen im Kontext des Alten Testamentes und des alten Orients*, Orbis Biblicus et Orientalis 244 (Göttingen, Germany: Academic Press Fribourg, 2012), 82.

31. Wälchli, *Gottes Zorn in den Psalmen*, 82.

32. My translation of "Der ursprüngliche Königspsalm Ps 110 nimmt dann mit der Zusage an den messianischen König 'Setz' Dich zu meiner *Rechten*!' das Stehen Gottes zur *Rechten* des Armen (Ps 109,31) wieder auf und erfüllt somit die Bitte des psalmisten aus Ps 108,7: Hilf mit Deiner *Rechten*!" Van der Velden, *Psalm 109*, 131.

from Psalm 108, God stands at the right hand of the poor in Psalm 109 and summons the king to his right hand in Psalm 110.

The loose sequence of events in Psalms 108–110 begins to develop a more detailed picture of the eschatological notions of the king and the kingdom that Psalm 108 introduced. Psalm 108 sets up the expectation that God will establish his kingdom through a mighty act of salvation in response to the king's request: "give salvation by your right hand and answer me!" (Ps 108:7 ESV). Psalm 108:8–11 then records an oracle in which God declares victory over Israel's enemies. God continues to support Israel in Psalms 109 and 110, which clarify how he gives salvation to Israel. Specifically, Psalm 109 demonstrates that God will stand at the right hand of the needy (109:31; cf. v. 22), and Psalm 110 shows that *Adonai* stands at the lord's right side, closely associating the lord with *Adonai*.[33] The association suggests that the lord has a connection to divinity, and the united subjugation of the world (by *Adonai* and the lord; Ps 110:5–7) is a clear eschatological answer in response to Psalm 108's request. The lord in Psalm 110 is a royal figure who unites with *Adonai* to destroy Israel's eschatological enemies.

Royal Priest

The theme of the royal priest appears implicitly in Psalm 108 and explicitly in Psalm 110. This royal priest theme has its roots in earlier Scripture, which gives credence to the idea that Psalm 108 implicitly communicates the theme of a royal priest. For example, 1 Samuel creates an expectation that the coming Davidic king would be a priest-king, or at the very least a king who sometimes functions in a priestly manner. In his book on Psalm 110, Matthew Emadi shows how 2 Samuel 6 highlights David's "priestly identity."[34] This identity is seen when David sacrifices animals (2 Sam 6:13) and wears the "linen ephod" (2 Sam 6:14 ESV with

33. Andrew Streett demonstrates a close connection between Ps 80:18 and Ps 110:1 because both psalms use the term" right hand" to describe how the king acts as God's viceregent. The king thus possesses the authority of God. Streett writes, "The significance of this connection is that Psalm 110, situated as it is in Book V reflecting the return from exile and a hope for a renewed Davidic covenant, looks back to the plea of Psalm 80 for a king with such high standing and adopts similar language to express the highest view of kingship in the Psalter along with Ps 2:7." Andrew Streett, *The Vine and Son of Man: Eschatological Interpretation of Psalm 80 in Early Judaism* (Minneapolis: Fortress, 2014), 85.

34. Emadi, "The Royal Priest," 148.

Exod 28:4; 29:5).[35] David also makes priestly sacrifices in 2 Samuel 24. David intercedes on behalf of Israel (2 Sam 24:17) and builds an altar to offer "sacrifices to Yahweh at the threshing floor of Araunah the Jebusite (2 Sam 24:18–25)."[36] Furthermore, David's sons also serve as priests (2 Sam 8:18). It is not impossible, therefore, that the future Davidic king described in Psalm 108 would also follow this priestly pattern. Indeed, David's intercessory prayer in Psalm 108:6–7 evokes this Davidic priestly tradition from 1 Samuel.

In Psalm 108:6–7, the king intercedes for his people. He requests that God would glorify himself over the entire world and rescue his "beloved ones" (108:6–7). In Psalm 108:8, God speaks from his "sanctuary" (בְּקָדְשׁוֹ); thus, the word of God comes from the sanctuary.[37] Moreover, Psalm 108:8–11 recounts God's word in the form of a divine oracle. The oracle consists of God's declaration of absolute victory over the nations surrounding Israel and her traditional enemy, Edom (Ps 108:10, 11).

The king's prayer for his people becomes the prayer of the people in Psalm 108:12–14. The king's voice (Ps 108:1–7) joins with the voice of the people: "give us help against the foe" (Ps 108:13). The transition from the individual interceder ("I") to the community of interceders ("us") links God's victory over the nations with the success of the people of Israel. With this transition, the king's prayer leads to a hope for comprehensive national victory as is described in God's oracular declaration of victory (Ps 108:8–11).

The absoluteness of God's victory combined with the transition from the individual intercessor to the community of intercessors contributes to an eschatological understanding of Psalm 108. Following Becker, Ballhorn points to Psalm 108:6 as evidence that the king's prayer for the people of Israel is an eschatological request to see the glory of YHWH.[38] In Psalm 108:6, the king prays that YHWH's glory would cover "the whole earth,", which will occur concretely when God destroys Israel's enemies (Ps 108:8–11). Since the king's voice joins with the people's voice to request that God would destroy Israel's enemies (Ps 108:13), God's eschatological glory includes Israel as a people and perhaps as a people of a new kingdom.

35. Emadi, "The Royal Priest," 148.

36. Emadi, "The Royal Priest," 145.

37. Ballhorn, *Zum Telos des Psalters*, 150.

38. Ballhorn, *Zum Telos des Psalters*, 150–51.

In relation to the king's eschatological request (Ps 108:6), Ballhorn identifies the sanctuary in Psalm 108:8 as the heavenly sanctuary: "And out of the temple, the heavenly sanctuary can come into being."[39] The heavenly sanctuary perhaps speaks of a transcendent reality (heavenly temple),[40] and it reiterates the priestly theme implied by the king's prayer, which is developed eschatologically in Psalm 110 (See Ps 110:3–4).

In Psalm 110:4, David's lord is called a priest according to the order Melchizedek, and in Psalm 110:3 his people are said to be clothed in holy garments (בְּהַדְרֵי־קֹדֶשׁ). The association of David's lord with the priesthood may have existed already in the consciousness of the Israelites. After all, 2 Samuel 8:18 states: "David's sons were priests" and David had interceded for his people (2 Sam 24:17). As Psalms 108 and 110 confirm, David's lord, or a royal figure like David, functions as a priest and intercedes for his people.[41] The designation of the Melchizedekian priesthood fits David's royal and priestly role, as Melchizedek was an archetypical king and priest (Gen 14:18).

The regal-priestly development in Psalm 108 and 110 is obviously complicated due to the enigmatic identity of the priest-king.[42] The canonical reading proposed by this book clarifies the matter somewhat because I have shown (and am showing) that Psalms 108–110 *together* develop coherent theological ideas. To read Psalm 110 alone hampers one's ability to determine the priest's identity. However, when one reads Psalms 108, 109, and 110 together, a clearer picture emerges. Typologically, Psalm 108 speaks of an eschatological king. Psalm 109 outlines the travails of this king, and Psalm 110 unveils the full picture of the king, who is associated

39. My translation of "Und aus dem Tempel kann das himmlische Heiligtum werden." Ballhorn, *Zum Telos des Psalters*, 151.

40. Ps 2 speaks of the heavenly rule of God and the earthly rule of God's anointed. In Ps 2:4, God is enthroned in heaven. Yet in Ps 2:6, God installs the king on Zion. The significance might be that God rules from his heavenly throne in and through the earthly throne of the Davidic king. This theme of heavenly and earthly realities runs through Scripture. In Exod 25:40, God commands Moses to build the sanctuary after the pattern of the heavenly sanctuary (cf. Ps 78:69; Heb 8:5). The borders of the nations are determined by the number of angels according to Deut 32:8. In Dan 10:13, readers learn that Persia has a spiritual prince that rules over it. In the Bible, earthly institutions often point to heavenly realities.

41. For an overview of the relationship between king and priest in ancient Israel, see de Vaux, *Ancient Israel*, 113–14.

42. Goulder (*Psalms of the Return*, 142) notes that some associate Ps 110 with a Davidic or Maccabean setting, while others read the psalm in connection with Joshua the high priest from Zech 6:9–14.

with *Adonai* and possesses an eternal priesthood.[43] In short, the priest is the eschatological, Davidic king who is associated with *Adonai* and the Melchizedekian priesthood.

The idea of a priestly leader has a wider biblical context. Moses, for example, intercedes for Israel in Exodus 32 and Numbers 14 in order to rescue Israel from God's wrath. During the Mosaic era, God clearly views Moses apart from the people of Israel. God is willing to destroy Israel and fulfill his covenant with Moses (Exod 32:10), but Moses pleads for God to rescue Israel to defend God's honor (Exod 32:11–14). In contrast, David leads Israel as a representative who stands in place of the people. When David sinfully takes a census of Israel, God does not discipline David directly. Rather, God disciplines the entire nation of Israel (cf. 2 Sam 24:13). David then intercedes for Israel and offers sacrifices to God (2 Sam 24:17, 25). After the sacrifices, God relents from his wrath (2 Sam 24:25). David is tied corporately to the people of Israel as a king who functions as a priest.

The association of a royal priest with his people also appears in eschatological passages such as Zechariah 6. In this chapter, the Branch will build a temple and sit on the throne (Zech 6:12–13). The Branch is either a priest or it is implied that a priest will sit with this Branch on the throne (Zech 6:13).[44] Although Zechariah does not present the king interceding for the people, the idea of sacrifice is present. In this case, the sacrifice appears to be the king himself (Zech 12:10). Joel, however, ties together the themes of intercession and eschatological salvation.

---

43. Ballhorn (*Zum Telos des Psalters*, 164) writes, "The poor person from Psalm 109 is enthroned as king in Psalm 110. On the one hand, the person addressed is enthroned at the right of the Lord and thus made king, and, on the other hand, he is also granted the priesthood" ("Der Arme aus Ps 109 wird in Ps 110 zum König inthronisiert. Zum einen wird der Angeredete zur Rechten des Herrn inthronisiert und somit zum König gemacht, zudem wird ihm das Priestertum zugesprochen").

44. Didymus calls the throne a "two fold throne, a royal one and a priestly one." Hence, he sees Zech 6:13 as speaking about a king who is also a priest. Didymus the Blind, *Didymus the Blind: Commentary on Zechariah*, trans. Robert C. Hill, Fathers of the Church 111 (Washington, DC: Catholic University of America Press, 2006), 128. Interestingly, Didymus connects Zech 6:13 to Ps 110:4 and identifies the priest-king as Melchizedek rather than as the Son of God. He does so because Heb 7:3 does not directly identify the Son of God with Melchizedek. Rather, Melchizedek resembles the Son of God. See Didymus the Blind, *Commentary on Zechariah*, 129.

Joel speaks of intercession as the means by which Israel will be saved in the future (cf. Joel 2:17).[45]

Psalms 108 and 110 are part of a tradition that associates kingship with priesthood. This association is particularly true of David, or of those in the Davidic line, which includes his sons in their own priestly roles (2 Sam 8:18). David's prayer in Psalm 108:7, thus, represents a biblical trajectory of a royal priest who saves his people. Like Zechariah, Psalm 110 also inserts the idea of a royal priest into the realm of eschatological salvation. Psalm 108 hints at it, but Psalm 110 celebrates a "lord" who is both a ruler and priest forever. In addition, Psalm 108 clarifies how God's ruler-priest will save his people: God will destroy Israel's enemies in response to the king's intercessory request. Then, Psalm 110 clarifies how the king and God engage in the eschatological battle with Israel's enemies: God will battle Israel's enemies as a co-belligerent with the priestly ruler (Ps 110:5).

The Enemy

The theme of the enemy also plays an important role in Psalms 108, 109, and 110. In Psalm 108, the nations that surround Israel threaten her well-being (108:8–11). Consequently, David pleads for God's help (Ps 108:7), and the people expect victory through God (Ps 108:14) because of his promise of victory (Ps 108:8–11). Furthermore, in Psalm 109, the wicked (109:2, 6) and accusers (109:20, 29; cf. v. 6) oppose David.[46] In response, David turns to God for rescue (109:21, 26) and trusts that God stands at the right hand of the needy (Ps 109:31). David's trust is notable because it starkly contrasts the wicked, who desire an accuser to stand at David's right hand (Ps 109:6).

Examining these psalms, Frank van der Velden locates Psalms 108–110's inner-coherence, at least in part, by the development of the enemy theme: "The decisive content-related connection of Psalms 108 to 110 seems thus to lie in the motif-transfer from the 'enemy peoples' of the time of the state [in Ps 108] to the opponents of the individual in Psalm

45. Joel 2:17 refers to a (then) present priestly intercession that saved Israel from destruction. Joel, however, prefaces his book by indicating that his teaching is not only for the present but also for the future (Joel 1:3). In this way, Joel provides a hermeneutical preface to his work, which invites readers to see his prophecy as having an already-not-yet perspective. See Seitz, *Joel*, 111–19.

46. Van der Velden identifies Ps 108's enemies with Ps 109's enemies. For him, Ps 108's *Feinde* refers metaphorically to foreigners, which concretely becomes the"*Frevlern* of Ps 109:2, 6, 7. See Van der Velden, *Psalm 109*, 131.

109 and from the Davidic king in Psalm 110 to the poor and needy individual of Psalm 109."[47] Van der Velden thus sees a transition from an enemy of the state in Psalm 108 to a personal enemy in Psalm 109. He also views Psalm 109's poor and needy figure as tying himself to the triumphant, victorious king in Psalm 110. Van der Velden, however, does not mention that the enemy also appears in Psalm 110 and that each psalm portrays a Davidic king who finds help from God in the midst of enemies.

The theme of a royal priest links Psalms 108 and 110, and the theme of the right-hand shows continuity between the three psalms. However, the theme of the enemy best explains why Psalm 109 appears between Psalms 108 and 110. Psalm 109's enemy theme carries forward and personalizes the enemy theme of Psalm 108.[48] Additionally, Psalm 109's enemy theme carries into Psalm 110, in which the enemy is finally defeated (Ps 110:6). In these ways, Psalm 109 binds itself to the psalms that flank it.

If Psalm 109's intention is to highlight the unchallenged victory of God through the royal figure, it would contribute less to the story of Psalms 108–110. However, the psalm highlights how the royal figure suffers and is threatened by enemies. Therefore, Psalm 109 adds a layer of nuance to the destiny of the future Davidic ruler: he will rule with God over Israel and fight as a co-belligerent against Israel's enemies, but the ruler's path to victory is fraught with suffering and threats.

Continuing the enemy theme, Psalms 108 and 109 highlight different aspects of the conflict with the enemy. In Psalm 108, the nation of Israel is under threat, and the king intercedes to God on its behalf. In Psalm 109, the king is under attack and prays to God for himself. Psalm 110 unites the concepts of people, king, and God into a single enigmatic figure, thereby drawing on important themes from Psalms 108 and 109. In Psalm 110 David describes the king's people as a freewill offering (Ps 110:4). In addition, the royal figure is not merely Israel's king, but he is also associated with *Adonai* (Ps 110:5). The king not only asks God for redemption, but *Adonai* also stands at the psalmist's right hand and

47. My translation of "Der entscheidende inhaltliche Zusammenhang der Psalmen 108 bis 110 scheint demnach in der Motivtransposition von den 'Feindvölkern' der staatlichen Zeit zu den Gegnern des einzelnen in Ps 109 und vom davidischen König in Ps 110 zum armen und schwachen einzelnen von Ps 109 zu liegen." Van der Velden, *Psalm 109*, 131.

48. Although Pss 108 and 110 portray the enemies as national enemies and Ps 109 as personal enemies, Ballhorn (*Zum Telos des Psalters*, 165) affirms the unity of message within Pss 108–110 by arguing that God elects and saves the king on the basis of the oppression he experiences in Ps 109.

shatters kings (Ps 110:5–6). Therefore, Psalm 110 brings to fruition ideas introduced in Psalms 108 and 109 and details the ultimate destruction of the eschatological enemies and their rulers (Ps 110:6 with Ps 2).

In Psalm 110, the royal figure fully expresses his intercessory role as a priest for his people. He also completely conquers the enemies who assault God's people in Psalm 108 and God's king in Psalm 109.

Under the Foot

The theme of being underfoot is also important in Psalms 108–110. In Psalm 108:10, God throws his shoe over Philistia, and in Psalm 108:14 God treads over Israel's enemies. Additionally, God declares that the lord will reign until his enemies become his footstool in Psalm 110:1. This theme draws on Ancient Near Eastern imagery in which a ruler makes his enemies a footstool.[49] While notable, the Ancient Near Eastern examples do not nullify the canonical meaning of putting an enemy under one's foot. Indeed, the idea of having one's enemy underfoot has a broader canonical context.

In Psalm 110:1, the footstool statement possibly alludes to language in Genesis 3:15, namely, "the damaged heel and head."[50] Psalm 110:6 confirms this allusion because it reads מָחַץ רֹאשׁ עַל־אֶרֶץ רַבָּה ("he will shatter the head over the wide earth"). Often, this clause is translated as "he will shatter chiefs" or its equivalent (ESV; cf. NIV 2011, NKJV). However, as James Hamilton notes, this clause

> could just as well be translated, "he will crush (*māhas*) the head (*rō's*, sg.) on the broad land" (cf. JPS, NAB, NJB, NLT, NRSV). This is a Davidic Psalm (110:1), and the use of the verb *māhas* (crush, shatter) and the term *rō's* in a number of head-crushing contexts in the OT (cf. Num 24:8, 17; Judg 5:26; 2 Sam 22:39; Job 26:12; Ps 68:22, 24; Hab 3:13) would seem to color the use of these terms in Ps 110.[51]

---

49. Othmar Keel, *The Symbolism of the Biblical World: Ancient Near Eastern Iconography and the Book of Psalms*, trans. Timothy J. Hallett (New York: Seabury, 1979), 255. In his discussion of Ps 110:1 and of the imagery of putting one's enemies underfoot, Keel illustrates and discusses the symbolism of putting one's feet over *nine* enemies (or even over nine bows). In Ps 108:8–10, God declares his possession of nine entities, which further suggests that Ps 108 draws on the Ancient Near Eastern motif of making one's enemies a footstool.

50. James Hamilton, "Skull Crushing Seed of the Woman," 37.

51. Hamilton, "Skull Crushing Seed of the Woman," 37.

The connection between Psalm 110 and Genesis 3 is likely. Essentially, Psalm 110:6 alludes to the promise in Genesis 3:15 that the woman's offspring would crush the head of the serpent's offspring (הוּא יְשׁוּפְךָ רֹאשׁ). Putting the allusions together, one can conclude that the lord will lay low his enemy by placing the enemy underfoot and crushing his head.

Psalm 110's allusions to Genesis 3 also appear to identify the unnamed enemy in Psalm 110 and, by extension, in Psalms 108 and 109 *as the seed of the serpent* (see Gen 3:15). The two-seed theology is prevalent in the Pentateuch: Cain and Abel, Noah and the world, Abraham and Sodom, Jacob and Esau, Israel and Egypt, and so on. Throughout Scripture, the seed of the woman battles the seed of the serpent. As part of this larger scriptural theme, Psalm 110 identifies the enemy as the serpent's seed, contributing to the overall eschatological picture of Psalms 108–110 and perhaps to the whole Psalter. Plausibly, the victory described in these psalms is the victory promised in Genesis 3: the serpent will finally be defeated when God's kingdom is established on earth.

King

God stands at the right hand of the king, the king is a royal priest whose voice overlaps with the prayers of his people, and the king conquers his enemies with the help of God. These previously discussed themes intertwine in Psalms 108–110 and provide a framework for understanding the identity of the king or royal figure in these psalms.

Psalm 108 portrays the king as a Davidic figure who prays for his people and for God's eschatological glory to be revealed (108:6). Psalm 110 explicitly identifies the royal figure (לַאדֹנִי) with a priest (Ps 110:4), and the royal figure will rule over a mighty kingdom (Ps 110:2, 5–6; cf. Ps 2).[52] Between these portrayals of the ruler, Psalm 109 illustrates the king's struggle. The national enemies of Psalms 108 and 110 are personalized in Psalm 109.

Enemies threaten the king to the extent that he identifies with the poor and needy: "For I am poor and needy" (Ps 109:22). As the king's voice overlaps with the voice of his people in Psalm 108 (vv. 12–14), so now in Psalm 109 the king identifies with his people by being "poor and

52. Peter Gentry and Stephen Wellum write "that the king will accomplish in his person the purpose that God had for the nation of Israel as a whole, to be a kingdom of priests. The king will embody the nation in himself." Peter J. Gentry and Stephen J. Wellum, *Kingdom through Covenant: A Biblical-Theological Understanding of the Covenants* (Wheaton, IL: Crossway, 2012), 422.

needy." The king's victory in Psalm 110 thus comes through a struggle, of which he states, "I vanish like a shadow in the evening. I am shaken off like a locust" (Ps 109:23).

Scepter

The theme of the scepter also plays an important role in Psalms 108 and 110 and further clarifies the identity of the future king. Psalm 108:9 affirms that "Judah is my scepter" (יְהוּדָה מְחֹקְקִי) and clearly alludes to Genesis 49:10: "The scepter shall not depart from Judah, nor the ruler's staff from between his feet, until tribute comes to him; and to him shall be the obedience of the peoples" (ESV). In addition, Psalm 108 possibly alludes to Numbers 24:17–19 through scepter-based language because Numbers 24 describes a scepter and its role in an eschatological victory over Moab and Edom, two of the enemies mentioned in Psalm 108:9–10.

Psalm 110:2 also develops the scepter theme, clearly alluding to Numbers 24.[53] Psalm 110:2 reads: "The LORD sends forth from Zion your mighty scepter. Rule in the midst of your enemies!" (ESV). Numbers 24:17–19 says,

> I see him, but not now; I behold him, but not near: a star shall come out of Jacob, and a scepter shall rise out of Israel; it shall crush the forehead of Moab and break down all the sons of Sheth. Edom shall be dispossessed; Seir also, his enemies, shall be dispossessed. Israel is doing valiantly. And one from Jacob shall exercise dominion and destroy the survivors of cities! (ESV)

The scepter comes from Zion (or "out of Israel") to "crush (מָחַץ) the forehead (פַּאֲתֵי) of Moab." As noted above, Psalm 110:6 reads "he will shatter (מָחַץ) the head (ראשׁ) over the wide earth" and alludes to Genesis 3:15. Moreover, Psalm 110:6 alludes to Numbers 24:17, speaking to the fulfillment of the biblical-theological trajectory of crushing the serpent's head. In so doing, Psalm 110 refers to the fulfillment of the first promise of salvation in Scripture (Gen 3:15).

The scepter theme also exists elsewhere in within the Psalter. Psalm 110:2 thus alludes to Psalm 2:9, "You shall break them with a rod of iron and dash them in pieces like a potter's vessel" (ESV) and Psalm 45:6, "Your throne, O God, is forever and ever. The scepter of your kingdom

---

53. Hamilton argues that Ps 110:2 brings to mind Num 24:17. See Hamilton, "Skull Crushing Seed of the Woman," 37. Ps 110:2, like Ps 108:9, alludes to Gen 49:10 although the linguistic connections are not as explicit (Ps 110 does not mention "Judah").

is a scepter of uprightness" (ESV).[54] In this sense, Psalm 110 accesses the theme of the scepter that not only appears at the gateway to the Psalter (Ps 2) but also within its hallway (Ps 45).

Conclusion

Psalms 108–110 share the themes of the right hand, the royal priest, the enemy, being underfoot, the king, and the scepter. With these themes outlined, this chapter concludes by narrating the story that Psalms 108–110 tell in order to show how the themes contribute to that story.

THE STORY OF PSALMS 108–110

Psalm 107 describes God's eschatological redemption of his people, Israel. They are drawn from all the corners of the earth (Ps 107:3), and they live in a place that is like a new Eden (cf. Ps 107:35). The next stage of the story is told through the three Davidic psalms that follow Psalm 107. Psalm 108 describes the new conquest of the land and the defeat of Israel's enemies. The king functions like a priest by praying on behalf of the people, but the war of conquest is not without difficulties. Psalm 109 chronicles these difficulties of the coming king. Through suffering and betrayal, however, God will bring the king to victory, a victory that Psalm 110 records. In this victory, the enemy of the king and of Israel is crushed underfoot, and readers discover that the lord and king is both priest and ruler. As a priest-king, he will rule with his scepter over the entire world.

Psalm 108 is a fitting introduction to this Davidic trilogy. It continues a sequence of events that Psalm 107 introduces and entertains key eschatological notions that Psalms 109 and 110 further develop. Read together, Psalms 108–110 tell a story of the king's conquest with YHWH's help, his difficulties during battles with the enemy, and, finally, his ultimate victory over the enemy. The head of the ancient enemy (cf. Gen 3:15) will be crushed, all things will once again be placed under humanity's feet (cf. Ps 8:7), and Eden will be restored (Ps 107:35).

CONCLUSION

This chapter demonstrates how Psalm 108 introduces eschatological notions into its canonical context (Psalms 108–110) as part of an eschatological trajectory set by Psalm 107. Willed types and pregnant meanings

54. Vesco, *Le Psautier de David*, 2:1054–55.

clarify how the editors of Psalms 108–110 could intend to communicate a clear message by grouping Psalms 108–110 while also honoring David's authorial intent within each of these psalms. This chapter also surveys the cohesive elements within Psalms 108–110, paying special attention to thematic connections. Together, these analyses show that Psalms 108–110 unite to narrate a story of conquest, conflict, and kingdom.

Conclusion

Psalm 108 introduces the eschatological notions of the king and of the kingdom into its canonical group (Pss 108–110) through its inclusion of a non-historically specific superscription, its quotation and paraphrase of earlier psalmic material (Pss 57 and 60), and its canonical placement in Book V of the Psalter.

By applying a biblical-theological and canonical approach to Psalm 108, this study provides a viable alternative to form-critical approaches to the psalm. It also shows that reading Psalm 108 as a discrete psalm without recourse to its earlier psalmic material (Pss 57 and 60) and its canonical context (Pss 107, 109–110) means that a reader will misunderstand the theological message of Psalm 108.

OVERVIEW

Chapter 1 presents this study's thesis along with three undergirding assumptions: (1) the Psalter is a book; (2) individual psalms should be read in sequence; and (3) the Psalter progressively tells a story along redemptive-historical lines.

Chapters 2 and 3 provide histories of interpretation of Psalm 108 and of research into inner-biblical exegesis and canonical approaches to the Psalter. Chapter 2 shows differences among interpreters' views of Psalm 108. Chapter 3 demonstrates how this work's approach engages inner-biblical exegesis and Psalter exegesis (a canonical approach) to clarify the meaning of Psalm 108.

Chapter 4 interprets Psalm 108 in its canonical context. It reveals how Psalm 108 participates in the narrative flow of the Psalter. The chapter concludes that Psalm 108 continues the story of eschatological redemption that began in Psalm 107, which records the eschatological return of Israel to the land. In continuation of this story, Psalm 108 speaks of the eschatological conquest of the land. In response to the king's prayer, God will go out with Israel's armies and conquer the land, and through the king's prayer, the kingdom comes.

Chapter 5 compares Psalm 108 with Psalms 57 and 60 to clarify the message that Psalm 108 conveys by its quotation and paraphrase of these two earlier psalms.

Chapter 6 highlights certain themes that Psalm 108 shares with Psalms 109 and 110, noting the development of these themes across the three psalms. Psalm 108 introduces the eschatological notions of the king and the kingdom to this Davidic triptych (Pss 108–110). Before discussing these psalms, this chapter also explores the theoretical tools of willed types and pregnant meaning to explain how the Psalter's editor(s) could have organized Davidic psalms into a sequence while honoring David's authorial intent.

AUTHOR AND EDITOR

This book discusses both the authors of individual psalms and the editor(s) of the Psalter. Because the authors and editor(s) play important roles in how one understands Psalm 108, a summary of this study's approach to the relationship between the authors and editor(s) is worthwhile to consider.

This book posits that the editor(s) skillfully organized the Psalter, placing psalms side-by-side and into groups in order to communicate theological ideas. In this sense, the editor(s) is a theologian who organizes individual psalms into distinct books. The authors of individual psalms are also theologians.

In the Old Testament, David's psalms are held in high esteem and are even considered the word of YHWH (see 2 Sam 23:2). In 2 Samuel, David is called God's "anointed" and "the sweet psalmist of Israel" (2 Sam 23:1 ESV), and 2 Samuel 23:2 reads, "The Spirit of the Lord speaks by me; his word is on my tongue" (ESV).[1] Moreover, David's spiritual reflections are theological in nature, as can be seen in Psalm 110. In this psalm, David hears two oracles of God (Ps 110:1, 4) and develops the theological implications of these oracles in poetic form (Ps 110:2–3, 5–7). David's words in Psalm 110 also reflect a mind that has meditated on the theological meaning of Genesis 14.[2]

1. Of this passage, Jan Jaynes Quesada writes, "The speaker is staking a fierce claim to his status as a channel for divinely inspired speech, which is the very definition of a prophet in ancient Israel." Jan Jaynes Quesada, "Is David, Too, among the Prophets? A Study of 2 Samuel 23:1–7," *Perspectives in Religious Studies* 44, no. 2 (2017): 255.

2. D. A. Carson, "Getting Excited about Melchizedek" (Sermon presented at The Gospel Coalition National Conference, Chicago, April 14, 2011), http://resources.

Furthermore, as a theologian, David writes Psalm 108 by intentionally drawing from his earlier writings. In Psalms 57 and 60, David recounts his conflict with Saul (cf. 1 Sam 24, 26) and others (cf. 2 Sam 8). Readers can identify the canonical backdrop to these psalms because David has identified it in the superscriptions. In Psalm 108, David selects portions of his two earlier psalms that communicate God's victory over the nations, writing a superscription that divests this earlier material of its historical specificity. Moreover, David recasts his experiences in Psalms 57 and 60 to speak typologically of the coming king in Psalm 108.

The editor(s) recognized that David was a theologian and read his psalms as works of theology. When the editor(s) placed Psalms 107, 108, 109, and 110 side-by-side, he did so as a result of discerning David's theological intent.[3] The editor(s), in this sense, is a biblical-theologian, working with theological poems and organizing them into a work of biblical-theology (the Psalter) to honor the authorial intent of these psalms and deepen and extend their meanings.

In Book V of the Psalter, Psalm 107 describes Israel's eschatological return to the land. In Psalm 108, the king requests that God would help Israel re-conquer the land. However, the path to victory is fraught with conflict (Ps 109). A divine priest-king is needed to finally bring about victory (Ps 110). Psalm 108 plays a crucial role in this biblical-theological story developed across Psalms 107–110. Specifically, Psalm 108 functions as a preface to Psalms 109 and 110 and introduces eschatological notions of the king and the kingdom that Psalms 109 and 110 further develop.

FUTURE RESEARCH

This book aims to contribute to the canonical study of the Psalter by clarifying how Psalm 108 and, by extension, other double psalms might be interpreted within this framework. For example, the method of this book could be applied to a study of Psalms 14 and 53 as well as Psalms 40:14–18 and 70.

Furthermore, portions of 1 Chronicles 16 appear in Psalms 96, 105, and 106. In this case, parallel material appears not only in the Psalter but also in two books of the MT. Research into the significance of 1 Chronicles 16 and its relationship to the Psalter from a canonical perspective might add further clarity to the meaning of these four texts.

---

thegospelcoalition.org/library/getting-excited-about-melchizedek.

3. Ps 107 has no superscription, and so David may not have written this psalm.

Finally, Psalms 9 and 10 as well as Psalms 42 and 43 share significant similarities, yet they are different psalms in the MT. The methods used in this study might clarify the theological purpose of these psalms.

FINAL WORD

My hope is that anyone who reads this study will come to a new appreciation of the book of Psalms as a work of theology. The editor(s) of the Psalter and the authors of individual psalms pursued a vision of God that has been handed down to readers to this day. May we take to heart the words of the psalmist who says, "Seek his face always" (Ps 105:4).

Bibliography

Alexander, J. A. *The Psalms: Translated and Explained*. 3 vols. New York: Baker and Scribner, 1850.

Allen, Leslie C. *Psalms 101–150*. Word Biblical Commentary. Nashville: Thomas Nelson, 2002.

Anderson, G. W. "The Psalms." Pages 409–43 in *Peake's Commentary on the Bible*. Edited by Matthew Black and H. H. Rowley. New York: Thomas Nelson, 1962.

Anderson, Gary A. "King David and the Psalms of Imprecation." Pages 29–45 in *The Harp of Prophecy: Early Christian Interpretation of the Psalms*. Edited by Brian E. Daley and Paul R. Kolbet. Notre Dame, IN: University of Notre Dame Press, 2015.

Augustine. *Exposition of the Psalms*. Translated by Maria Boulding. Vol. 5. New York: New City, 2003.

Auwers, Jean-Marie. *La Composition Littéraire du Psautier: Un État de la Question*. Cahiers de la Revue biblique 46. Paris: Gabalda, 2000.

Ballhorn, Egbert. *Zum Telos des Psalters: Der Textzusammenhang des Vierten und Fünften Psalmenbuches (Ps 90–150)*. Bonner Biblische Beiträge 138. Berlin: Philo, 2004.

Barker, Joel. "Brevard S. Childs and the Canonical Approach." Pages 359–79 in *Prevailing Methods after 1980*. Vol. 2 of *Pillars in the History of Biblical Interpretation*. Edited by Stanley E. Porter and Sean A. Adams. Biblical Studies Series 2. Eugene, OR: Pickwick, 2016.

Barnes, W. E. *The Psalms with Introduction and Notes*. Vol. 2. London: Methuen, 1931.

Bates, Matthew W. *The Birth of the Trinity: Jesus, God, and Spirit in New Testament and Early Christian Interpretations of the Old Testament*. Oxford: Oxford University Press, 2015.

Beale, G. K. "The Cognitive Peripheral Vision of Biblical Authors." *Westminster Theological Journal* 76, no. 2 (2014): 263–93.

Becker, Joachim. *Israel deutet seine Psalmen: Urform Und Neuinterpretation in den Psalmen*. Stuttgarter Bibelstudien 18. Stuttgart: Verlag Katholisches Bibelwerk, 1967.

Beckwith, Roger T. "The Early History of the Psalter." *Tyndale Bulletin* 46, no. 1. (1995): 1–27.

Bingham, D. Jeffrey, and Clayton N. Jefford, eds. *Intertextuality in the Second Century*. The Bible in Ancient Christianity 11. Boston: Brill, 2016.

Bird, T. E. *A Commentary on the Psalms*. Vol. 2. London: Burns Oates & Washbourne, 1927.

Borger, James Todd. "Moses in the Fourth Book of the Psalter." PhD diss., Southern Baptist Theological Seminary, 2002.

Botha, Phil J. "Psalm 108 and the Quest for Closure to the Exile." *Old Testament Essays* 23, no. 3 (2010): 574–96.

Bourguet, Daniel. "La Structure des Titres des Psaumes." *Revue d'Histoire et de Philosophie Religieuses* 61, no. 2 (1981): 109–24.

Brueggemann, Walter. "Bounded by Obedience and Praise: The Psalms as Canon." *Journal for the Study of the Old Testament* 16, no. 50 (1991): 63–92.

———. *The Message of the Psalms: A Theological Commentary*. Minneapolis: Augsburg, 1984.

———. *Spirituality of the Psalms*. Minneapolis: Fortress, 2002.

Brueggemann, Walter, and William H. Bellinger Jr. *Psalms*. New York: Cambridge University Press, 2014.

Carr, David M. *Writing on the Tablet of the Heart: Origins of Scripture and Literature*. New York: Oxford University Press, 2015.

Carson, D. A. "Getting Excited about Melchizedek." Sermon presented at The Gospel Coalition National Conference, Chicago, April 14, 2011. https://www.thegospelcoalition.org/conference_media/getting-excited-melchizedek/.

Childs, Brevard S. *Introduction to the Old Testament as Scripture*. Philadelphia: Fortress, 1979.

———. *Isaiah: A Commentary*. The Old Testament Library. Louisville, KY: Westminster John Knox, 2001.

Clifford, Richard J. *Psalms 1–72*. Abingdon Old Testament Commentary. Nashville: Abingdon, 2002.

———. *Psalms 73–150*. Abingdon Old Testament Commentaries. Nashville: Abingdon, 2003.

Clines, David J. A., ed. *The Dictionary of Classical Hebrew*. Sheffield: Sheffield Academic, 1993.

Cobb, W. F. *The Book of Psalms: With Introduction and Notes*. London: Methuen, 1905.

Cole, Robert L. *The Shape and Message of Book III*. Journal for the Study of the Old Testament Supplement Series 307. Sheffield: Sheffield Academic, 2000.

Collins, John J. *Introduction to the Hebrew Bible*. Minneapolis, MN: Fortress, 2004.

Cole, Robert Luther. *Psalms 1–2: Gateway to the Psalter*. Sheffield: Sheffield Phoenix, 2013.

Cook, Stephen L. "Apocalypticism and the Psalter." *Zeitschrift für die alttestamentliche Wissenschaft* 104, no. 1 (1992): 82–99.

Creach, Jerome F. D. *Yahweh as Refuge and the Editing of the Hebrew Psalter*. Sheffield: Sheffield Academic, 1996.

Dahood, Mitchell. *Psalms III: 101–150*. Anchor Yale Bible Commentaries. Garden City, NY: Doubleday, 1970.

De Beaugrande, Robert-Alain, and Wolfgang Ulrich Dressler. *Introduction to Text Linguistics*. New York: Longman, 1981.

DeClaissé-Walford, Nancy. *Reading from the Beginning: The Shaping of the Hebrew Psalter*. Macon, GA: Mercer University Press, 1997.

DeClaissé-Walford, Nancy, Rolf A. Jacobson, and Beth Laneel Tanner. *The Book of Psalms*. New International Commentary on the Old Testament. Grand Rapids: Eerdmans, 2014.

Delitzsch, F. *Psalms*. Vol. 5 of Keil, C. F., and F. Delitzsch. *Commentary on the Old Testament*. 10 vols. Peabody, MA: Hendrickson, 2006.

De Vaux, Roland. *Ancient Israel: Its Life and Institutions*. Translated by John McHugh. London: Darton, Longman, and Todd, 1961.

Didymus the Blind. *Didymus the Blind: Commentary on Zechariah*. Translated by Robert C. Hill. Fathers of the Church 111. Washington, DC: Catholic University of America Press, 2006.

Dines, Jennifer M. *The Septuagint*. Edited by Michael A Knibb. London: T&T Clark, 2004.

Drinkard, Joel F. Jr. "Right, Right Hand." Page 5:724 in *The Anchor Bible Dictionary*. Edited by David Noel Freedman. 6 vols. New York: Doubleday, 1992.

Duhm, D. Bernhard. *Die Psalmen*. 2nd ed. Kurzer Hand-Kommentar zum Alten Testament 14. Tübingen, DE: J. C. B. Mohr, 1922.

Dyer, Bryan R. "Esau in Romans and Hebrews." Pages 209–26 in Stanley E. Porter, *Sacred Tradition in the New Testament: Tracing Old Testament Themes in the Gospels and Epistles*. Grand Rapids: Baker Academic, 2016.

Eaton, John. *The Psalms: A Historical and Spiritual Commentary with an Introduction and New Translation*. New York: T&T Clark International, 2003.

Emadi, Matthew Habib. "The Royal Priest: Psalm 110 in Biblical-Theological Perspective." PhD diss., The Southern Baptist Theological Seminary, 2016.

Estes, Daniel J. "Psalms." Pages 141–211 in *Handbook on the Wisdom Books and Psalms*. Grand Rapids: Baker Academic, 2005.

Fishbane, Michael A. *Biblical Interpretation in Ancient Israel*. New York: Oxford University Press, 1985.

Flint, Peter W. "Dead Sea Scrolls, Psalms." In *The Lexham Bible Dictionary*. Edited by John D. Barry. Bellingham, WA: Lexham, 2012.

Fokkelman, J. P. *The Crossing Fates*. Vol. 2 of *Narrative Art and Poetry in the Books of Samuel*. Dover, NH: Van Gorcum, 1986.

Gentry, Peter J. "The Text of the Old Testament." *Journal of the Evangelical Theological Society* 52, no. 1 (2009): 19–45.

Gentry, Peter J., and Stephen J. Wellum. *Kingdom through Covenant: A Biblical-Theological Understanding of the Covenants*. Wheaton, IL: Crossway, 2012.

Gerstenberger, Erhard S. *Psalms Part 2, and Lamentations*. The Forms of the Old Testament Literature 15. Grand Rapids: Eerdmans, 2001.

———. "Der Psalter als Buch und als Sammlung." Pages 3–13 in *Neue Wege der Psalmenforschung*. Edited by Klaus Seybold and Erich Zenger. Herders Biblische Studien 1. New York: Herder, 1994.

Gill, John. *An Exposition of the Old Testament*. Vol. 4. 1810. Repr., Paris, AR: Baptist Standard Bearer, 2005.

Goldingay, John. *Psalms 90–150*. Baker Commentary on the Old Testament Wisdom and Psalms. Grand Rapids: Baker Academic, 2008.

Goulder, M. D. *The Psalms of the Return (Book V, Psalms 107–150)*. Vol. 4 of *Studies in the Psalter*. Journal for the Study of the Old Testament Supplement Series 258. Sheffield: Sheffield Academic, 1998.

———. *The Psalms of the Sons of Korah*. Journal for the Study of the Old Testament Supplement Series 20. Sheffield: JSOT Press, 1982.

Grant, Jamie A. *The King as Exemplar: The Function of Deuteronomy's Kingship Law in the Shaping of the Book of Psalms*. Atlanta: Society of Biblical Literature, 2004.

Gregory of Nyssa. *Gregory of Nyssa's Treatise on the Inscriptions of the Psalms*. Translated by Ronald E. Heine. New York: Oxford University Press, 1995.

Griffiths, Paul J. *Religious Reading: The Place of Reading in the Practice of Religion*. New York: Oxford University Press, 1999.

Grogan, Geoffrey W. *Psalms*. Two Horizons Old Testament Commentary. Grand Rapids: Eerdmans, 2008.

Gunkel, Hermann. *Die Psalmen*. 5th ed. Göttingen, Germany: Vandenhoeck & Ruprecht, 1968.

———. *Die Psalmen: Übersetzt und erklärt*. 4th ed. Handkommentar zum Alten Testament 2. Göttingen, DE: Vandenhoeck & Ruprecht, 1926.

Hamilton, James. "Psalm 107: Thank the Lord for His Steadfast Love." Sermon presented at the Kenwood Baptist Church, Louisville, KY, July 23, 2017. https://kenwoodbaptistchurch.com/sermons/thank-the-lord-for-his-steadfast-love/.

———. "The Skull Crushing Seed of the Woman: Inner-Biblical Interpretation of Genesis 3:15." *Southern Baptist Journal of Theology* 10, no. 2 (2006): 30–54.

Hays, Richard B. *The Conversion of the Imagination: Paul as Interpreter of Israel's Scripture*. Grand Rapids: Eerdmans, 2005.

———. *Echoes of Scripture in the Gospels*. Waco, TX: Baylor University Press, 2016.

———. *Echoes of Scripture in the Letters of Paul*. New Haven, CT: Yale University Press, 1989.

Hirsch, E. D. *Validity in Interpretation*. New Haven, CT: Yale University Press, 1967.

Ho, Peter C. W. *The Design of the Psalter: A Macrostructural Analysis*. Eugene, OR: Pickwick, 2019.

Holladay, William Lee. *The Psalms through Three Thousand Years: Prayerbook of a Cloud of Witnesses*. Minneapolis: Fortress, 1993.

Holmes, Michael W. "Intertextual Death: Socrates, Jesus, and Polycarp of Smyrna." Pages 51–61 in *Intertextuality in the Second Century. Edited by D. Jeffrey Bingham and Clayton N. Jefford*. The Bible in Ancient Christianity 11. Leiden: Brill, 2016.

Hossfeld, Frank-Lothar, and Erich Zenger. *A Commentary on Psalms 51–100*. Vol. 2 of *Psalms*. Edited by Klaus Baltzer. Translated by Linda M. Maloney. Hermenia. Minneapolis: Fortress, 2005.

———. *A Commentary on Psalms 101–150*. Vol. 3 of *Psalms*. Edited by Klaus Baltzer. Translated by Linda M. Maloney. Hermeneia. Minneapolis: Fortress, 2011.

Howard, David M. Jr. "A Contextual Reading of Psalms 90–94." Pages 108–23 in *The Shape and Shaping of the Psalter*. Edited by J. Clinton McCann. Sheffield: JSOT Press, 1993.

———. *The Structure of Psalms 93–100*. Biblical and Judaic Studies 5. Winona Lake, IN: Eisenbrauns, 1997.

Jacquet, Louis. *Les Psaumes et le Coeur de l'Homme: Etude Textuelle, Littéraire et Doctrinale*. Gembloux, Belgium: Duculot, 1979.

Jamieson, Robert, A.R. Fausset, and David Brown. *A Commentary, Critical and Explanatory, on the Old and New Testaments*. Grand Rapids: Zondervan, 1940.

Joüon, Paul. *A Grammar of Biblical Hebrew*. Translated by T. Muraoka. Rome: Pontifical Biblical Institute, 1996.

Keel, Othmar. *The Symbolism of the Biblical World: Ancient Near Eastern Iconography and the Book of Psalms*. Translated by Timothy J. Hallett. New York: Seabury, 1978.

Kissane, Edward J. *The Book of Psalms: Translated from a Critically Revised Hebrew Text with a Commentary*. Dublin: Browne and Nolan, 1964.

Knauf, Ernst Axel. "Psalm LX und Psalm CVIII." *Vetus Testamentum* 50, no. 1 (2000): 55–65.

Koehler, Ludwig, Walter Baumgartner, and Johann Jakob Stamm. *The Hebrew and Aramaic Lexicon of the Old Testament*. Translated and edited under the supervision of Mervyn E. J. Richardson. 4 vols. Leiden: Brill, 1994–1999.

Koenen, Klaus. *Jahwe wird kommen, zu herrschen über die Erde: Ps 90–110 Als Komposition*. Bonner Biblische Beiträge 101. Weinheim, Germany: Beltz Athenäum Verlag, 1995.

König, Eduard. *Die Psalmen eingeleitet, übersetzt und erklärt*. Gütersloh, Germany: Bertelsmann, 1927.

Kraus, Hans-Joachim. *Psalms 60–150*. Translated by Hilton C. Oswald. Minneapolis: Augsburg, 1989.

Kristeva, Julia. "Word, Dialogue, and Novel." Pages 64–91 in *Desire in Language: A Semiotic Approach to Literature and Art*. New York: Columbia University Press, 1980.

Leuenberger, Martin. *Konzeptionen des Königtums Gottes im Psalter: untersuchungen zu komposition und redaktion der theokratischen Bücher IV–V im Psalter*. Abhandlungen zur Theologie des Alten und Neuen Testaments 83. Zürich: Theologischer Verlag Zürich, 2004.

Lewis, C. S. *Reflections on the Psalms*. New York: Mariner, 2012.

Longman, Tremper III, and Raymond B. Dillard. *An Introduction to the Old Testament*. 2nd ed. Grand Rapids: Zondervan, 2006.

MacIntyre, Alasdair. *After Virtue*. 3rd ed. Notre Dame, IN: University of Notre Dame Press, 2007.

Maillot, Alphonse, and André Lelièvre. *Les Psaumes: Traduction Nouvelle et Commentaire*. Vol. 3. Geneva: Labor et Fides, 1969.

Mays, James Luther. "The Place of the Torah-Psalms in the Psalter." *Journal of Biblical Literature* 106 (1987): 3–12.

———. *Psalms*. Interpretation. Louisville, KY: John Knox Press, 1994.

McCann, J. Clinton. "Books I–III and the Editorial Purpose of the Hebrew Psalter." Pages 93–107 in *The Shape and Shaping of the Psalter*. Edited by J. Clinton McCann. Sheffield: JSOT, 1993.

———. Preface to *The Shape and Shaping of the Psalter*. Edited by J. Clinton McCann. Sheffield: JSOT, 1993.

———. ed. *The Shape and Shaping of the Psalter*. Sheffield: JSOT, 1993.

McKelvey, Michael G. *Moses, David and the High Kingship of Yahweh: A Canonical Study of Book IV of the Psalter.* Piscataway, NJ: Gorgias, 2014.

Meek, Russell. "Intertextuality, Inner-Biblical Exegesis, and Inner-Biblical Allusion: The Ethics of a Methodology." *Biblica* 95, no. 2 (2014): 280–91.

Millard, Matthias. *Die Komposition des Psalters: Ein formgeschichtlicher Ansatz.* Forschungen zum Alten Testament 9. Tübingen: Mohr, 1994.

Mitchell, David C. *The Message of the Psalter: An Eschatological Programme in the Book of Psalms*. Sheffield: Sheffield Academic, 1997.

Moo, Douglas J., and Andrew David Naselli. "The Problem of the New Testament's Use of the Old Testament." Pages 702–46 in *The Enduring Authority of the Christian Scriptures*. Edited by D. A. Carson. Grand Rapids: Eerdmans, 2016.

Mowinckel, Sigmund. *The Psalms in Israel's Worship*. Translated by D. R. Ap-Thomas. 2 vols. Oxford: Basil Blackwell, 1962.

———. *Psalm Studies*. Translated by Mark E. Biddle. History of Biblical Studies. Atlanta: Society of Biblical Literature, 2014.

Moyise, Steve. *Paul and Scripture: Studying the New Testament Use of the Old Testament*. Grand Rapids: Baker Academic, 2010.

Murphy, Roland E. "Reflections on Contextual Interpretation of the Psalms." Pages 21–28 in *The Shape and Shaping of the Psalter*. Edited by J. Clinton McCann. Sheffield: JSOT, 1993.

Oesterley, W. O. E. *The Psalms: Translated with Text-Critical and Exegetical Notes*. Vol. 2. London: Society for Promoting Christian Knowledge, 1939.

Perowne, J. J. Stewart. *The Book of Psalms: A New Translation with Introductions and Notes*. 3rd London ed. Vol. 2. Andover, MA: Warren F. Draper, 1879.

Phillips, George. *The Psalms in Hebrew: With a Critical, Exegetical, and Philological Commentary*. Vol. 2. London: John W. Parker, 1846.

Pietersma, Albert. "Septuagintal Exegesis and the Superscriptions of the Greek Psalter." Pages 443–75 in *The Book of Psalms: Composition and Reception.* Edited by Peter W. Flint and Patrick D. Miller Jr., Boston: Brill, 2005.

Porter, Stanley E. *Sacred Tradition in the New Testament: Tracing Old Testament Themes in the Gospels and Epistles*. Grand Rapids: Baker Academic, 2016.

Quesada, Jan Jaynes. "Is David, Too, among the Prophets? A Study of 2 Samuel 23:1–7. *Perspectives in Religious Studies* 44, no. 2 (2017): 249–59.

Rashi. *Rashi's Commentary on Psalms*. Translated by Mayer I. Gruber. Brill Reference Library of Judaism 18. Boston: Brill, 2004.

Rendtorff, Rolf. *The Canonical Hebrew Bible: A Theology of the Old Testament*. Translated by David E. Orton. Tools for Biblical Study Series 7. Leiderdorp, the Netherlands: Deo, 2005.

Robertson, O. Palmer. *The Flow of the Psalms: Discovering Their Structure and Theology*. Phillipsburg, NJ: P & R, 2015.

Rodd, Cyril S. *Psalms 73–150*. Epworth Preacher's Commentaries. London: Epworth, 1964.

Rogerson, J. W., and J. W. McKay. *Psalms 101–150*. Cambridge Bible Commentary. New York: Cambridge University Press, 1977.

Sailhamer, John H. *The Meaning of the Pentateuch: Revelation, Composition and Interpretation*. Downers Grove, IL: InterVarsity Press, 2009.

Sanders, James A. *Canon and Community: A Guide to Canonical Criticism*. Philadelphia: Fortress, 1984.

———. *Torah and Canon*. Philadelphia: Fortress, 1972.

Schaefer, Konrad. *Psalms*. Berit Olam. Collegeville, MN: Liturgical, 2001.

Segal, Benjamin J. *A New Psalm: The Psalms as Literature*. New York: Gefen, 2013.

Seitz, Christopher R. *Joel*. International Theological Commentary. New York: Bloomsbury T&T Clark, 2016.

Shemaryahu, Talmon. "Pisqah Be'emṣa' Pasuq and 11 QPsa." *Textus* 5 (1966): 11–21.

Snearly, Michael K. *The Return of the King: Messianic Expectation in Book V of the Psalter*. Library of Hebrew Bible/Old Testament Studies 624. New York: Bloomsbury T&T Clark, 2016.

Sommer, Benjamin D. "Exegesis, Allusion and Intertextuality in the Hebrew Bible: A Response to Lyle Eslinger." *Vetus Testamentum* 46 (1996): 479–89.

Stanley, Christopher D. *Paul and the Language of Scripture: Citation Technique in the Pauline Epistles and Contemporary Literature*. Society for New Testament Studies Monograph Series 69. Cambridge: Cambridge University Press, 1992.

Streett, Andrew. *The Vine and the Son of Man: Eschatological Interpretation of Psalm 80 in Early Judaism*. Minneapolis, MN: Fortress, 2014.

Terrien, Samuel. *The Psalms: Strophic Structure and Theological Commentary*. Grand Rapids: Eerdmans, 2003.

Theodoret of Cyrus. *Commentary on the Psalms: Psalms 73–150*. Translated by Robert C. Hill. Washington, DC: Catholic University of America Press, 2001.

Tournay, Raymond Jacques. "Psaumes 57, 60 et 108: Analyse et Interprétation." *Revue Biblique* 96, no. 1 (1989): 5–26.

———. *Seeing and Hearing God with the Psalms: The Prophetic Liturgy of the Second Temple in Jerusalem*. Translated by J. Edward Crowley. Journal for the Study of the Old Testament Supplement Series 118. Sheffield: Sheffield Academic, 1991.

Tucker, W. Dennis Jr. *Constructing and Deconstructing Power in Psalms 107–150*. Atlanta: SBL, 2014.

———. "Empires and Enemies in Book V of the Psalter." Pages 723–31 in The Composition of the Book of Psalms. Edited by Erich Zenger. Bibliotheca Ephemeridum Theologicarum Lovaniensium 238. Leuven, Belgium: Uitgeverij Peeters, 2010.

———. "The Role of the Foe in Book 5: Reflections on the Final Composition of the Psalter." Pages 179–91 in *The Shape and Shaping of the Book of Psalms: The Current State of Scholarship*. Edited by Nancy L. deClaissé-Walford. Atlanta: SBL, 2014.

Vaillancourt, Ian James. "The Multifaceted Savior of Psalms 110 and 118: A Canonical Exegesis." Sheffield: Sheffield Phoenix, 2019.

Van der Velden, Frank. *Psalm 109 und die Aussagen zur Feindschädigung in den Psalmen*. SBB 37. Stuttgart, Germany: Verlag Katholisches Bibelwerk, 1997.

VanGemeren, Willem A. *Psalms*. Rev. ed. Pages 21–1011 in *The Expositor's Bible Commentary*. Vol. 5. Edited by Tremper Longman III and David E. Garland. Grand Rapids: Zondervan, 2008.

Vesco, Jean-Luc. *Le Psautier de David: Traduit et Commenté*. 2 vols. Paris: Cerf, 2006.

Vos, Gerhardus. "Eschatology of the Psalter." *Princeton Theological Review* 18 (1920): 1–43. https://commons.ptsem.edu/id/princetontheolog1811arms-dmd002.

Wälchli, Stefan H. *Gottes Zorn in den Psalmen: Eine Studie zur Rede vom Zorn Gottes in den Psalmen im Kontext des Alten Testamentes und des alten Orients*. Orbis Biblicus et Orientalis 244. Göttingen, Germany: Academic Fribourg, 2012.

Wallace, Robert E. *The Narrative Effect of Book IV of the Hebrew Psalter*. Studies in Biblical Literature 112. New York: Peter Lang, 2007.

Wallace, Howard N. *Psalms*. Sheffield: Sheffield Phoenix, 2009.

Waltke, Bruce K., and Michael Patrick O'Connor. *An Introduction to Biblical Hebrew Syntax*. Winona Lake, IN: Eisenbrauns, 1990.

Walton, John H. "Psalms: A Cantata about the Davidic Covenant." *Journal of the Evangelical Theological Society* 34, no. 1 (March 1991): 21–31.

Wardlaw, Terrance Randall. *Elohim within the Psalms: Petitioning the Creator to Order Chaos in Oral-Derived Literature*. Library of Hebrew Bible/Old Testament Studies 602. New York: Bloomsbury, 2015.

Weber, Beat. *Werkbuch Psalmen II: Die Psalmen 73 Bis 150*. Stuttgart, Germany: W. Kohlhammer GmbH, 2003.

Weiser, Artur. *The Psalms: A Commentary*. Translated by Herbert Hartwell. 5th ed. Old Testament Library. London: SCM, 1962.

Wenham, Gordon J. *Psalms as Torah: Reading Biblical Song Ethically*. Grand Rapids: Baker Academic, 2012.

Wesley, John. *Wesley's Notes on the Bible*. Grand Rapids: Francis Asbury, 1987.

Whybray, Norman. *Reading the Psalms as a Book*. Electronic ed. Journal for the Study of the Old Testament Supplement Series 222. Sheffield: Sheffield Academic, 1996.

———. *Reading the Psalms as a Book*. Journal for the Study of the Old Testament Supplement Series 222. Sheffield: Sheffield Academic, 1996.

Willgren, David. *The Formation of the "Book" of Psalms: Reconsidering the Transmission and Canonization of Psalmody in Light of Material Culture and the Poetics of Anthologies*. Forschungen zum Alten Testament 2. Reihe 88. Tübingen, Germany: Mohr Siebeck, 2016.

Wilson, Gerald Henry. *The Editing of the Hebrew Psalter*. Society of Biblical Literature Dissertation Series. Chico, CA: Scholars, 1985.

———. *Psalms*. Vol. 1. NIV Application Commentary. Grand Rapids: Zondervan, 2002.

———. "The Shape of the Book of Psalms." *Interpretation* 46 (1992): 129–42.

Zenger, Erich. "The Composition and Theology of the Fifth Book of Psalms, Psalms 107–145." *Journal for the Study of the Old Testament* 80 (1998): 77–102.

——. "The God of Israel's Reign over the World (Psalms 90–106)." Pages 161–90 in *The God of Israel and the Nations: Studies in Isaiah and the Psalms*. Collegeville, MN: Liturgical, 2000.

——. "Psalmenexegese und Psalterexegese: eine Forschungsskizze." Pages 17–65 in *The Composition of the Book of Psalms*. Edited by Erich Zenger. Bibliotheca Ephemeridum Theologicarum Lovaniensium 238. Leuven, Belgium: Uitgeverij Peeters, 2010.

Subject & Author Index

Scripture Index

Old Testament

New Testament

Septuagint

Dead Sea Scrolls and Related Texts

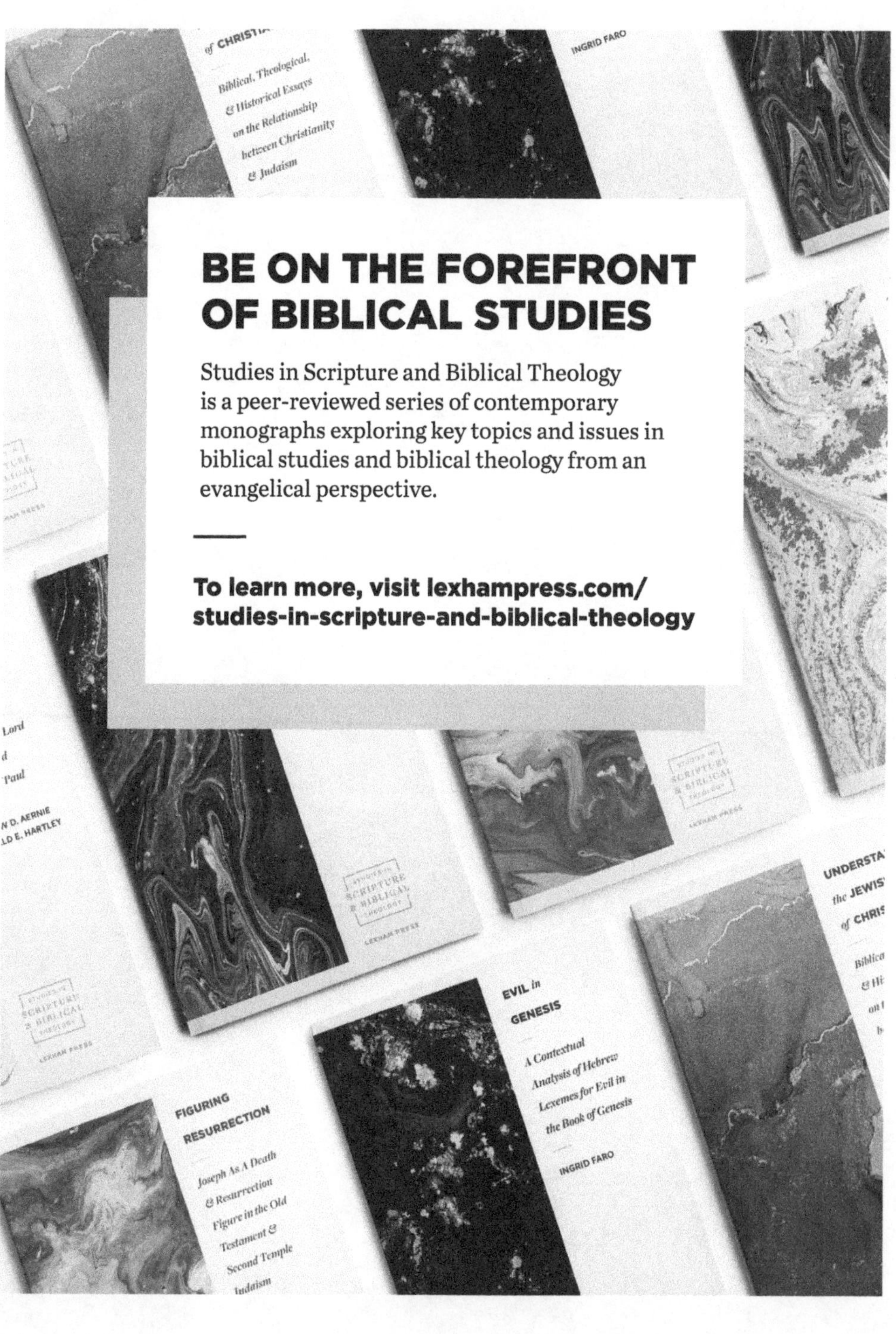

BE ON THE FOREFRONT OF BIBLICAL STUDIES
Studies in Scripture and Biblical Theology is a peer-reviewed series of contemporary monographs exploring key topics and issues in biblical studies and biblical theology from an evangelical perspective.
To learn more, visit lexhampress.com/studies-in-scripture-and-biblical-theology
EVIL in GENESIS
A Contextual Analysis of Hebrew Lexemes for Evil in the Book of Genesis
INGRID FARO
FIGURING RESURRECTION
Joseph As A Death & Resurrection Figure in the Old Testament & Second Temple Judaism
Biblical, Theological, & Historical Essays on the Relationship between Christianity & Judaism